UNDERSTANDING
the
PRINCIPALSHIP

UNDERSTANDING
the
PRINCIPALSHIP

Metaphorical Themes, 1920s-1990s

Lynn G. Beck and Joseph Murphy

Foreword by
Thomas J. Sergiovanni

TEACHERS
COLLEGE
PRESS

Teachers College, Columbia University
New York and London

Support for this research was provided by the National Center for Educational Leadership (NCEL) under U.S. Department of Education Contract No. R117C8005. The views in this report are those of the authors and do not necessarily represent those of the sponsoring institution or of the universities in the NCEL Consortium—The University of Chicago, Harvard University, and Vanderbilt University.

Published by Teachers College Press, 1234 Amsterdam Avenue
New York, New York

Library of Congress Cataloging-in-Publication Data

Beck, Lynn G.
    Understanding the principalship : metaphorical themes,
1920's-1990's / Lynn G. Beck and Joseph Murphy.
        p.   cm.
    Includes bibliographical references (p.   ) and index.
    ISBN 0-8077-3208-7 (alk. paper). — ISBN 0-8077-3207-9 (pbk.)
    1. School principals.   2. School management and organization.
3. Metaphor—History—20th century.   I. Murphy, Joseph, 1949-
II. Title.
LB2831.93.B43   1993
371.2'012—dc20   92-28071

ISBN 0-8077-3208-7
ISBN 0-8077-3207-9 (pbk.)

Printed on acid-free paper
Manufactured in the United States of America

99 98 97 96 95 94 93   7 6 5 4 3 2 1

To my mother,
Charlice Gillespie,
with love and gratitude

To L. C.

Where is the wisdom we have lost in knowledge?
Where is the knowledge we have lost in information?

T. S. Eliot, Chorus from *The Rock*

Contents

Foreword

Books are tools of the trade for academics. Thanks to publishers, dozens of unsolicited books cross my desk each year. Many more manage to accumulate. Figuring out what to do with them can be a problem. I have a three-category system that makes the job easier for me. Some of the books go directly to a table in the reception area of the Department of Education. If I'm lucky, I will never see them again. Others go to the bookshelf in the part of my office where I work most often. After a while the ideas in nearly all these books get used up, and out the books go to the reception area. The survivors eventually find their way over to the bookshelf that holds my personal collection.

This book by Lynn G. Beck and Joseph Murphy will begin its life on my work shelf but is destined to wind up on my personal shelf, along with other books that are either pioneering for their time or have enduring value. I would put this book in the first category. It is pioneering for having opened a new line of inquiry and for having established an appealing invitation to other researchers to join in.

As the title suggests the book seeks to study the inner life of school administration as revealed in the metaphors that have appeared in the literature from 1920 to the present. The topic of metaphor is hardly new to school administration, but this book is unique for its historical approach. Beck and Murphy's research strategy is simple enough. Conducting an exhaustive review of the literature, the authors provide a decade-by-decade analysis of the metaphors used by writers to describe the role of the principalship. They chart, as well, the unfolding social movements and key historical events that influenced schooling during each of the decades and then bring the two together in search of explanations for why certain metaphors appeared and what they meant.

The research strategy is both appealing and compelling. As the reader travels through this metaphorical journey the principal as Values Broker of the 1920s is transformed into the Scientific Manager of the 1930s, the Democratic Leader of the 1940s, the Theory-Guided Administrator of the 1950s, the Bureaucratic Executive of the 1960s, the Humanistic Facilitator of the 1970s, and the Instructional Leader of the 1980s. The changing metaphors for the principalship, the authors discover, represent recurrent shifts from value-based conceptions to technical conceptions and back again.

Beck and Murphy point out that the study of metaphor provides a deeper, richer, and potentially more accurate look at the principalship than other methods, and they are right. Metaphors transform the phonetic to the semantic by revealing the governing idea structures, values, and practical theories of those who use them. But metaphors are as much prisons as frames. The realities they create not only guide us but hold us in bondage. Escaping requires that the undergirding value structures of metaphors used be made explicit and examined critically. Beck and Murphy's book helps to do just that.

Metaphors are also powerful means for shaping the realities of others and thus dominating. Some language systems are more legitimate than others, having been anointed by authority. Schools officially sanction a language of teaching and learning through curriculum documents, statements of objectives, job descriptions, teacher evaluation systems, and inservice programs. How the official language system defines teaching effectiveness, for example, may be at odds with effectiveness as defined by the teacher's personal language. Further, if new evaluation procedures and instruments using a different language system were introduced, teachers thought to be effective initially would no longer be seen as such. Winning and losing, it appears, are functions of the language used. Those who control this language determine the winners and losers.

Beck and Murphy provide many examples of how anointed language dominates. They point out that over the years the writings of academics have served as vehicles for introducing new concepts into the parlance of practice. Academic writing is anointed by university degree requirements, state certification requirements, and society's reverence for the printed word.

Beck and Murphy write in a way that invites and stimulates readers to consider their own explanations for findings. They note, for example, the sheer volume of different metaphors that exist and the quick shifting of metaphors as the decades progress. Perhaps school administration is a field frantically in search of its own identity and perhaps the school is indeed vulnerable to forces from the outside. Equally tenable, in my view, is that school administration is a field with a fleeting official identity and an enduring personal and private identity. What might we discover, for example, if we dug into the private metaphorical lives of principals? We would, I wager, discover fewer and more enduring metaphors.

The expression "food for thought" may be a bit overworked, but it is a good description of Beck and Murphy's book. You will not be disappointed if you accept their invitation to join them in an exciting conversation.

Thomas J. Sergiovanni

CHAPTER ONE

Using a Metaphorical Perspective

While I first felt sheepish about taking up the problem of metaphor in the social sciences, I now feel more bullish. At the least we should have been tossed on the horns of the following dilemma which I believe fundamental to the understanding of culture. However men may analyze their experiences within any domain, they inevitably know and understand them best by referring them to other domains for elucidation. It is in that metaphoric cross-referencing of domains, perhaps, that culture is integrated, providing us with the sensation of wholeness. And perhaps the best index of cultural integration or disintegration, or of genuineness or spuriousness in culture for that matter, is the degree to which men can feel the aptness of each other's metaphors.

D. W. Fernandez, 1986, p. 25

In the early history of American schooling, principals were nonexistent—"the administration of schools was hardly differentiated from teaching" (Campbell, Fleming, Newell, & Bennion, 1987, p. x). Teachers in one-room schools throughout this country simply performed the necessary administrative, clerical, and janitorial tasks associated with schooling (Pierce, 1935; Sheets, 1986). As schools grew, however, the complexity of these tasks increased, requiring a single person to assume responsibility for them (Campbell et al., 1987; Messinger, 1939). This person, designated as the "principal teacher," continued to function in the classroom but also served as "the controlling head of the school" (Pierce, 1935, p. 11).

The single word *principal*, referring to this controlling head, appeared in the Common School Report of Cincinnati in 1835 and in the writings of Horace Mann in 1841 (Pierce, 1935). In the second half of the nineteenth century and into the early decades of the twentieth century, principals' primary duties were "the performance of minor administrative tasks, . . .

discipline, . . . some teaching" (Cooper, 1979, p. 272), plant and building maintenance, and some personnel supervision (Pierce, 1935). Reports to school boards during the late 1800s suggest that time allocated to these various areas and specific details of the tasks varied greatly from school to school and from system to system (Pierce, 1935).

In the 1920s, the Department of Elementary School Principals and the Department of Secondary School Principals were established within the National Education Association. The creation of these departments signaled the official recognition of the position of principal by a national body of professional educators. This acknowledgment opened the door for many things. Special university-based training programs, for example, developed to equip people for administrative positions (Cooper & Boyd, 1987; Tyack & Hansot, 1982). At the school level, the public began to hold principals responsible for the effectiveness of schools (Tyack & Hansot, 1982). Teachers expected principals to assist them in gaining a voice in how schools should be run, to guide them toward better instructional methods, and to order the school environment so that effective instruction could occur (Clark & Lotto, 1982; Lindquist, 1933). Additionally, central office personnel assumed that principals would serve as their link to individual schools (Cubberley, 1923; Morris, Crowson, Porter-Gehrie, & Hurwitz, 1984). In the midst of these changes, educational theorists began to do research on the role of the principal and other school administrators (Campbell & Gregg, 1957; Cubberley, 1923; Elsbree & McNally, 1951; Griffiths, 1959, 1982).

DEVELOPMENT OF THIS STUDY

In this book, we report on the results of one research effort on the principalship. Our goal was to develop a more robust understanding of the principalship than is generally available. We decided early on that traditional methods used to inform us about the principalship, while useful, conveyed a disturbingly thin base of information about this role (see Bridges, 1982). To be sure, there was no shortage of material, but we found it to be highly descriptive and repetitive in nature. While we accumulated knowledge about the role and the men and women who populated it, we did not feel as if we understood the principalship. In short, we found that the field had produced a good deal of "ameaningful" thought (Dokecki, 1990, p. 155)—information long on description but short on meaning. When we examined some of the emerging methodological approaches being employed in the study of school-level administrators (see, for example, Donmoyer, 1985; Lotto & Murphy, 1990; Taylor, 1986a, 1986b), we caught a glimpse of what we were seeking. In total though, we were still left with a longing for a deeper and more penetrating understanding of the principalship.

We concluded that we needed to get beyond micro-level descriptions, to transcend discussions of how principals behaved on the job, the career patterns they followed, the ways they were evaluated, and so forth. We looked for a different way to frame our investigation—one that would provide a little distance from the descriptions of routine activities, allow our understanding to accumulate over time, get at the deep structures of the role, focus on the personal and interpersonal dimension of the job, and place our understanding of educational leadership within the broader socio-political and historical context in which schools operate and principals manage and lead.

We allowed ourselves to be guided by the work of Bronfenbrenner (1979), who discusses this broader context as follows:

> It is clear that the concept of role involves an integration of the elements of activity and relation in terms of societal expectations. Since these expectations are defined at the level of the subculture of culture as a whole, the role, which functions as an element of the microsystem, actually has its roots in the higher-order macrosystem and its associated ideology and institutional structures.
>
> It is the embeddedness of roles in this larger context that gives them their special power to influence—and even to compel—how a person behaves in a given situation, the activities she engages in, and the relations that become established between that person and others present in the setting. (p. 86)

Borrowing from our colleagues in the helping professions, we came to believe that we needed an approach to inquiry that was more attuned to the humanities than to the sciences, that would allow us to avoid "the dualisms of knowledge-action and theory-practice" (Dokecki, 1990, p. 159; see also Foster, 1986) and permit us to conduct a world view (*Weltanschaung*) study (Dokecki, 1990). We settled on a strategy of constructing meaning by examining the language used in talking about being a principal. Because we wanted to get beyond self-conscious structural analysis—to tap into language that conveyed the essence of the principalship in more evocative ways—we went beyond explicit statements about the principalship and looked at implicit conceptions of the role as conveyed in the metaphorical language of educational literature. We came to the same conclusion in our analysis of the principalship that Owens and Steinhoff (1989) reached in their study of organizations: "Metaphorical thinking provides a different way of knowing about organizations as an alternative to conventional methods of enquiry into the phenomenon of social order" (p. 13).

Furthermore, following Ogbu's (1981) suggestion, we decided to examine the principal's role historically, to see how understanding of this role has changed over time and been influenced by societal context. Beginning at 1920, the year when the Department of Elementary School Principals was established, we undertook a decade-by-decade analysis of the metaphors used by educational writers in the empirical, theoretical, and practical literature on the principalship. We discovered that conceptions of the principalship have evolved over time, resulting in dramatically different role expectations in each of the last seven decades. As we explored these changing expectations against an overlay of educational and political history, we concluded that many of the changes grew not out of a proactive response to the needs of children and teachers in this country's schools, but rather out of a reactive response to political and historical events, to trends emanating from universities and research centers, to ideologies of organizing, and to public opinion—or as Campbell and his colleagues (1987) noted in their recent history of educational administration, "major movements in the field of educational administration, like those in education more generally, reflect deeper social trends" (p. 6; see also Callahan, 1962; Callahan & Button, 1964).

Our study is thus informed by a comprehensive, historical, analytical approach. We conducted a review of practical and theoretical literature on educational administration and extracted metaphors used in relationship to principals' roles and work. Building on the work of Bredeson (1988), we considered metaphors to include actual and suggestive comparisons, and, for the purpose of this book, we defined metaphor as a form of linguistic communication that acts as explanation or reflection of one idea in terms of another. Some of the authors offering metaphors were practicing principals commenting on their own experiences; others were professors involved in administrative training programs and/or the study of the principalship; still others were teachers offering their perspectives on principals; and a few authors reviewed were not in the field of education.

We discovered consistent themes in the metaphorical perspectives of the diverse authors we reviewed, suggesting that metaphors do, indeed, reflect shared meanings and that a study of metaphors can provide insight into the evolution of conceptions of principals' work. We also found considerable evidence to support the position that these metaphors helped influence the role of building-level administrators.

In the remainder of this introductory chapter we briefly discuss the concept of metaphor in general and then ground our study in the work that preceded it. The introduction is followed by a series of six chapters, arranged chronologically from the 1920s to the 1980s, offering the results of our metaphorical analysis and our thinking about these results. We look at the dominant metaphors of each decade and analyze them according to the following framework:

1. Dominant metaphorical themes
2. Dominant tone(s) of the metaphors
3. Values that dominate each decade
4. Conceptions of the principal's relationships to community, school boards, teachers, and students
5. Standards against which the work of the principal is evaluated

We discuss these results as they relate to developments and changes in politics, history, and general and scholarly thought about education. In the eighth chapter, we present an analysis of how we believe emerging metaphors will shape and direct our understanding of the role of the principal. In the final chapter, we propose ways that our analysis might be useful to educational theorists. Information on procedures employed in the study is contained in the Appendix.

METAPHORICAL ANALYSIS AS A PATH TO UNDERSTANDING

Metaphors serve at least two functions in language.[1] They clarify the meaning of abstract concepts by comparing them to concrete, easily understood ones—in Fernandez's (1986) terms, they have "the profundity of a concrete immediacy" (p. 7)—and they create mental pictures by likening a person or thing to something that evokes an emotional response. Metaphors are thus related to both cognitive and affective ways we perceive and order our world. Miller and Fredericks (1988), reflecting on the work of Lakoff and Johnson (1980) and Law and Lodge (1984), argue that metaphors "are worthy of serious study because they must reflect a 'fundamental core' of shared meaning. . . . Metaphors are not simply random events but are important ways of structuring and extending experience" (pp. 263–264).

In literal language, the sentence structure itself gives meaning to the sentence. The sentence is bound by the truth that is expressed within it. Finding and understanding the literal meaning in a sentence does not require any knowledge beyond the rules of language, the conditions of the utter-

---

1. We would like to acknowledge the assistance provided by Sandra Herman and Laura Berman in developing this section.

ance, and shared background assumptions (Searle, 1979). When using metaphorical language, however, the truth conditions of meaning are not determined by the truth conditions of the sentence. The hearers must draw upon something more than just their understanding of the rules of language, the conditions of the utterance, and shared background assumptions. Metaphors require the hearer to "call something to mind" (Searle, 1979, p. 99). Thus metaphors expand the meanings of ideas and offer insights that in literal language might be nonsense. For example, "love is blind" in our literal language would lead the listener to believe that love is an object or being that is, although capable of sight, blind. In metaphorical terms, "love is blind" refers to the indefinable quality of love that prevents persons who are "in love" from seeing objectively that which they love.

Metaphors allow a speaker to name a subject for communication and then frame it, or perhaps reframe it, within the bounds of a second concept. With the framing or reframing, an idea can take on many more characteristics or attributes than it may have had in its literal form (Ortony, 1979). Metaphors, in this sense, actually have the potential to generate new meanings and ideas between speaker and listener (Schön, 1979, p. 255). By helping people to communicate their personal realities with other speakers, metaphors help people begin to organize and support their cultural domain. A person can share with others insights about "how things are" and receive recognition in the process (Black, 1979, p. 40).

Metaphor is an important linguistic form because it offers a speaker a discrete symbol system for encoding a continuous discourse of experiential information. It is a compact way to represent thoughts, beliefs, and perceptions, and it also provides an opportunity to create ideas linguistically that have no current literal vocabulary for their communication (Ortony, 1979). With metaphor a speaker can be creative, vivid, emotional, and representational in her or his language (Paivio, 1979). Additionally, and perhaps most important, metaphor allows a vivid transfer of ideas that may not have a counterpart in objective words. When this happens, we communicate not at the concrete, linear level, but at the holistic, conceptual one. And we receive and encode ideas as images, with perhaps several layers of meaning.

Metaphor is a piece of our conceptual system. It is a language form grounded in experience (Manning, 1979) and provides a lens through which we view our experiences and ideas. Using metaphor enables a speaker to offer a view of a complex, often abstract experience or idea by referring to an experience or idea more readily understood. Brown (1976) states that stereoscopic vision is needed to comprehend metaphor fully. He also notes, in a later work (1989), that metaphors which reside at a deep or root level of meaning are a primary frame of reference for the ways in which we construct or know the world. These metaphors reside at the subconscious level and appear to be requisite to perception. Brown argues that people must first see "all knowledge as a construction" and "truth as a matter of the context in which it is embedded"; then they can begin to see the possibilities of how they frame or know anything (1989, p. 125).

Peter Manning (1979) relates the concept of metaphors as revealers of constructed understanding to organizational theory. He says, "If organization is a label with a set of domain assumptions about the semantic space in which it operates, and a set of implicit meanings that are tacitly assigned to behaviors, then it cannot be a concrete, unequivocal, phenomenologically invariant thing" (pp. 660–661). If it is true that organizations are the constructed reality of those who belong to them and assign meaning and behaviors to them (see Lotto & Murphy, 1990, for a review), then anything that helps scholars understand this reality is worthy of study. Language, because it is a primary revealer of beliefs about organizations and their members, is a phenomenon that helps to uncover constructed reality. It is evident, therefore, that anyone seeking to understand organizations such as schools or important stakeholders in organizations, such as principals, must consider language (Manning, 1979).

METAPHORICAL STUDY IN EDUCATIONAL ADMINISTRATION

Historical periods in school administration carry labels that, with reasonable accuracy, capture the social role and underlying value prescriptions for those occupying leadership positions. (Kerchner, 1988, p. 381)

Several scholars of school organizations in recent years have begun to recognize that a study of language can lead to a better understanding of organizational processes.[2] Bolman and Deal (1989) suggest that metaphors reveal much about the culture of an organization and that a study of metaphors can shed light on the meanings that organizational members attach to events, processes, and roles. Bredeson (1988) has shown how metaphors can "broaden perspectives, enhance understanding, and provide insight into the organization, operation, and administration of schools" (p. 293). At a more practical level, he demonstrates how the metaphors principals use influence the way they think about their roles and shape the

_____

2. We would like to acknowledge our debt to Peter Patina (1988) whose earlier work in this area helped shape the ideas presented in this section. This section of the chapter is taken from Beck and Murphy, Searching for a Robust Understanding of the Principalship, _Educational Administration Quarterly_, copyright © 1992. Reprinted by permission of Sage Publications, Inc.

activities they perform (see also Sergiovanni, Burlingame, Coombs, & Thurston, 1980).

Blumberg (1984), Gudgeon (1989), Petrie (1990), Schlechty (1990), and Sykes and Elmore (1989) all reveal how organizational metaphors shape our understanding of the nature of our professions, the core technologies of educational and child care, and the roles and responsibilities of organizational stakeholders. For example, through the use of powerful metaphors, Schlechty (1990) provides an insightful analysis of how the language we use to capture schooling shapes organizational behavior. He notes that when we view schools as tribal centers, the role of the principal is that of chief priest. When the language of schools is that of the factory, the principal's role is that of manager of the industrial center. When the metaphor of school-as-hospital predominates, the principal functions more as a chief of staff. In the school-as-knowledge/work organization, the role of the principal is to lead leaders and to nurture the conditions in which others can thrive. Other students of organizations (Murphy, 1992; Seeley, 1980) have shown the ways in which schooling metaphors influence how educators comprehend the various environmental stakeholders, for example, parents and regulatory agencies.

An interesting perspective on the use of metaphors in organizational analysis is offered by Smircich (1983). She proposes that the figurative language used by organizational members grows out of a "root metaphor" (p. 347), which she equates with the organization's culture. This root metaphor is understood and accepted on a subconscious level by organizational stakeholders. Smircich proposes that scholars must seek to uncover these root metaphors if they are to understand properly organizational symbols and images. Owens and Steinhoff (1989) build their theory of educational cultures on this concept. They argue that understanding schools requires knowing their cultures, an endeavor that necessitates uncovering "the assumptions—unspoken, taken for granted in the preconscious—that give rise to the organizational culture" (p. 6). Continuing the work of Smircich (1983), they suggest that discovering the root metaphor of the organization is a precursor to a comprehensive understanding of the symbolic expressions that reflect a school's culture. (See Steinhoff and Owens, 1989, for a discussion of their instrument and study examining this theory.)

The ways metaphors affect our understanding of organizations and their cultures is a focus of Morgan's (1986) classic work, *Images of Organization*. He writes that "theories and explanations of organizational life are based upon metaphors that lead us to see and understand organizations in distinctive yet partial ways" (p. 12). His statement points to the ways metaphors both expand and limit our perspectives. They expand them in that they link objective ideas with images rich in connotations; paradoxically, they also limit them in that they tend to lead to a "one-sighted insight" (p. 12) or to a "highlighted interpretation" (Patina, 1988, p. 22; see also Bredeson, 1985, 1987). Both Morgan and Patina indicate that this limited insight or interpretation "tends to force others into a background role" (Patina, 1988, p. 13). Perrin (1987) also articulately discusses the ways metaphors influence our thinking by simultaneously expanding and limiting understanding.

> Metaphor opens us to experience in certain ways and closes us in others. It invites us to participate in the constitution of reality while, at the same time, barring us from the consideration of rival alternatives. (p. 265)

Bates, in his article "Toward A Critical Practice of Educational Administration" (1984), offers views similar to those of Morgan (1986), Perrin (1987), and Patina (1988) and stresses the importance of metaphorical studies in educational administration. Noting that "organizational paradigms are not only formal structures of thought but are also constituted by the language, rhetoric, and practices of the organizational community" (p. 262), he calls for educational scholars to engage in "observation, analysis, and reflection on the metaphorical currency negotiated and exchanged within [and about] the school" (p. 267) in order to develop sound and useful administrative theories. Bates especially stresses the importance of discovering metaphorical patterns and subsequent shifts in these patterns. He argues that "shifts in the fundamental metaphors which we use . . . have far-reaching repercussions" (p. 264). He also notes the critical importance of perceiving and understanding contradictory or conflicting metaphors that might be operating simultaneously.

> Conflicts of metaphor are sources of great debate and tension within educational systems and schools. But the tension is not simply a semantic one. The metaphors which people use are often representative of the kind of future—the social movement—to which they are consciously or unconsciously committed. (p. 265)

Owens and Shakeshaft's (1987) reflections also highlight the value of metaphorical studies in educational administration. In a presentation to the University Council for Educational Administration, they support the premises of Smircich (1983), Morgan (1986), and others. Noting that educational metaphors "give rise to the personal views, beliefs, and values that individuals hold" (p. 21), Owens and Shakeshaft argue that metaphors determine "the ways in which an individual reacts and [shapes] the future behavior of the individual in response to various situations that will arise in everyday life" (p. 21).

Aspin (1984), Elliot (1984), and Taylor (1984) emphasize that the study of metaphors is appropriate and useful in understanding processes and beliefs in education. Aspin suggests that an understanding of the communication process is important in understanding how metaphors affect conceptions of education. He stresses that the meaning of images in educational discourse must be understood in relationship to the meaning they have for those who offer and receive them. Elliot points out the relationship between metaphor and theory. He suggests that metaphors used in discussions of education have a "deep affinity" (p. 53) with the favorite theories of those who use them. Metaphorical language thus helps to structure a theoretical perspective or paradigm, and an analysis of metaphors can help to reveal the theoretical persuasion of an author. Taylor agrees that metaphors and theories are linked. He argues that students of education wishing to gain a complete understanding of their field must study not only literal but also imaginative, or metaphorical, language, because this language "represents one of the ways in which many kinds of discourse—including discourse about education—are ordered and structured" (p. 20).

Several researchers, building on the theoretical perspectives noted in the preceding paragraphs, have examined the language used by various professional groups within education. The language of teachers is the focus for Munby (1986, 1987). In two studies, he examines metaphors used by teachers as they discuss their work and discovers several distinct patterns of metaphors that affect the teachers' construction of professional reality. Collins and Green (1990) examine the metaphors used by both teachers and students as they construct their understanding of the meaning of classroom experiences. Their data underscore the point made by Morgan (1986) and Perrin (1987): Metaphors expand and limit the understanding of reality held by teachers and students. Morgan and Perrin conclude their works by challenging educators to consider the metaphors they use and the ways in which these metaphors influence their construction of classroom reality.

Collins and Green's (1990) article opens a volume of *Theory Into Practice* devoted to examining the influence of metaphors on teachers' understanding of their work. Two articles in this volume discuss metaphors that convey certain conceptions about the teacher's role in the education process. Cohen and Lotan (1990) focus on the "teacher as supervisor of complex technology" (p. 78), and Berliner (1990) explores the concept of the teacher as classroom executive. Metaphors that influence teachers' understanding of their work are discussed by Marshall (1990a, 1990b) and Shuell (1990). The former notes problems inherent in the classroom-as-workplace metaphor, while the latter examines the benefits of picturing teaching and learning as a problem-solving process. The work of Carter (1990), Munby and Russell (1990), Tobin (1990), and Weade and Ernst (1990) focuses on metaphorical studies as tools for improving the practice of teaching.

Bredeson (1985, 1987, 1988) and Kelley and Bredeson (1987) examine metaphors utilized by principals. Bredeson's basic conclusion is that

> The metaphors of principals—whether expressed verbally or hidden in values, behavior patterns, or administrative structures—reveal a great deal about the shared cultural associations of the principals as well as provide a profile of individual creativity and adaptability to the role of principal. (1985, p. 38)

In the 1985 report, Bredeson identifies three major themes that dominate the language of the principals he interviewed. These are survival, maintenance, and vision. He relates these to the activity of principals, noting that most administrators operate out of a maintenance metaphor, with tasks directed at continuity and nurturing the status quo. Bredeson suggests that principals who are struggling with their work are more likely to use survival metaphors and that those who offer "the most hope" that the profession can truly influence education are the ones who think and speak of their work in terms of a vision metaphor. These principals can think "holistically" and can "use imagination . . . to think beyond accepted notions" (p. 43). Kelley and Bredeson (1987) compare the ways two principals use metaphors and other symbolic language in managing their schools. They discover some distinct patterns in the ways both leaders communicate. They recommend further study into principals' personal or idiosyncratic symbols, into the impact of the school culture on principals' use of symbols, and into the effect of symbols associated with role expectations on practitioners' metaphorical grids.

Hanson (1984) conducted a study of metaphors in educational administration research. Her investigation into the writing of five widely published educational scholars is concerned with determining these authors' underlying views that may be discerned from the metaphors used in their writing. Miller and Fredericks (1988) offer a number of arguments for the usefulness of metaphorical analysis in qualitative educational research. First, they note that metaphors reveal the "pervasive ways by which people make sense of their experience" (p. 269). Thus, an analysis of metaphors helps to uncover the "conceptual systems" (p. 270) that guide and influence educators in their work. Second, they propose that metaphorical analysis assists in the construction of "thick description" (p. 270) of events and roles in educational settings. Third, they state that studies of metaphors "can be viewed as adjuncts to conventional triangulation strategies" (p. 270) and, finally, that "metaphor analysis may suggest hypotheses that can be analyzed further in other research settings" (p. 271). They join Morgan (1986), Owens and Shakeshaft (1987), Munby (1986, 1987), Bredeson (1985), Kelley and Bredeson (1987), and others in affirming that the language associated with schooling and with school leadership is an important indicator of underlying beliefs and assumptions.

CONCLUSION

The research presented in this book builds on a rich tradition. Historically, metaphors have been recognized in the humanities as important revealers of meaning. Recently, social science has begun to recognize the importance of metaphorical analysis. The study reported in this book builds on concepts from the methodologies, conclusions, and implications of metaphorical investigations cited in this chapter. We accept the premises that a study of organizational metaphors, at a micro-level, allows us "to discover our frames and the generative frames implicit within our frames" (Schön, 1979, p. 266) and "that the metaphoric assertions men make about themselves or about others influence their behavior" (Fernandez, 1986, p. 6) and determine their "attitudes toward the world, people, events, and action" (Bates, 1984, p. 264). We also propose, however, that, on a more macro-level, historical analysis of language serves the purposes of revealing the frames that were held both by principals and by those writing about them, of assessing changes in perceptions and beliefs that have occurred in the twentieth century, of creating a deep base of understanding of this important educational leadership role, and of informing future studies on the principalship. Responding to challenges offered by Bates (1984) and Kelley and Bredeson (1987), we provide a systematic and systemic examination of the role symbols associated with the principalship. We attempt not only to offer a comprehensive analysis of "the metaphors behind the metaphors" in writings about the principalship over seven decades, but also to suggest possible influences on these conceptualizations and beliefs and some possible effects of these beliefs on educational practice. This work, with its emphasis on a comprehensive understanding of the principalship and of forces guiding it and emanating from it, is intended to complement the work that has just been cited as well as other types of studies of leadership that are context bound and, in a sense, limited in the type of understanding they produce.

CHAPTER TWO

The 1920s and the 1930s

In Chapters 2 through 7, we present the results of our historical analysis of metaphors about the principalship, beginning in this chapter with an investigation of the 1920s and 1930s. The examination of each decade opens with an outline of the results of our examination. We use these outlines to structure the discussion of our findings and to frame the analysis of the possible influences on beliefs about and expectations for principals during each decade.

THE TWENTIES

In the early part of this century, two forces apparently merged to shape the principalship: "common sense-tempered, pseudo-religious beliefs" about education's purposes and "the contemporary force of scientific management" (Glass, 1986b, p. 126; see also Tyack & Hansot, 1982). The metaphors of the 1920s reflect both of these influences. They suggest, though, that the view of principals as leaders chiefly concerned with promoting traditional spiritual and civic values in schools and communities dominated the thinking of this decade (see Figure 2.1).

DOMINANT METAPHORICAL THEMES

Four themes are evident in metaphors associated with the principalship in the 1920s.

1. The work of the principal is linked with absolute, spiritual truths and values.
2. The principalship is a role energized by a zeal for education and guided by principles of scientific management.
3. The principal is expected to be a social leader in the community.
4. For all of these reasons, the role is vested with dignity and importance.

FIGURE 2.1 Analysis of Metaphors of the 1920s

Dominant Metaphorical Themes
The work of the principal is linked with absolute, spiritual truths and values.
The principalship is a role energized by a zeal for education and guided by
    principles of scientific management.
The principal is expected to be a social leader in the community.
For all of these reasons, the role is considered to be a noble, honorable one.

Dominant Tone
Optimistic because of grounding in spiritual values and science

Dominant Values
Absolute values—both traditional and spiritual
Principles of scientific management
Accepted social values

Relationship to Others
To superintendents—
    Member of an educational team
To teachers—
    Presiding officer
    Organizer
    Guide
To students—
    Transmitter of values
    Teacher
    Disciplinarian
To the community—
    Public servant

Standards for Evaluation
Success is assumed if values held and methods used

Principal as Spiritual Leader

Educational writers of this decade, continuing a trend established by
the earliest chroniclers of school management (see Mason, 1986), make
ample use of religious imagery in their discussions of education and of the
people charged with administering education in local schools. Johnston,
Newlon, and Pickell (1922), for example, write that educational leaders
"with delicate direction . . . and a sense of mastery, can make moments burn
with meaning and become eternal. The cultivation of love of truth, love of
right, and appreciation of the beautiful, is the choicest task of the educator"

(p. 27). Efforts to accomplish this task are viewed as a "movement" (p. 41), and opposition is labeled "sacrilegious" (p. 154).

Principals, the leaders in this movement, are often spoken of in religious terms. Johnston and his colleagues (1922) write of the "spiritual" (p. 18) side of the administrative task. Cubberley (1923) notes "the great spiritual importance" (p. 561) of the principal's work and speaks of it in terms of "service" (p. 561). Johnson (1925) writes, "He is no Moses to bring down the tables of law from the mountaintop" (p. 63). Even though this is a negative comparison, the choice of this kind of image to describe the principal suggests that the office has certain "priestly" or "prophetic" dimensions. And Cubberley (1923) forthrightly likens the principal to "the priest in the parish" (p. 26). These images combine to paint a picture of the principal as one whose role is linked to timeless truths and values. Mason (1986), after analyzing school administration textbooks from the early twentieth century, confirms that this is, indeed, a facet of early conceptions of the principal. He notes that, "it is . . . within the realm of possibility that the nineteenth- and early-twentieth-century schoolmen had glimpsed the beatific vision which St. Thomas Aquinas had taught was the joint product of faith and reason at work" (p. 17). Mason describes this vision as "the vision of perfection . . . the true, the good, and the beautiful" (p. 17) and notes that a belief in the perfectibility of humans inspired early administrators. (See also Tyack, 1974, for a discussion of these motivating beliefs in early-twentieth-century education.)

Principal as Scientific Manager

Conjoined with the metaphor of the principal as a spiritual leader is the picture of the principal as a scientific manager who uses the best of modern methods and discoveries to create and manage an efficient and productive school. This view of the principal is perhaps best articulated in the writings of Cubberley who, in 1923, stresses the importance of "learning system and perfecting organization" (p. 47). Burton (1929) also supports this conception of the role in his description of the principal as a "leader of technical workers" (p. 538). And Pierce (1935), writing about the "supervisory activities of the principal established since 1920" (p. 81), notes that intelligence and achievement tests used in World War I and the formation of the Department of Elementary School Principals in 1920 influenced expectations of this role.

> The former resulted in putting into the principal's hands tools for making scientific studies of his supervisory problems; the latter provided a stimulus for making the studies and a medium for publishing results. Principals,

as a consequence, were able to base procedures on factual data to an extent not previously possible, and their supervision for the first time assumed the characteristics of a science. (p. 81)

Interestingly, this image of the principal as scientific manager apparently did not conflict with the metaphor of the principal as a spiritual leader. Cubberley, a chief advocate for scientific management in education, also likens the principal to a priest, and Johnston and colleagues (1922) point out that this role has both "spiritual and technical sides" (p. 18). Tyack and Hansot (1982) also note that "small town pietism and science" (p. 114) come together in both the training and the work of the school administrator. They offer an explanation of this unusual merger by pointing out that the religious zeal associated with education in the 1800s and early 1900s was in large measure reflective of the belief that "God had selected America as a redeemer nation" (p. 21). Distinctly American values such as education as a vehicle to help the nation "fulfill its destiny" (Tyack & Hansot, 1982, p. 23), the scientific management principles proposed in the early part of the century by Frederick Taylor (1911) and others are viewed as entirely consonant. Tyack and Hansot (1982) discuss these beliefs in detail, noting that

> Jean Quandt has shown how much the earlier millennial character of Protestantism [linked at this point in time with education] became fused with the evolutionary thought of many social scientists, imparting to the latter group a continuing faith in moral absolutes, an optimism about social destiny, and an energizing call to action. "The process of secularization," she observes, "entailed a partial transfer of redemptive power from religious to secular institutions." In the case of the new educational scientists, the older providential view of redemption became subtly transmuted into a view of social evolution which held that people could control and improve their world by conscious means, notably through education. (p. 116)

Eaton (1986) also writes about the comfortable coexistence of conceptions of the principal as both spiritual leader and scientific manager. He notes that Cubberley's works on administration (1914, 1916, 1923, 1927), while oriented toward discussing administration as a systematic, scientific practice, contain language suggesting that "the common school quest is the search for the Holy Grail, and the knight in shining armor is the school superintendent or principal whose purity in the quest for school efficiency and human perfection is not overshadowed by the godly Sir Gwayne" (p. 32). Evidently, those who believed in the divine call of American educators viewed scientific management as a divinely sanctioned method to help them achieve their goals.

Principal as Social Leader

In addition to being spiritual and scientific leaders, principals of the twenties are also expected to be social leaders. Gist (1924), quoted in Messinger (1939), writes that one principal believed "that it [was] essential that he be trained well socially, dance well, and do well on the golf course, be a good public speaker and good mixer" (p. 97). Johnston and colleagues (1922) agree, calling for the principal "to develop helpful social contacts" (p. 204) and to "cease to live an isolated life" (p. 205). Cubberley (1923), writing of the principal, notes that "no other person in the community can so immediately mould its life and shape its ideals" (p. 36).

Principal as Dignified Leader

For all of these reasons, the role of the principal is considered to be one of "dignity and importance" (Longshore, 1927, quoted in Messinger, 1939, p. 140). She or he is considered to be a "presiding officer" (Johnson, 1925, p. 103) and a "high class professional leader" (Burton, 1929, p. 538). Some of the strongest statements about the importance of the principalship are offered by Cubberley (1923), who writes, "We are not likely to overestimate the importance of the office of school principal" (p. 28). He elaborates on this statement with these words:

> The knowledge, insight, tact, skill, and qualities of helpful, professional leadership of the principal of the school practically determine the ideals and standards of achievement of both teachers and pupils within the school. . . . a strong and capable principal can develop a strong school even in cities where the general supervisory organization is weak and the professional interest of teachers is low. (p. 28)

Cubberley sums up this view of the principal's importance with his oft-quoted, "As is the principal, so is the school" (p. 15).

Interestingly, this statement and the belief that the principal plays a critical role in the success or failure of the school have appeared in the educational literature of every decade. The bases of this importance, though, and the expectations of the actions that a principal must take in order to fulfill the role effectively have varied. In the twenties, the principalship is important because it is vested with spiritual and social significance, and it is a role that has access to the techniques of scientific management that, if practiced, will create effective schools for teachers and students.

DOMINANT TONE OF THE METAPHORS: OPTIMISTIC

Cubberley's bold assertions about a principal's ability to affect the course of a school are made with great confidence. He apparently has no doubt that educational leaders, using scientifically "proven" methods, can succeed. Certainly, when we consider that principals in the twenties are viewed as high priests of educational truths, as first-order scientific managers, and as competent and popular social leaders, it is easy to understand why optimism is the dominant tone of this decade's metaphorical statements about the principal's role and work. Burton's (1929) statement provides an example of the confidence that pervades the literature of this period: "[The principal] must believe in modern supervision and secure the training for it. The great difficulty is time, *but this can be corrected with reasonable ease*" (p. 538; emphasis added). Other authors reinforce this view by not including extensive discussions of major dilemmas, role conflicts, and frustrations of the principalship, and by focusing on the noble dimensions of the job, on the spiritual foundations of the role, and on the availability of science and technology to guide principals as they confront the routine problems associated with running schools. The lengthy discussions of the positive dimensions of the role, the rather abbreviated discourses on the difficulties, and the framing of much of the discussion of problems in terms of "opportunities for personal growth and for community service" (Cubberley, 1923, p. 32) differ dramatically from the writings of later decades.

DOMINANT VALUES

What are the values that inform conceptions of the principal's role during the 1920s? Earlier discussion of the dominant metaphorical tone suggests three broad classifications of values that influence both education in general and the principalship in particular.

Absolute Traditional and Spiritual Values

Considered to underlie and inspire the work of educators were absolute values, both traditional and spiritual. A tacit acceptance of these values is found in virtually all the literature of this period, and many writers quite clearly embrace them. Johnson (1925), for example, argues that "training in ethical character" (p. 174) is a chief responsibility of schools and their teachers and administrators. He notes that such training will lead to "an individual's ability to distinguish clearly between right and wrong and the will to do right" (p. 182). As with most chroniclers of the period, Johnson seems to assume that readers share his views of right and wrong, and he does not discuss these abstractions in detail. He does note, though, that "right" includes concepts such as honesty, responsibility, clean speech, and good sportsmanship. Johnston and his colleagues (1922) in turn emphasize such values as "love of truth, love of right, and appreciation of the beautiful" (p. 27). Cubberley (1923) discusses the values associated with education in the following way:

> In teaching the youth of our nation the principles which lie at the foundation of liberty guided by law, and the difference between freedom and license; in training them for self-control; in developing in them the power to shoulder responsibility; in giving them a sense of the greatness of that democratic nobility in which we all may share; in instilling into them the importance of fidelity to duty, truth, honor, and virtue; in arousing in them a desire to be clean and strong, both in mind and body; and in unifying diverse elements and fusing them in the national mould, . . . our schools are rendering a service seldom appreciated and not likely to be overestimated. (p. 561)

Principles of Scientific Management

The second set of values undergirding conceptions of the principalship in the 1920s relates to science and to methods of scientific management. Actually, much of the writing from this period testifies to the importance placed on these methods and techniques. Cubberley (1923), Johnston and colleagues (1922), and Johnson (1925) devote considerable portions of their writings to ways principals can more effectively manage such details of their jobs as teacher meetings, plant management, and efficient use of time. Values such as "educational efficiency" (Cubberley, 1923, p. 15), appropriate delegation of responsibility (Johnson, 1925), the systematic handling of records (Johnston et al., 1922), "a scientific approach to . . . curriculum building" (Johnston et al., 1922, p. 346), and "management and control of his [school] in accordance with the larger lines of policy" (Cubberley, 1923, p. 18) are important to the educational leaders of this decade.

Accepted Values of the Community

The third set of values is related to the belief "that the school touches the community" in important ways and that "the principal links the school and its internal affairs with those in the community" (Johnston et al., 1922, p. 354). Cubberley (1923) discusses this role and the values related to it.

> The principal must remember that he holds a particularly responsible position as a model in his community. . . . He must, in his dress, his manner, his speech, and his bearing so conduct himself that he will easily win and hold the respect of [teachers, pupils, and the community]. (p. 26)

Cubberley notes that this requires attention to physical appearance, avoidance of any questionable activity (e.g., "He must not frequent places where gentlemen do not go" [p. 27]), reliability, and humor. Johnson (1925) and Gist (1924) also stress that the principal must understand, accept, and work with the values of the community.

THE PRINCIPAL'S RELATIONSHIP TO OTHERS

A view of administrators as transmitters of sacred values within scientifically managed schools tells us little about the relational aspects of the principal's job in the 1920s. The literature from the period suggests that the principal assumes a variety of roles depending on the person or groups with whom she or he is dealing.

To Superintendents

Principals' relationships to superintendents and boards of education in the twenties are described by Johnson (1925), Cubberley (1923), Koos (1924), and Pierce (1935) in terms that suggest that these roles are linked more by commitment to education than by bureaucratic regulations and procedures. Johnson (1925) sees the principal as an advocate for the school. He writes, "His intimate acquaintance with the problems of . . . education as presented by his own school places upon him the responsibility for influencing, through proper channels, those who are in charge of the larger policies of the entire school system" (pp. 6–7). Cubberley (1923) seems to take a more hierarchical view when he states, "It is primarily the function of the superintendent to think and to plan and to lead; it is primarily the function of the principal to execute plans and to follow and to support" (p. 19; see also Callahan & Button, 1964). Cubberley, however, describes various administrators' actual relationships in terms of "whole-hearted cooperative team work" (p. 21). He discusses several specific situations in which a principal and a superintendent might disagree, and in each he stresses that discussions "done at a time that is opportune, and done without bitterness and in apparent good spirit" (p. 32) will lead to the greatest chance of a satisfactory, productive outcome. Pierce (1935), reflecting on the relationship between the principal and superintendent from 1900 to 1930, confirms that the two are linked, in large measure, informally by their cooperative attitudes.

> Theoretically, the general supervisor has been, from the beginning the superior line officer of the principal; actually he has rarely exercised his prerogatives except in routine matters. . . . The data show that the principal succeeded in establishing himself as the supervisory head of his school prior to 1900, and that for two decades thereafter the district superintendent was relatively ineffective in influencing the work of principals. . . . The beginning of a scientific attitude on the part of principals and general supervisors, about 1920, gave them a common ground on which to work out co-operative procedures. (pp. 104–105)

Koos (1924) also focuses on "cooperation" (p. 116) as the attitude expected to link principals, superintendents, and boards of education if the school is "to render the high type of social service which we are coming to demand of it" (p. 115).

To Teachers

The principal of the 1920s is portrayed as having a multifaceted relationship with the teachers in her or his school. Johnson (1925) emphasizes that the principal is the "presiding officer" (p. 103) of the faculty, which should be led "in an effective yet democratic manner" (p. 103). He underscores the importance of delegating responsibilities to the faculty and supporting their development "in every possible way" (p. 87). Johnson (1925), Cubberley (1923), and Johnston and his colleagues (1922) all stress that the principal has the responsibility to organize the curriculum, to guide teachers toward effective methods, and to supervise the actual teaching process. Cubberley emphasizes that this latter activity involves the evaluation and rating of teachers. Perhaps the most apt description of principals' relations with teachers was penned by Callahan and Button (1964), who describe the system of school administration in the 1920s as "benevolent authoritarianism" (p. 85).

To Students

From students' perspective, the principal is described as "a good teacher" (Johnston et al., 1922, p. 349) who understands curriculum content, values, and skills that education should teach. Johnston and his colleagues, in the tradition of John Dewey, stress that a good principal should, by example, by the provision of opportunities, and by direct teaching, help young people become good citizens. Frederick Johnson (1925) argues that the principal should focus on teaching young people such attitudes as taking personal responsibility for their actions, respecting the property rights of others, good sportsmanship, and cleanness of speech. With respect to students, the principal is also considered to be the person within the school responsible for "discipline and control" (Cubberley, 1923, p. 265; see also Johnson, 1925).

To the Community

Within the community, the principal of the 1920s is viewed as a public servant in an important and prestigious position (Cubberley, 1923; Gist, 1926; Johnson, 1925). Johnston and his colleagues (1922) maintain that the principal is in a position to "instill in the minds of the youth of today a real appreciation and understanding" (p. 380) of democracy. They believe that principals can encourage the arousal of "a new national spirit" and the "genius of the American people" (p. 380) to ensure the ongoing success of "the basic institutions of a free, happy, and united people" (p. 380). Johnson (1925) stresses that the school is "an agency which society undertakes to secure its own perpetuation" (p. 5) and that this "places upon the principal the need of considering his relations to the community as a whole" (p. 5). He emphasizes that the principal must consider service to the community as one of the purposes of education. Gist (1926) stresses that principals should "possess a vision of a real democracy outside of the school and of a miniature republic within" (p. 160) and that they should help pupils develop as citizens and as democratic leaders. And Cubberley (1923) notes that

> Few who serve a city have such opportunities for such constructive work. Many of our cities have men and women who have served twenty-five to thirty years or more as the principal of one school building and whose work has in consequence deeply moulded the lives of a generation of the people. (p. 35)

STANDARDS FOR EVALUATION

The literature of the 1920s says little explicitly about how the principal's work is to be evaluated. Implicit in most of the writings of this era is the belief that a well-managed school that transmits solid values and well-developed social and academic skills attests to a job well done. Also implied is the assumption that principals can achieve this kind of school if their efforts are built on principles of "efficient organization, 'scientific' facts, methodological values, [and] . . . religious values" (Tyack & Hansot, 1982, p. 116). If these principles are followed, the likelihood of success is apparently considered to be so great that there is little need to establish standards against which to judge performance.

THE THIRTIES

Views of the principalship revealed by the metaphorical language in the literature of the 1930s seem to have grown naturally out of the thinking of the 1920s. In both decades, an emphasis on scientific management as a tool of effective principals is evident. In the twenties, however, this emphasis merged with a focus on the spiritual side of the educator's work. In the thirties, the spiritual emphasis is much less evident, and the conception of schooling as a business and of the principal as an executive with several key duties can be found throughout the literature (see Figure 2.2).

DOMINANT METAPHORICAL THEMES

The metaphors associated with the principalship during the 1930s suggest an increasingly entrenched view of education as a business enterprise and of principals as executives or managers. Three dominant themes emerge from our analysis of data from this period.

1. The principal's primary tasks are administrative, not instructional. She or he is considered to be an executive within the school.
2. Organization within the school and supervision of those implementing this organized plan are the key dimensions of the principal's administrative activities.
3. The principalship is becoming established as a profession separate from, but related to, teaching.

Principal as Executive

The first theme, the view of the principal as a school executive, grows logically out of the belief that education is a business and that principles

FIGURE 2.2 Analysis of Metaphors of the 1930s

Dominant Metaphorical Themes
The principal's primary tasks are administrative, not instructional.
Organization and supervision are the key dimensions of her or his work.
The principalship is becoming established as a profession apart from teaching.

Dominant Tone
Practical even to the point of becoming trivial

Dominant Values
Educational research
Principles of scientific management
Business efficiency and economy in schools

Relationship to Others
To superintendents—
  Representative
  Interpreter and administrator of policies
  Assistant
To teachers—
  Authority
  Trainer
  Supervisor
To students—
  Organizer of the learning authority

Standards for Evaluation
Comparison to surveys on issues of efficient and economical management

effective in the marketplace translate easily into the school (Callahan, 1962; Tyack & Hansot, 1982). Such beliefs are not unique to this decade. Callahan (1962) notes that numerous forces have influenced "the origin and development of the adoption of business values and practices in educational administration" (preface). He suggests that this process began about 1900 "and had reached the point by 1930, that, among other things, school administrators perceived themselves as business managers, or as they would say, 'school executives' rather than as scholars and educational philsophers" (preface). He argues that school administrators forsook traditional educational values for "the attitudes, ethics, and methods of corporate America" (Campbell et al., 1987, p. 32, commenting on Callahan, 1962). The abundant business imagery used to describe the work of principals in the thirties certainly supports Callahan's contention that the view of principal as executive is entrenched and widely accepted during this decade.

The work of George Strayer (1930), Professor of educational administration at Teachers College in New York City, provides a good example of the business imagery so common during this decade. He writes of the importance of "the professional training of school executives" (p. 376) and argues that this will result in businesslike outcomes such as standardized methods of "pupil accounting" and "introduction of 'sound business administration' in budgeting, plant planning and maintenance, and finance" (p. 378). Indeed, as Campbell and his colleagues (1987) note,

> An analysis of early twentieth-century college programs for school managers illustrates the great attention educators began to pay at that time to accounting procedures, budget preparation, all forms of record keeping, public relations, the production of annual reports, and the adoption of other managerial trappings normally associated with the corporate world. (p. 39)

Others who emphasize the business manager dimensions of the principalship include Lindquist (1933), who states that a principal should be chosen "with a view to his ability as an administrator" (p. 72), and Cox and Langfitt (1934), who write that "there is a very high correlation between the administrative competency of a principal and his personal solvency" (p. 673).

Principal as Bureaucratic Organizer and Supervisor

Two activities of the principal—organization and supervision—are heavily emphasized in the literature of this period. The overall organization of a hierarchy within the educational system is a concern of leading thinkers of this period, and organization of a hierarchy within individual schools becomes a concern of principals. Tyack and Hansot (1982) describe the first activity as "the bureaucratization of American public schooling" (p. 129) and note that "by creating hierarchically stratified and functionally differentiated school structures and by stating definite qualifications for office holding [educational theorists] hoped to design school systems in which expertise and efficiency were the governing principles" (p. 129). Dorsey (1930), Lindquist (1933), and Messinger (1939) all highlight the organizational activities of principals within schools. Dorsey states that the principal "holds the most important place" (cited in Messinger, 1939, p. 130) in the educational hierarchy. Lindquist (1933) writes that work within schools must be organized so "that interplay of the mind is facilitated, initiative is rewarded, and cooperation is encouraged" (p. 133). Messinger (1939) enumerates and prioritizes the duties of school-level executives, emphasizing that the principal must be personally organized in her or his daily activities if the school is to be well organized.

Principal as Professional

In addition to organizing within schools, principals of the thirties are also concerned with organizing as a profession. Pierce (1935) notes that the activities of a special group for principals in the National Education Association have done much to contribute to the sense that the principalship is a profession distinct from teaching. Tyack and Hansot (1982) point out that university-based educators have also contributed to the sense that principals are professionals by establishing special courses of study intended to prepare educational leaders. Interestingly, these special preparation programs, while contributing to a sense of professionalism, also reinforce the belief that the job of the principal is essentially an executive or managerial one. Newlon (1934), citing Murphy (1931), notes that the most common topics of these university preparation programs are finance; business administration; organization and administration of the curriculum and the school; and management of school records and reports.

Regardless of the forces operating to create this sense of professionalism, principals in the 1930s, according to Cayce (1931), are recognizing that they are able to function most effectively when they connect with one another. In 1931, he writes that "the past ten years have witnessed tremendous change. Today . . . principals in city, state, or nation are organizing for the professional improvement of their own work" (quoted in Messinger, 1939, p. 1).

DOMINANT TONE OF THE METAPHORS: PRACTICAL

Educational writers of the 1930s are primarily concerned with the practical dimensions of the principalship. Of special interest is "'social engineering,' a strategy of identifying practical problems and finding practical solutions empirically tested" (Tyack & Hansot, 1982, p. 153). Callahan (1962), Tyack and Hansot (1982), and Newlon (1934) all conclude that the leaders in educational administration in the 1930s focus their research efforts on practical issues such as fiscal and business administration, personnel, building and equipment management, and "similarly applied fields such as construction costs, school bonds, the single salary schedule, and techniques of child accounting" (Tyack & Hansot, 1982, pp. 153–154).

Newlon's (1934) work is especially revealing of the practical emphases of this era. His content analysis of 18 textbooks on educational administration finds that

> Over four-fifths of eight thousand pages are devoted to the purely executive, organizational, and legal aspects of administration. Almost the entire emphasis is on the "how" of administration. There is virtually no discussion of the "why," [with] little critical examination of educational and social implications of the structure and procedures. (p. 90)

Bair's (1934) doctoral dissertation (cited in Callahan, 1962) also offers evidence that preparation work for principals and other school administrators is "heavily weighted toward the financial-mechanical aspects of education" (p. 200).

Callahan (1962) suggests that this focus on practical issues of education becomes, at times, a "descent into trivia" (p. 240). He cites, for example, work by Cooper (1933) and Payne (1931), where the authors discuss scientific approaches to saving money in the purchasing of supplies such as toilet tissue, paper clips, and theme papers. Tyack and Hansot's (1982) work supports the contention that a concern with practical issues often leads principals into rather mundane activities. They cite Ayer's (1929) discussion of principals' activities, which stresses such routine behaviors as checking on mail, typing correspondence, and operating mimeograph machines.

DOMINANT VALUES

The dominant educational values of this period are related to science and business and include

1. The discovery of "truth" through research
2. The application of "truth" through scientific management
3. The realization of "truth" in objective educational outcomes

These affect the principal in that she or he is expected to embrace the first value and to engage actively in the second in order to realize the third in the school.

Discovery of "Truth" Through Research

The value placed on research during this period is discussed articulately by Tyack and Hansot (1982). They describe the work of several key figures who preach "the gospel of science" to educators (p. 145). One of these, Frank Cody, served as superintendent of the Detroit schools from 1919 to 1942. Tyack and Hansot report that, as far back as 1920, Cody argued "that research gave educators a 'method which will in time solve every problem, hold a key for every lock'" (p. 145). They suggest that, by the thirties, this kind of thinking had become widely accepted, that "educational research [had become] institutionalized" (Tyack & Hansot, 1982, p. 156) as a key part of the schooling process.

Application of "Truth" Through Scientific Management

Principals are expected to recognize the value of the research discoveries and to utilize them, as much as possible, within their schools. Strayer (1930) calls for "the application of the scientific method to the problems of administration" (p. 376). Lindquist (1933) stresses that effective principals have "faith in the teacher and in the scientific method as a growth producing way of living" (p. 133), and he maintains that this faith should motivate and guide their work.

Realization of "Truth" in Efficiency

In 1930, George Strayer celebrated the "introduction of 'sound business administration'" (p. 378) and became one of many to herald the fact that scientifically discovered management principles have resulted in "business efficiency" in education (Tyack & Hansot, 1982, p. 158). According to Campbell et al. (1982), evidence of this outcome is highly valued as educators seek to justify their activities to "business and community spokespeople [who criticize] teachers for their lack of efficiency and . . . journalists [who voice] disapproval about education inefficiency and [inquire] why massive investments in public schooling [produce] such poor educational results" (p. 33).

Both the pursuit of efficiency and various attempts to demonstrate its attainment are evident in much of the literature of this period. Cooke (1939), Cooper (1933), Newlon (1934), and Payne (1931) write of efforts to maximize the fiscal and human resources in schools. Indeed, Callahan (1962) chooses the image of a "cult" to emphasize that cost and time efficient management has become almost a religious pursuit for principals and other educational leaders.

THE PRINCIPAL'S RELATIONSHIP TO OTHERS

To Superintendents

When discussing the role of principals in relationship to the superintendents under whom they work, writers picture principals as "representative[s]," "interpreter[s] and executor[s] of . . . policies," and "assistant[s]"

(Reavis, Pierce, & Stullken, 1931, p. 12). Principals are responsible for implementing policies made by others, and they are accountable for the ways in which they do this. Both their power and their responsibilities are also, at least theoretically, determined by the superintendents. Parker (1986) notes that textbooks from the thirties and early forties (e.g., Cox & Langfitt, 1934; Koos, Hughes, Hudson, & Reavis, 1940) indicate that

> Realistically, administrative power was granted to the principal by the superintendent and the school board; and in effect, the superintendent controlled the duties of the principalship. Thus the superintendent could make of the principalship anything from its being a clerical position to its having carte blanche concerning educative influences of a school. (p. 57)

A fair amount of the clerical work engaged in by principals is evidently for the purpose of providing central office officials with evidence of efficient administration in individual schools (Pierce, 1935). Cubberley (1923) offers a number of metaphors to describe the relationship between the principal and the superintendent.

> The relationship is analogous in the business world to that of the manager of a town branch of a public utility to the general superintendent of the business; to that of the manager of a single department to the general manager of the department store; to that of the superintendent of a division of a railroad to the president of the company; or to that of the colonel of a regiment to the commanding general of an army. (p. 18)

The literature of the thirties suggests that the kinds of relationships pictured by Cubberley in the early twenties had become widely accepted a decade later.

To Teachers

The concept of the principal as the superintendent's representative in the school carries over to descriptions of the expected relationship between the principal and the teachers in the school. Military and business images are often used in picturing these relationships. Dorsey (1930, cited in Messinger, 1939, p. 130) states that the principal "holds the most important place in the whole line of educators because he receives and trains the recruits." In this context, "the recruits" refer to teachers for whom the principal is responsible. Pierce (1935) reports "the principal's right to give and enforce orders to his teachers" (p. 36) and describes the principal as the one "in authority to advise, direct, and support teachers in their work" (p. 36).

Lindquist (1933) notes that the principal is responsible for organizing the work environment for teachers, and Reavis and his colleagues (1931) and Pierce (1935) write of the expectation that the principal will supervise the work of teachers to ensure that they do an effective job.

To Students

Surprisingly, little is written about principals' relationship to either students or their families. Insights offered by Powell, Farrar, and Cohen (1985) may help to explain this void in the literature. In their chapter exploring the origins of the modern high school, they note that administrators of the 1930s, thinking of students as products of the school system, feel that the system will work efficiently if students are classified according to their potential and placed in a course of study commensurate with their abilities. Clearly, the view that education's purpose is efficient production of people who can fit into social and vocational "niches" (p. 247), and the belief that educators should sort students into tracks so that most can pass, are not conducive to principals' viewing pupils as individual people worthy of interest and involvement. (See Oakes, 1985, for a comprehensive discussion of the history and implications of tracking.)

A few writers of the thirties do obliquely mention expectations about administrators' relationships with students. Dorsey (1930, cited in Messinger, 1939, p. 130) states that the elementary principal holds "the great responsibility of educating the children in the use of the tools of all learning and in attitudes, appreciation, and habits," but he sees the principal executing this responsibility by working with and through the school hierarchy. Lindquist (1933) offers similar observations, claiming that the job of educating children will occur if the work of teachers, principals, and supervisors is organized to facilitate learning. The belief that students' needs will be met within schools that are scientifically organized and managed seems, during this decade, to have prompted educational writers to focus on ways to understand and implement management techniques rather than on needs of students or teachers.

STANDARDS FOR EVALUATION

In the 1930s, research is viewed as the activity that can provide tools for educational improvement, and educational improvement is framed in terms of sound business and fiscal management. This research and the concepts of sound management provide the standards against which the principal's work can be judged.

Tyack and Hansot (1982), Callahan (1962), and Campbell and his colleagues (1987) all note that almost all the research of this era took the form of surveys. They suggest that these surveys provided a means for the public "to compare one system with others" (Tyack & Hansot, 1982, p. 160), as well as an important avenue for assessing the work of individual principals and the quality of the profession as a whole. For example, Campbell and colleagues (1987) note that "survey reports often identified the need for more knowledgeable, better trained administrative personnel" (p. 174). Callahan (1962) reports that surveying the costs of running a school provided concrete figures against which administrators could rate their work or be rated by those to whom they were accountable. Tyack and Hansot (1982) describe a survey conducted in 1929 by Hollis Caswell. They note that "his list of questions about recommended reforms was the standard template of changes desired by administrative progressives" (p. 166), and they suggest that responses to these questions became a kind of checklist against which an administrator's work was measured. Parker (1986) stresses that rating scales and checklists were other methods for evaluating the work of educators. He cites Frederick Ford, who, in 1938, writes that "practically every educational effort should be measured" (p. 50), and notes the work of Dennis Cooke (1939), who "devised performance checklists with which to evaluate principals" (Parker, 1986, p. 53).

CONCLUSION

The metaphors of the twenties suggest that principals are expected to link their schools with spiritual and social values and with principles of scientific management. Principals are viewed in that decade as "high class professional leaders" (Burton, 1929, p. 538) whose work has "great spiritual importance" (Cubberley, 1923, p. 563) and who render "not a small local but a great national service" (p. 563). In the thirties, with the waning of interest in the spiritual side of schooling and the burgeoning fascination with and faith in business principles (Callahan, 1962; Tyack & Hansot, 1982), conceptions of the principal's role shift. Instead of being a broker of values, she or he becomes a middle manager within an educational bureaucracy (Cooper & Boyd, 1987).

CHAPTER THREE

The 1940s

The adjective *democratic* is used repeatedly in the educational literature of the 1940s to describe the expected leadership style of principals. This adjective refers both to the style of management that is considered desirable and to the American, democratic ideals that provide a kind of ethical code to guide educators. Evidently, the demands imposed by World War II, the realities of life in a post-war, "modern" world (Association for Supervision and Curriculum Development [ASCD], 1944), and the personnel management principles of Chester Barnard (1938), Elton Mayo (1933, 1945), and other human resource theorists (see Bolman & Deal, 1989) came together to influence conceptions of principals as "democratic" leaders in this decade. Figure 3.1 outlines the results of our analysis of the metaphors of the 1940s, revealing both the dominant metaphors of the decade and the beliefs and values that they convey.

DOMINANT METAPHORICAL THEMES

Four major themes can be detected in the language used to discuss administrative leadership during the 1940s.

1. During the war, the principal is viewed as the school's leader on the homefront.
2. The principal is expected to demonstrate democratic leadership so that students and teachers can lead peaceful and productive lives. This expectation is related to a belief that schools have important social purposes to fulfill.
3. In fulfilling these roles, the principal is expected to be a curriculum developer, a group leader and coordinator, and a supervisor.
4. The principal is viewed as the school's public relations representative within the community.

FIGURE 3.1   Analysis of Metaphors of the 1940s

Dominant Metaphorical Themes
During the war the principal is viewed as the school's leader on the
   homefront.
The principal is expected to demonstrate democratic leadership so that
   students and teachers can lead peaceful and productive lives.
In fulfilling the school's social roles, the principal is expected to be a
   curriculum developer, a group leader and coordinator, and a supervisor.
The principal is viewed as the school's public relations representative within
   the community.

Dominant Tone
Distinctively American with an emphasis on social issues

Dominant Values
Faith in humanity's ability to solve social problems
Commitment to equality of educational opportunity
Belief in democracy

Relationship to Others
To superintendents—
   Colleague
   Co-leader
To teachers—
   Sharer of responsibility
   Equal
   Facilitator of group leadership
To students, parents, and community—
   Co-planner

Standards for Evaluation
Wise use of resources
The degree to which principal leads democratically

Principal as Leader on the Homefront

The first theme, the expectation that the principal should be a leader in
the war effort, can be seen in much of the practical literature written for
principals. Yearbooks of the National Education Association's Department
of Elementary School Principals published during this decade contain a host
of articles dealing with topics such as "A Make-Believe Air Raid" (Millard,
1944), "Handwork Stimulated by a War Emergency" (Wramp, 1944),

"Patriotic Exercises" (Adams & Korber, 1943), and "Air-Raid Drills as Citizenship Experiences" (Limpus, 1943). The 1944 ASCD Yearbook reports that, during the early years of this decade, teachers and principals developed courses including "Rationing, Vocations for Victory, Health Services on the Home Front, the Freedoms We Defend and Seek, . . . Sharing Our Food for Victory, The Geography of Rationing, . . . Victory Gardens, The Freedoms, and Understanding Our Enemies" (p. 14), and implies that administrators are, in large measure, responsible for the effectiveness of these courses. Gregg (1943) underscores the view of the principal as a leader in the war effort.

> Never was there a time when it was more imperative that the secondary school principal have a clear conception of the purposes of his school, and more particularly of its role in a nation at war. . . . Every leader . . . has not only the professional, but also the patriotic responsibility of an all out effort to make his school function in such a way that the nation and youth of his community will be served in the most effective way. (p. 7)

His use of military terms such as "besieged" (p. 7) further reinforces the connection between the principalship and the war effort.

Principal as Democratic Leader

This military imagery is generally associated with democratic rather than authoritarian leadership, a perspective that usually meant that teachers, students, and parents should participate with principals in decision making (Giles, 1945; Koopman, Miel, & Misner, 1943; Koos, Hughes, Hudson, & Reavis, 1940; Parker, 1986). Several factors seem influential in shaping principals' leadership styles in this direction. One is the focus in business on personnel development as a wise practice (Barnard, 1938; Campbell et al., 1987). A second is the "enormous growth in size and specialization of school organization," leading to the belief that it is, "in effect, no longer advantageous for school leaders to maintain an autocratic or 'top down' style of management" (Campbell et al., 1987, pp. 52–53). Most important of all, however, is the inescapable reality of World War II. The horrors of totalitarianism and anti-Semitism and the reality of possible nuclear destruction lead educators to call for leadership that will help young people and school employees live in such a way that peace and democracy will prevail, not just in this country but throughout the world (ASCD, 1947; Campbell et al., 1987; Parker, 1986; Van Til, 1946). All of these factors combine to create a call for principals to model the underlying principles of democracy to prepare students to lead their lives in accordance with those beliefs, and to promote a high quality of living for all citizens.

This expectation of democratic leadership from principals is related to an explicit belief about the purposes of schooling—that "democratic socialization should be the unitary objective of education" (Parker, 1986, p. 59). Parker discusses the evolution of this belief, noting that Jesse Newlon's (1934) *Educational Administration as Social Policy* is an early volume calling for educational leaders to embrace the social purposes of their work. Parker notes that, in the 10 years following the publication of this influential text, a number of school administration textbook writers joined Newlon's camp, including Doughtery, Gorman, and Phillips (1936) and Koopman, Miel, and Misner (1943). Campbell and his colleagues (1987) also offer helpful insights concerning the development of the view that an explicit function of schools is to transmit important values of the larger society. They note that human relations ideas drawn from research in the social sciences and business (e.g., Mayo, 1945; Roethlisberger, 1941; Roethlisberger & Dickson, 1939) and accepted beliefs about democratic leadership in schools (e.g., Dewey, 1916, 1946; Department of Elementary School Principals, 1943) combine, in the context of war and post-war circumstances, to foster widespread interest in the social dimensions of educational leadership. A different perspective on the reconceptualization of education's dominant purpose is offered by Powell and his colleagues (1985), who note that "by 1940 . . . schools were fast approaching universal coverage, enrolling two thirds of those who were old enough to attend, roughly six and one half million students" (p. 276). The expanded enrollment, according to Powell and colleagues prompted educators to develop curricula with a distinctly social emphasis, courses that were "more human, practical," and "fun" (p. 276). These courses, promoted by educational leaders such as Charles Prosser (1939), were less demanding academically and more conducive to easy success by the masses.

The literature of the 1940s is replete with rich examples of metaphorical language used to describe the view that democratic leadership is expected of principals and that this expectation is, indeed, related to a belief in the social purposes of schooling. For example, the 1947 ASCD Yearbook opens with these words:

> Far too many people in America, both in and out of education, look upon the elementary school as a place to learn reading, writing, and arithmetic. These were the only purposes of the . . . school during the frontier days of our country. Times have changed. America is no longer a rural, frontier society. It is a highly industrialized urban society. Democracy

and the civil liberties that we have come to take for granted in this country are backed against the wall all over the world. *Education, if it is to continue to be a force for improving the lives of people, must reexamine its purposes; it must take on broader and deeper purposes aimed directly at lifting the quality of living for all kinds of people.* These objectives must be tuned to modern times and modern demands. They must meet the challenge facing our world. (p. 9; emphasis added)

Van Til (1946) discusses how these redefined purposes affect principals and other school leaders.

We in American schools, granted honourable discharges from wartime curriculums, turn back to the task of education for democratic living in a society where the power of billions of wild horses has been turned loose. . . .

We must equip young people to respect the worth of the individual, to work together for common purpose, and to apply the method of intelligence to the difficulties we face in living together, to the controlling of our material environment, and to the use of our mounting scientific and mechanical inventions and discoveries for the welfare of mankind. In short, our major function should be to help young people understand and practice the democratic way of life in a technological age. (pp. 1–2)

The writers of this decade stress that principals, by developing a democratic orientation in their administrations, can move schools toward achieving these newly defined purposes. Parker (1986) notes that

Generally, school administration textbook writers after 1940 portrayed teachers as relative equals of administrators, as necessary to execute administrative policy, and as valuable contributors to cooperative procedures which, they said, produced better plans and programs than one person alone could. (p. 60)

Harry Study (1945), writing in an ASCD Yearbook entitled *Group Planning in Education,* calls for principals to include teachers, parents, and students in planning educational experiences. Taggart and Evans (1946a) call for administrators to work primarily through faculty committees. And a 1948 Report from the National Conference of Professors of Educational Administration (NCPEA) calls for administrators to practice "reliance on the cooperative use of intelligence in the solution of problems common to the group" (cited in Graff & Street, 1957, p. 130).

Principal as Curriculum Developer, Group Coordinator, and Supervisor

Three specific dimensions of this democratic leadership dominate the literature of this decade. Principals are expected to

1. Lead in the development of a curriculum that goes beyond traditional subject matter and focuses more heavily on social issues
2. Function as group coordinators and involve students, parents, community members, and especially teachers in decision making
3. Supervise the implementation of group-directed activities

A 1944 ASCD Yearbook entitled *Toward a New Curriculum* underscores the first of these dimensions. Its authors suggest that administrators should consider incorporating programs that focus on the proper expression of emotion; health, home, and financial management; expressive arts; conservation; family relations; work habits; and community service options. Kilpatrick and Van Til (1947) stress the importance of a curriculum that meets the social needs of all students. They call for "an education in life for living" (p. 6) and argue that this will require curricula stressing "learning to do" rather than "learning about" (p. 8).

Principals in the 1940s are also expected to function as group leaders or coordinators. For example, the NCPEA's statement issued in 1949 that "the administrator is a facilitating and serving agent to the learning situation . . . when teacher and pupil come together in common education purpose" (cited in Graff & Street, 1957, p. 132) clearly emphasizes this dimension of the principal's role. Study (1945) describes a model program in Springfield, Illinois, in which "everyone is in on the plan for an extended day program" (p. 125). Parker (1986), discussing educational administration texts of this period, notes that a number of them (e.g., Cooke, 1939; Douglass, 1945; Koopman et al., 1943; Koos et al., 1940) promote the idea that "group policy-making is an essential element in democratic administration" (Koopman et al., 1943, p. 50). Finally, Campbell and colleagues (1987), commenting on the prevailing thought of this period, note that scholars "generally agreed that educational leadership should be a non-coercive and less-directive process and that teacher involvement in many aspects of school decision making should be encouraged" (p. 52).

In addition to painting a picture of the principal as a curriculum developer and a group leader, the literature of the forties emphasizes the principal's role as a supervisor, committed to ensuring that jointly made decisions are carried out. In his review of educational administration texts from this era, Parker (1986) makes an important observation about a shift in the commonly held understanding of the principal's supervisory responsibility. He notes that, by the forties, the concept of supervision had changed from an "inspectorial and state-mandated" activity to an activity focused "on the improvement of teaching and cooperatively undertaken by administrator and teacher" (p. 52). This alteration is entirely consistent with the transformation occurring simultaneously in the purposes of education. When education was considered to be a business with efficiency, economy, and the production of educated students as ends, the principal was viewed as a middle manager of the process (see Chapter 2 for a discussion of this view; see also Schlechty, 1990, for a discussion of the school-as-factory metaphor). When education is viewed as a social endeavor, with human development and the promotion of democracy as ends (the school-as-hospital metaphor; see Schlechty, 1990), the supervisory role shifts from directing and managing to facilitating and helping. Ransberger (1946) offers an extensive discussion of the educational leader as supervisor, which confirms this change. She describes the ideal supervisor/leader: "He is a friend, discovering in each individual with whom he works a personality worthy of recognition and understanding" (p. 18). Koopman and colleagues (1943), promoting the idea that supervision is a tool to help teachers, suggest that this activity should be thought of as a consultative service rather than as supervision. Others writing during this era—Gregg (1943) and Yauch (1949)—also support this conception of the principal's supervisory role.

Principal as Public Relations Representative

A final theme that emerges from an analysis of the metaphors of the 1940s is the expectation that the principal should serve as a kind of public relations representative of the school. Ransberger (1946) discusses this belief, noting that "the supervisor is the key liaison officer between the schools and the community" (p. 24). Farmer (1948) emphasizes that "the community relations of the principal cannot be neglected if he expects to carry on a successful educational program" (p. 88). And Reber (1948) stresses that the "principal of today, if he is to provide a sound educational program, must show paramount concern for a need of community understanding" (p. 73).

Generally, these authors do not conceive of the principal's public relations activity as a defense of the school. Rather, they and others (e.g., ASCD, 1947; Prall, 1944; Rogers, 1945) seem to view engagement in public relations activities as a way for principals to promote their schools' work for social progress by forging a bond between the school and the community. Campbell and his colleagues (1987) do note, however, that principals of this era needed to develop "conflict resolution skills" as they faced "conservative opposition to progressive education and to the public school emphasis on 'life adjustment' skills rather than academic content" (p. 55).

DOMINANT TONES OF THE METAPHORS

Describing the tone of the metaphors of the 1940s in a few words has proven to be an exceedingly challenging task. Nearly every adjective we considered to describe the writing of this period seemed quite general and not particularly evocative. In the end, we decided that two words—"American" and "social"—best capture the overall tone of the language used in this decade.

The "American" Tone

Three categories of metaphors led us to select our "American" label: military images, frontier images, and images that associate either schooling or school leadership with democracy. Imagery of the first type is especially prevalent in writing of the period during and immediately following the war years. The 1945 ASCD Yearbook, for example, uses military language in its discussion of organizational philosophy. The yearbook authors conclude their volume with a belief statement in which they write of school leaders' responsibility to "sustain and extend [social] gains" that "are compatible with the freedoms for which we are fighting" (p. 154). They describe educators' work in terms of "patriotic duty," and they note ways schools can be effective in the "attack on wartime problems" (p. 152). Van Til (1946) uses similar imagery in his discussion of the challenges facing educational leaders after the war. He describes "knowledge of the emerging social sciences" as "weapons" that "may yet prevail" (p. 1), and he notes that school leaders have been "granted honorable discharges from wartime curriculums" (p. 2). He also repeatedly describes the challenge facing educators as a "struggle" (e.g., pp. 2, 3). In a similar vein, with the country in the midst of war, Gregg (1943) writes of principals being "besieged" and stresses that it is "imperative" that they recognize their "patriotic responsibility" (p. 7). The 1944 ASCD Yearbook calls for schools to develop qualities needed in "the resourceful, self-controlled soldier" (p. 192).

In addition to its general association with "Americanism" and the way it reflects the impact of the war on American thought, this military language also provides an interesting metaphorical transition between the organizational ideologies of the twenties and thirties and those of the late forties and fifties. In the earlier decades (especially in the thirties), beliefs in businesslike efficiency and economy as good educational ends and in scientifically specified hierarchies as means to achieving these ends are reflected in metaphorical language associated with business and bureaucracy. In the late forties and early fifties, however, schools are viewed not primarily as businesses, but rather as institutions to promote democracy and the welfare of students, their families, other members of the local community, the state, the nation, and even the world (ASCD, 1947; Parker, 1986). Group planning with a flattening of the hierarchies of authority is emphasized in much of this literature. Military imagery nicely links these two different emphases. On the one hand, it stresses concepts of hierarchy, "duty," and developing "the resourceful, self-controlled person who respects leadership" (ASCD, 1945, p. 154), which are dominant in the writing of the thirties. On the other hand, it is related to patriotism, the promotion of democracy, and a commitment to the ideal of equality for all, concepts that are prevalent in the writing of the late forties and fifties.

Another set of metaphors that led to our characterization of the language of this decade as "American" are those that discuss educational leadership in terms of exploration and attacking new frontiers. Van Til (1946) offers one such example when he titles his discussion of post-war educational leadership "Exploring Educational Frontiers" (p. 1). He describes the process by which "educators are slowly discovering how to help young people" as "scarcely explored territory in education" (p. 15). Ransberger (1946) also writes of leadership as the challenge of "thinking of frontier areas" (p. 17). Parker (1986) calls school "the pioneer of society" (p. 39). Arndt (1945) describes a goal of educational planning as "broadening [the] horizons" (p. 116) for students and others affected by schools. And Crow and Crow (1947) write that educational leaders must "look forward to the achievement of worthy educational goals" and "set the pace for future progress" (p. 53).

The final group of "American" images are those that frame the principal's role as a promoter of democracy. Koopman and colleagues, for example, state that the purpose of their text, *Democracy in School Administration* (1943), is to help administrators "translate democracy into action" (p. v). Ransberger (1946) maintains that the ideal educational leader has "an abiding faith in the destiny of the democratic way of life" (p. 21). The 1949 ASCD Yearbook emphasizes that principals and other administrators need to use "democratic values" (p. 1) as a guide to decision making. Further, the 1948 National Conference of Professors of Educational Administration discusses ideal administrative activity as "democratic educational leadership" and notes that this kind of leadership will contribute to "the continuous improvement of our democratic society" (cited in Graff & Street, 1957, p. 130).

The Social Tone

A second set of metaphors related to and heavily intertwined with these democratic ones highlights the social purposes of schooling and the social responsibilities of school leaders. Koopman, Miel, and Misner's

(1943) administrative credo clearly expresses this social emphasis. At the end of their text, they note that administrators must consider possibilities such as

> The substitution of group control for individual control . . .
> The utilization of group reactions in administration of education . . .
> The facing of social studies . . .
> Provision for the needs of all groups simultaneously (p. 322)

The National Conference of Professors of Educational Administration issued a philosophy statement in 1949, which stresses, among other things, that "administration is the stimulating force to the process for which a social organization is created" (cited in Hagman & Schwartz, 1955, p. 303). The 1945 ASCD Yearbook notes that the school and its leaders "must carry on group enterprises directed to the continued improvement of the quality of living for the people for whom it is concerned" (p. 10). Kilpatrick and Van Til's (1947) work is representative of the thinking in this era. Arguing that "man's nature is social," they call for intercultural education "to combat and correct the evils of bias, prejudice, and discrimination" and to ensure "that all the pupils shall live well together" (pp. 4, 5).

DOMINANT VALUES

The values that undergird conceptions about education and educational leadership as presented in the literature of the 1940s are consistent with those values that permeate business, politics, and other areas of American life during this time. Three such values dominate writings about school administration.

1. Faith in humanity's ability to solve social problems
2. A commitment to equality, especially in the area of educational opportunity
3. A belief that democracy is practically and philosophically the best and most moral form of government

Faith in Humanity's Potential

Metaphorical language capturing the first of these values—faith in humanity's ability to solve problems—laces the books and articles of this period. Brubacher and colleagues, in *The Public Schools and Spiritual Values* (1944), claim that schools must recognize and promote spiritual values in order to create a better quality of life. Their arguments are predicated on the assumption that humans are capable of creating this better life. They reflect on educational and social advances and note that "man himself made his own advances . . . by using his sensitivity, his insight, and his wit" (p. 33). In a similar vein, the numerous works on the importance of "the cooperative use of intelligence" and "cooperative action" (NCPEA, 1948, p. 6; see also ASCD, 1945, 1948; Koopman et al., 1943; Koos et al., 1940) either explicitly or implicitly emphasize the faith of educators and others in humanity's ability to solve society's problems.

Education is believed to be one key that can both foster this faith in students and help them unleash this ability (Hanna, 1948; NCPEA, 1948). Educational leaders are expected to facilitate this developmental process in their schools. Caswell (1946) nicely captures this link between faith in people's potential and the expectation that leadership should tap this ability when he writes that "our best high schools have developed and have been able to improve themselves most when their professional leaders have most willingly and generally utilized democratic and educative processes and techniques of administration" (p. 255).

Commitment to Equal Educational Opportunity

The second value—the belief in the equality of all people and the concomitant belief that all need and deserve the opportunity to be educated—is especially evident in post-war literature. Caswell (1946), for example, stresses that education should be designed "to make democracy work for all men" (p. 66), and he argues that schools must be "the people's institution devoted to teaching and understanding of public issues to the mass of citizens" (p. 67). Kilpatrick and Van Til (1947), in a volume on intercultural education, write:

> An increasing number among us positively reject . . . discrimination as being fundamentally opposed to democracy, to ethics, and to any adequately sensitive religion. Our Declaration of Independence, as if to anticipate and forbid all such discriminations, declares that "all men are created equal"—not equal in body or in mind but equal in their rights before the law. (p. 2)

The authors of the 1947 ASCD Yearbook claim that some appropriate goals of post-war education involve teaching young people to

> Understand the problems of other people;
> Judge an individual by his actions, rather than the social, religious, political, national, or racial group to which he belongs;

Respect the dignity and worth of each individual;
Defend the rights of minority groups. (p. 204)

Again, principals are expected to embrace these goals and the value systems that inspire them and to see that their schools move toward offering excellent educational opportunities to all (see, for example, ASCD, 1947; Brubacher et al., 1944; Ransberger, 1946; Taggart & Evans, 1946a, 1946b).

Belief in Democracy and Morality

The final value that permeates the thinking of this decade is a commitment to democracy as the best governing system for nations, for businesses and other organizations, and for schools. Kilpatrick and Van Til (1947) describe educational goals in the following manner:

> The pupils as they grow older shall build a clear understanding of what democracy means, historically and ethically—what Jefferson and Franklin and Lincoln stood for; how democracy means respect for human personality where found; how equality of rights and of opportunity is an essential part of democracy; how America has in historic fact helped to spread democracy as an ideal through the world—and that all shall learn to accept such a democracy in very fact as the American way of life and learn to live it personally. (pp. 5–6)

The 1947 ASCD Yearbook stresses that "the child should emerge from the elementary school with a depth of ideals formed with the general framework of freedom and democracy" (p. 11). As noted in earlier sections, principals are expected not only to accept these beliefs, but to model them in their leadership style within their schools (Koopman et al., 1943; Koos et al., 1940).

THE PRINCIPAL'S RELATIONSHIP TO OTHERS

The belief in the appropriateness of democratic administration in schools deeply affects the conception of principals' relationships with superintendents, teachers, parents, students, and members of the community.

To Superintendents

Discussions of the relationship between principals and superintendents offered by Brubacher and colleagues (1944) in the Seventh Yearbook of the John Dewey Society indicate that principals and superintendents view their relationship as more collegial than hierarchical. The authors emphasize that a cooperative attitude or "spirit" between superintendents and principals will do more to ensure a successful school than a rigidly specified "structural form" (p. 206). Taggart and Evans (1946b), discussing relationships between district and school-level administrators, write:

> There should be an absence of an inflexible hierarchical system of relationships between superior and inferior officers. . . . Leadership is a shared responsibility of all staff members. . . . It operates from the bottom up rather than from the top down. (p. 109)

Corey (1945) stresses that all leaders in school situations must work together. He calls for the administrator to think of himself as "leader" rather than as "director." Study (1945), a school superintendent in Springfield, Missouri, writes of a model program in his city where he, principals, teachers, parents, and students work together to make and implement policy.

To Teachers

Wilhelms (1946), Koopman and colleagues (1943), and Koos and colleagues (1940) are among those who write specifically about principals' relationships with teachers during this era. Wilhelms (1946) notes that teachers have always, in one sense, been policy makers in schools in that they function as the "primary makers of curriculum and choosers of philosophy" (p. 121) and he suggests that principals consider the formal "institution of this casual policy-making" (p. 121). Koos and his colleagues (1940) stress that "teachers should share in the exercise of administrative control over the schools" (p. 481). Koopman and colleagues (1943) emphasize that "group policy making is an essential element in democratic administration" (p. 10). Yauch (1949) offers a strong statement of his conception of the appropriate principal–teacher relationship when he writes, "The principal and the teacher meet on equal ground . . . each having equal authority in what is proper and what is not" (p. 114). Miller (1942) also advocates teacher involvement in decision making. He cites a statement by Strayer, a former proponent of scientific management who had become a proponent of democratic leadership: "Participation by teachers is indispensable to the best development of the public schools" (p. 24).[1]

---

1. For additional evidence of this expectation, see also Campbell and colleagues' (1987) discussion of NEA publications from the 1940s: *Elementary Schools: The Frontline of Democracy, Learning the Ways of Democracy, Education and the People's Peace, Cooperation: Principles and Practices,* and *Leadership at Work.*

To Students, Parents, and the Community

Study (1945), Caswell (1946), McSwain (1945), and contributors to the 1949 ASCD Yearbook are among those who stress that principals should share control, not only with other professionals in the field, but also with students, parents, and other community members. Study (1945) describes what he believes to be a model educational program, where the prevailing attitude is that "post war planning is everybody's job" (p. 126). The 1949 Yearbook focuses on improving teaching by involving students and parents in decisions about the curriculum. In discussing the principal's role in relation to the larger school community, Campbell and colleagues (1987) note that the democratic and human relations emphases of this period lead to an increased concern with community relations and that this in turn means involving parents and other community members in school decision making.

STANDARDS FOR EVALUATION

The literature of the forties suggests that the work of principals should be evaluated according to two standards.

1. During wartime, school leaders are expected to use the available limited resources as wisely as possible.
2. During and especially after the war, they are expected to model democracy in their schools by leading and facilitating group decision making.

Principals are evaluated, at least implicitly, by the way they fulfill these expectations. Interestingly, they both focus on the product and the process of leadership and in so doing encompass both types of standards for evaluation that dominated the early decades. In the twenties, the standards were vague and basically process-oriented. Principals were doing their job if they were using the then popular principles of scientific management to link students with such noble values as truth, beauty, and right moral conduct. In the thirties, principals were doing an effective job if the school was run economically, efficiently producing products of well-educated children able to function and succeed in the world outside the classroom. Throughout the decade of the forties there is an emphasis on values—the values of equality and democracy. Principals are expected to promote these values in a number of ways. In the early part of the decade, there is a continued emphasis on economy, but it is related to survival, not to success. Schools need to contribute to the country's efforts by using the resources they have as efficiently as possible.

Use of Resources

An emphasis on effective use of resources (which in the literature can be material, natural, temporal, or human) as an evaluative standard against which principals' work will be measured fills the school administration literature of the 1940s. Walters's "Better Half a Loaf Than None" (1943), in the Twenty-Second Yearbook of the Department of Elementary School Principals, describes a model principal who leads his school in learning to make maximal use of the physical plant. Bassett and Cooper's "Teaching Pupils to Care for Public Property" (1943) in the same yearbook offers a similar ideology, stressing that effective educators will encourage and demonstrate wise stewardship of material resources. The expectation that educational leaders will be involved in wise use of resources is richly conveyed by Miel (1944), when she notes that principals are expected to promote rationing in the curriculum. Her discussion suggests that principals can, at least in part, be evaluated by the manner in which these courses are brought into the curriculum and by the response of students to them. Caswell (1946), writing about education and about those who lead educational efforts, states:

> Secondary education should be committed to teaching youth that we have adequate resources to meet the economic and social needs of all our people and that these resources must be used for this purpose. When men realize that part of their condition is due to mismanagement of natural resources and to the joint disregard for selfish interests, they will require their resources to be used wisely. (p. 68)

Fitzpatrick (1945), a principal in Boulder, Colorado, reports on a model program in which he, the teachers, and students learn to care for natural resources by instituting a school-wide cleanup day. An entire ASCD Yearbook, *Large Was Our Bounty: Natural Resources and the Schools* (1948), is devoted to how educational leaders can guide schools into an awareness of ways to promote "a wise husbanding and appropriate use of resources" (p. 146).

Promotion of Democracy

Since the central theme of much of the writing on the principalship in this decade is that democratic leadership is both ideologically correct and practically effective (see, for example, ASCD, 1945, 1948; Caswell, 1946; Koopman et al., 1943; Koos et al., 1940; Parker, 1986), it is not surprising that the wise use of time and human resources as criteria of effective leadership is, in much of the literature, related to the belief that effective principals will promote democracy and equality. Van Til (1946) is one author who emphasizes the ideological rightness of democratic stewardship, suggesting that such leadership can be seen in administrators who are aware of "the needs, problems, and tensions of the young people within whom learning is to take place" (p. 4), and who possess "a philosophy of guiding values which [will determine] purposes of learning experiences" (p. 4). He states that those outside schools can judge the work of those within by the extent to which the latter demonstrate this awareness of needs and by their philosophical commitment to meet them. Study (1945), who also agrees with the ideology of democratic leadership, indicates that principals' commitment to this concept will be evidenced by their inclusion of teachers, students, and parents in planning processes. Hanna (1948), who believes that participatory leadership is the most efficient type and that administrators can be judged by the way their schools function, writes: "Certainly the mark of a democratic school, the characteristic which best distinguishes it from other schools, is the effective use of democratic group process at all levels" (p. 19).

Discussions by Campbell and colleagues (1987) of educational administration in the 1940s also identify the assumption that a smoothly run school and democratic leadership will occur together and that evidence of either or both will testify to the principal's effectiveness. They note John Dewey's belief that democratic leadership reflects good administrative abilities. They argue that wartime culture and the post-war reality of a teacher shortage combine in the forties to forge links among democratic leadership, teacher morale, and school effectiveness. They reason that, after the war, teachers and other school employees expect to be involved in planning and that those principals who emphasize participatory decision making will be more likely to attract and retain good teachers.

CONCLUSION

In the 1920s, principals were considered to be a link among spiritual values, the "truths" of scientific management, and their schools. In the thirties, both the language and the content of educational writings suggest that the spiritual emphasis waned and that the principal came to be viewed as a business executive, a kind of manager within the school. In the forties, the principal is once again expected to link the school with values and beliefs.

This time, however, the values are less religious and otherworldly than those of the twenties and more oriented toward a democratic commitment to the worth, dignity, and equality of all the people of this world. The Seventh Yearbook of the John Dewey Society (Brubacher et al., 1944) clearly defines the kind of values principals are expected to promote. Its authors call these values "spiritual" but clarify their secular use of this term.

> The term spiritual . . . carries no explicit or necessary reference to religious or divine authority or sanction. . . . As we thus uphold the spiritual in experience, it is the good life we seek, the life good to live; and we seek it for all and as far as is humanly possible to effect it on terms of equality for all. (p. 8)

Interestingly, comments offered by Powell, Farrar, and Cohen (1985) suggest that these ostensible values may not, in fact, be reflective of the underlying ideologies of this decade. They agree that the stated educational values revolve around democracy, equality, and meeting social needs, but suggest that educators' real concern is how to efficiently and economically move masses of students through the system. Administrators' commitment to shared decision making then becomes more of a tactical response to cultural pressure than the result of deeply held values, and their embracing of socially oriented curricula is motivated by a desire to offer courses that most students can pass. Powell and his colleagues claim that the rhetoric about faith in humanity masks

> an odd combination of despair over the intellectual capacities of most young Americans and hope for the saving potential of schools . . . [and that the rhetoric in 1930s and 1940s] was full of promises about the democratic content of popular education, but also full of implied pessimism about the people's capacity for thought and for thoughtful democratic participation. (p. 279)

In stressing the paradox of hope and despair that exists in education in this era, Powell, Farrar, and Cohen suggest that much of the lofty language used in the literature of this decade masks educators' reluctance to confront the challenging task of merging genuine equality of educational opportunity with quality academic programs. This premise would certainly help explain why discussions of group planning (e.g., Corey, 1945; Study, 1945; Wilhelms, 1946; Yauch, 1949) fail to address the following questions: What happens when no consensus is reached? What happens if hostility or divisiveness derails the whole planning effort? It would also help explain the fact that many educational writers, although they speak in glowing terms about quality and equality (e.g., Cottrell, 1946; Koopman et al., 1943; Van Til, 1946), fail to address the reality that children of color, children of immigrants, and children from low socio–economic backgrounds are not being offered the same type of education as their white, middle-class, college-bound counterparts. This growing frustration over the discrepancy between rhetoric and reality sets the stage for *Brown* v. *Board of Education* (1954) and for much of the tumult that occurred in the years following that decision.

CHAPTER FOUR

The 1950s

The decade of the 1950s is one of great change in the field of educational administration (Boyan, 1963; Campbell et al., 1987; Culbertson, 1988; Griffiths, 1959, 1988; Howard, 1958; Tyack & Hansot, 1982; Woodruff, 1958). Several factors are apparently influential in propelling principals, teachers, supervisors, and academicians toward a new understanding of the role of leadership in education. Griffiths (1959, 1988) and Culbertson (1988) suggest that one factor critically important to changes in commonly held conceptions of the role of school administrators is the administrative theory movement. In their estimation, this movement, which began in the late 1940s and continues to exert considerable influence on the thinking of scholars through the 1950s, advocates that educational leaders develop and test theories in the same manner as researchers working in biology, mathematics, physics, and other scientific disciplines.

A second factor, closely related to the theory movement, that helps dramatically reshape the understanding of the principalship in the 1950s is the opening of schooling to a host of environmental issues—an openness that leads Woodruff (1958) to conclude: "The ivory tower is gone. The school and the community are now inseparable" (p. 90). For example, Tyack and Hansot (1982) and Campbell and colleagues (1987) devote considerable portions of their respective works to discussing the impact of the 1954 *Brown* v. *Board of Education* decision on the practice of educational administration. Campbell and colleagues (1987) call this decision a "watershed event" (p. 82) and suggest that it was spawned in a social and political environment that "appears to be related to, and perhaps even to have helped produce, the open-systems approach to administration" (p. 81).

Howard (1958) and Norton (1957) note a host of circumstances that influence the changing understanding of the role of education and school leaders in the 1950s. These include a proliferation of university-based administrator training courses; increased linkages between professionals from different locations and disciplines; the centralization of society and the increasingly large role played by the United States on the international scene; the rapid advance of technology; the development of more complex and more crowded schools and school systems; and a continued interest in the human relations side of business and schooling. The impact of these forces is evident in the metaphors used by educational writers in discussions of the principalship (see Figure 4.1).

DOMINANT METAPHORICAL THEMES

Our analysis of the metaphorical language in the educational literature of the 1950s suggests that the above factors lead to several beliefs and expectations about the role and work of principals during this decade.

1. The principal is expected to be a skilled administrator. In meeting this expectation, she or he is supposed to combine skills related to teaching and managing and to utilize insights and theories drawn from educational, psychological, sociological, and business research.
2. The principal is expected to defend the work of educators, answering critics of educational practices with empirical data that demonstrate the effectiveness of the practices in question.
3. A special concern of the principal is the effective and efficient use of time. This concern leads to a focus on the importance of principals' analyzing and prioritizing their tasks and delegating responsibility and work when possible.
4. The interest in efficient administration leads many writers to focus on minute (at times even trivial) details of school operation (e.g., methods for handling daily attendance slips, change of classroom procedures, effective ways to introduce a new secretary to teachers and students, and so forth; see Kyte, 1952).

Principal as Administrator

The word *administrator* is a straightforward role label. It is also, though, a word with connotative meaning that qualifies it as a metaphorical title. It is defined in the New American College Dictionary (1981) as "one who administers, executor"; *administer* is defined as "manage as an agent, conduct; superintend; make application of; supply; dispense." These definitions clearly suggest that administration usually involves carrying out the will of some person, implementing some policy, or making application of some fact, theory, or belief. The many references to the principal as administrator, when read in conjunction with the content of much of the literature in which they are found, suggest that principals of the fifties are expected to

FIGURE 4.1 Analysis of Metaphors of the 1950s

Dominant Metaphorical Themes

The principal is expected to be a skilled administrator combining practical
skills and theoretical insights.

The principal is concerned with being able to answer critics with empirical
data that demonstrate the effectiveness of the practices in question.

A special concern is the effective and efficient use of time.

The concern with efficient administration leads many writers to focus on
minute (at times even trivial) details of school operation.

Dominant Tones

Objective and academic
Detailed and specific

Dominant Values

Faith that social scientists can discover "confirmed empirical laws"
Belief in the value of theories
Commitment to objective thought
Belief in university-based preparation programs

Relationship to Others

To superintendents—
  Theoretically, colleague equal in status with different responsibility
  Practically, subordinate, responsible for management details within the
    school
To teachers—
  Theoretically, supportive, democratic, instructional leader and link between
    the classroom and the scientific study of education
  Practically, director of methodology and curricula
To nonprofessional staff—
  Theoretically, delegator and democratic leader
  Practically, person responsible for clerical and custodial activities
To parents—
  Leader who invites parents to become involved in school activities because
    of the "proven" benefits of involvement
To students—
  Friendly, personable leader, closely involved in a multitude of student-
    related activities
To the academic community—
  Person expected to link the school with the academic world, applying
    theories and discovered principles in administration and providing data to
    researchers and theorists

Standards for Evaluation

Few standards for practicing principals; success assumed if principals lead objectively and rationally according to principles emanating from universities

Beginning of call for principals to complete academic preparation programs
successfully, prior to entry into the profession

administer their schools by making application of insights derived from empirical and theoretical work being done in the field of educational administration by scholars grounded in the various behavioral science disciplines (Campbell, 1981).

The ideas that principals are expected to be administrators and that the task of administration includes studying the work of university-based scholars and applying principles derived from this work to school management can be seen in a number of pieces written during the fifties. Dunn, LeBaron, and Young (1952), for example, in their article "The Principal Pacesetter" in the Thirty-First Yearbook of the Department of Elementary School Principals, suggest that an excellent principal will be "a capable administrator" (p. 42). For these authors, capable administration means seeking ways to apply insights gained from human relations research to school management, with the goal of promoting effective teaching techniques in the context of a school that is seen as "a democratic organization" (p. 41) with "well-adjusted" (p. 41) students and teachers.

The title of Yeager's (1954) work, *Administration and the Teacher*, indicates that its author considers administration to be synonymous with educational leadership. In this work, replete with references from social science, education, and business, Yeager offers extensive discussions of the ways that theories and research reports can and should affect administrative practices. *The Elementary School Principalship* (NEA, 1958) is devoted entirely to ways school leaders might use research conducted by the NEA as "a point of departure" (Woodruff, 1958, p. 93) for developing sound theories and practices. Contributors to this yearbook focus on various areas where research can inform practice, including the organization of the school; the principal's schedule, workload, and financial status; and preparation for the principalship.

In a similar vein, Hunt and Pierce (1958), in *The Practice of School Administration*, write:

> On carrying out the central responsibility for the instruction of children and youth, the administrator utilizes cooperative effort involving a wide range of people, views the child as an individual within a social context, and *makes available through the findings of research and scientific evaluation the source materials and techniques essential to a purposeful curriculum-instructional program.* (p. v; emphasis added)

The link between effective administrative practice and a principal's awareness and use of scholarly theories and reports of empirical studies is emphasized throughout Hunt and Pierce's work. They also focus on the importance of "training on the doctorate level, apprenticeship experience, and continuous professional study" (p. 244) to develop in principals the abilities and "competencies" (p. 19) that will enable them to assess and apply administrative theory wisely.

The expectation that successful principals will consciously develop good work habits by using insights, theories, and ideas about effective administration can also be seen in the Department of Elementary School Principals' publication, *So Now You're a Principal! A Guide for the Elementary School Administrator in His Initial Principalship* (1958). The opening section of this volume, "The Principal and Principle," focuses on the idea that principals can face the challenges of their work by using "a set of professional principles . . . as guides for making specific decisions" (p. 3). The authors of this volume suggest that these principles should be based, to a great extent, on "advancement[s] of . . . knowledge" (p. 4) in education and other related disciplines, and they claim that each administrator should seek to gain "knowledge of his chosen field of work . . . [and that] the principal must acquaint himself with many other disciplines. In short, he must be a broadly educated person" (p. 5).

In her article, "Ideas for the Administrator," Elizabeth Hone (1953) focuses on the ways principals can employ learning theories to assist science teachers. Witty (1955), Durrell (1955), Dawson (1955), Carlson and Northrup (1955), and Morris (1955) take similar approaches in their discussions of the ways principals should and can use research findings to help classroom teachers offer more effective instruction in reading. Witty (1955) writes of what he considers to be a model "developmental reading program" (p. 13), and Durrell (1955) offers suggestions to principals about ways to interpret the results of research reports on reading readiness. Dawson (1955), Carlson and Northrup (1955), and Morris (1955) review research on ability grouping and suggest ways these results might guide class organization strategies and the selection of effective materials.

Huggett's (1950) comments on the value of research to educational leaders who are seeking to develop effective hiring practices provide still another example of the importance placed on research and related theory in this decade. In a chapter called "Acquiring an Efficient Staff," Huggett methodically examines issues related to hiring and supervising teachers and other staff and offers several suggestions, based on research, for predicting the success of prospective employees. For example, he advises principals that

> Studies show little correlation between academic marks and success in teaching. These statistical reviews thus agree closely with the experiences of most administrators. College marks seem to mean very little in the prediction of teaching success. Reports on student teaching and other

activities with children do, though, have considerable predictive value. (p. 80)

Huggett also recommends a scientific approach for evaluating interviews with teacher candidates. He notes that administrators often instinctively rate prospective employees and suggests that they consider using a "rating scale" (p. 83) in order to systematize and objectify the process.

Principal as Defender of Educational Practice

A challenge that apparently affects conceptions of the principal's role in the fifties is an increasing amount of criticism of instructional and administrative strategies. Principals of this decade seem to feel compelled to answer these criticisms with empirical data that support their actions and those of the teachers they lead. This challenge and response can be seen in the writings of practitioners and educational theorists who discuss ways principals can respond effectively to actual or potential critics.

One example of the expectation that principals should use research to defend their actions—or lack thereof—can be found in the discussion of "The Principal's Average Workweek," authored by the NEA Research Division (1958). The authors of this report conducted extensive survey research in an effort to ascertain the average amounts of time principals allocated to certain tasks. They contrast these results with principals' preferred time allotments and conclude that the "chief hindrance" to principals' ability to engage in supervision of teachers is "the lack of clerical help" (p. 104). They propose that school-level administrators make boards of education aware of the demands on principals' time and of the factors that help and hinder leaders in meeting their many obligations.

Zirbes (1952) also stresses the importance of principals' being aware of and using evidence from research to promote and defend new methods of teaching. Describing the principal's job as "explaining progress" (p. 30) and "demonstrating [the] values of modern practice . . . analytically and objectively" (p. 32) by the "presentation of various types of data" (p. 30), she calls on principals to keep abreast of the many insights and theories coming from the academic world. Indeed, Zirbes believes that an awareness of the ideas coming from the science of education is essential for successful leadership.

> The days in which a principal's job was simply the smooth running of a school are gone. The very basis for school policies and practices must be reconsidered in the light of professional advances, and principals must keep abreast. The lagging principal can neither lead teachers nor develop esprit de corps for forward adjustments and inservice growth. (p. 35)

Additionally, Zirbes argues that research can help principals in their task of managing the ever-expanding connections between the school and its larger environment, including representing the school in the community. Stressing the value of "impersonal" data in convincing the public of the value of administrative practices and teaching methods, she writes:

> Public understanding needs to be developed by reference to comparisons in which new values are made explicit. Comparisons should emphasize modern concern for developmental guidance, consideration of individual differences, individual needs, and individual progress at individual rates. The old round-the-class recitation with its place-keeping and turn-taking is still held in high esteem by persons who have never stopped to analyze its deficiencies and its ineffectiveness in comparison with modern procedures in which every pupil actually does more and learns more. (p. 29)

Carr (1957) also believes that educational leadership should be aware of the newest research advances in the fields of teaching, learning, and administration. He agrees with Zirbes that this knowledge can be used by principals and others both to educate the public and to answer criticism when it does occur. He writes:

> It is the duty of educational leadership not only to elicit public opinion but also to enlighten it. And the corollary is that the leader must himself be objective, a competent master of the relevant evidence, and completely honest in his endeavor to see that on school problems all the people have all the facts all the time. (p. 8)

Principal as Efficient Manager of Time

A special area of concern in the educational administration literature of the fifties is the efficient use of the principal's time. Many writers who deal with this issue focus on the importance of the principal's delegating work and responsibilities to teachers or to other members of the school staff. A vivid example of the concerns over time management and effective delegation methods is contained in the 1954 Yearbook of the Department of Elementary School Principals, *Time for the Job*. The preface in this volume notes that "many principals have indicated grave concern about 'lack of time for the job'" and suggests that the development of several competencies will enable the principal to "tackle [this] problem." These include analyzing "his job and his way of working on the job"; learning to practice "good planning and organization, through delegating responsibilities"; "getting adequate clerical help"; "recognizing that efficiency in handling the jobs that must be cared for saves time [and that] inefficiency wastes it"; and identifying "the areas which job studies show are time-consuming areas for principals [and seeking to] . . . improve [their] ability to work effectively in these areas."

This volume opens with a report of time studies conducted on a sample of 25 elementary school principals (Lewis, Grant, King, Reynolds, & Robinson, 1954). The authors of this report suggest that the data they collected can

1. be the basis for principals to consider . . . the possibilities for delegating or sharing activities related to the principalship . . .
2. . . . provide a factual basis for helping the board of education, parents, and other interested persons understand the specific nature of the principal's job . . .
3. . . . provide a factual basis for demonstrating the need for clerical help, the need for an assistant principal. (p. 19)

The remaining articles in this volume (Department of Elementary School Principals, 1954) attend to the ways a principal might use this information "to organize his many tasks so that he will find time to do them all efficiently" (p. 94), thus reinforcing the fact that time management is a chief concern of principals of this decade.

Yeager (1954) similarly supports the ideas that principals should use their time efficiently and that an awareness of management and organizational principles or theories is important for effective time management. In *Administration and the Teacher*, he focuses primarily on the "guiding principles" (p. 419) that should govern administrators' interactions with teachers. These principles involve such administrative concerns as "salary schedule making" (p. 365), "group action" (p. 419) of the faculty, and "accepted limitations of freedom in teaching" (p. 444). Although Yeager discusses the ways these principles might influence an administrator's action in rather general terms, he also offers some specific thoughts about the ways that they might affect the principal's time management. For instance, in his discussion on group action, he offers a number of specific suggestions of administrative responsibilities that might be delegated to teachers. For example,

(1) homeroom activities, (2) assembly programs and use of auditorium, (3) club activities, (4) health and physical education policies and activities, (5) student council, (6) commencement, (7) dramatics, (8) school publications, and (9) noon-hour supervision. (p. 423)

Yeager sees two benefits to this delegation of responsibilities: It is consistent with beliefs in the value of shared decision making, beliefs that continue to be popular in this decade (see Chapter 3); and it will enable principals to concentrate their time and attention on activities and decisions that they alone should handle.

The Department of Elementary School Principals' (1958) guidebook for beginning principals also underscores the belief that efficient time management (which includes shared or delegated responsibility) is a central feature of effective administration. This book explores 17 areas of concern for principals (e.g., supervision of the clerical and janitorial staff, maintenance and management of school records and reports, handling discipline problems, hiring and supervising substitute teachers, and so forth). In their discussion of techniques for successfully handling these various areas, the contributors to this volume offer numerous suggestions for resourceful use of time. For instance, in discussing the opening day of school, the authors suggest that principals delegate their usual responsibilities so that they are "free to observe how the opening of school is proceeding, and . . . available to cope with emergencies" (p. 12). When discussing communication within the school, the contributors very specifically note the importance of a definite schedule to aid principals and other personnel in efficiently handling teachers' bulletins.

> It is helpful to set up a regular schedule for handling the bulletin. For example, all items to be included in the bulletin on Wednesday must be in the office by 4 p.m. on Tuesday. The bulletin is typed, run off, and copies placed in the teachers' boxes the following morning. Community announcements can be geared to such a schedule. (p. 15)

Furthermore, contributors to the section devoted to the handling of records emphasize that the two central considerations for developing a system in this area are "requirements of the school system and the *amount of time*" (p. 25, emphasis in original) school personnel can devote to this task.

Principal as Overseer of Minute Details

In addition to exploring time management, much of the discussion in the educational literature of the fifties focuses on ways principals can apply educational theories and principles to quite minute issues of school management. Kyte (1952), for example, develops his administrative principles, in large measure, from

> research studies in the principalship and in supervision conducted by principals and others enrolled in the author's graduate research seminars

    . . . and intensive study and critical integration by graduate students and by the author of the published literature and unpublished research studies dealing with the work of the school principal. (p. *iv*)

One might expect these data to yield insights with far-reaching implications. Kyte, however, applies these principles in highly specific ways. He opens his work by offering three sets of theoretical statements about administration under the headings: "Principles of Organization Affecting the Principal" (p. 4), "Principles of Operation Affecting the Principal" (p. 6), and "The Functions of the Principal" (p. 11). He then discusses the application of these theories in great detail. For example, in discussing ways school administrators might use these principles of organization and operation in their supervision of the custodian, Kyte goes so far as to give specific statements that, in his opinion, should be used to introduce the custodian to the children. In a chapter devoted to "Routine Duties of Teachers" (pp. 190–204), he looks at likely topics of teachers' lunchtime discussions and suggests that principals structure the lunch period so that the conversations "take on a friendly aspect which improves the whole 'tone' of the school" (p. 197). Furthermore, in a section on the school library, he suggests not only the numbers and categories of books that should be included, but also the specific periodicals to which the school should subscribe.

    The high level of detail in Kyte's book is interesting when viewed in conjunction with his scholarly presentation of principles and theoretical discussions of the principal's functions. It vividly depicts the widely divergent nature of the metaphors used in the 1950s to describe principals and their work. Kyte, like numerous other authors of this decade, pays homage to the academic, scientific study of administration, stressing the importance of educational theory. Furthermore, he emphasizes that scholarly principles should guide leaders as they fulfill their professional responsibilities. The bulk of his book, though, belies this interest in theory, for most of his attention is focused on detailed, minute, and often mundane details of school management.

    An article by Marshall Jameson, a principal in Grosse Pointe, Michigan (1957), provides another example of the interest in detailed application of general concepts of administration. He focuses on ways principals can encourage the talents and creative abilities "of custodians, engineers, clerks, and secretaries" (p. 58). Like Kyte (1952), Jameson begins his article with a general statement about the importance of "including custodial and clerical staff in policy determination, decision making, and planning and operational responsibility" (p. 58). He then becomes quite specific in discussing how principals might apply this democratic philosophy. For instance, he suggests that principals seek to include nonprofessional staff on committees dealing with issues such as the "room mother's tea" and "outdoor flag

ceremonies" (p. 59). Jameson also recommends that the custodial and clerical staff be included in faculty meetings, which "always begin with a coffee
and chat session, allowing the staff to become better acquainted" (p. 58),
for, in his view, these sessions help "to maintain a harmonious blending of
. . . efforts and [help all involved] to reap the benefit of total group consideration" (p. 58).

Woodruff (1958) also moves rather abruptly from a broad discussion of
general principles of school administration to very detailed suggestions
regarding the application of these principles. In her article on the principal's
encouragement of parent participation, she offers a number of theoretical
statements on such topics as factors to be considered in promoting parental
involvement; the line "between lay and professional services" (p. 22); and
values underlying the call for parents to join with principals and teachers on
a number of projects. In the midst of this theoretical discussion, however,
Woodruff offers a list of 12 specific activities in which parents might assist
(e.g., "serving on a curriculum committee of teachers and parents"; "setting
up a card catalog system in the school library" [p. 24]). Like a number of
other writings of the fifties, Woodruff's discussion of principals' administrative concerns demonstrates that educational leaders in this decade, although
concerned with the theoretical basis for promoting instructional excellence,
are primarily concerned with small, even trivial, details of school management.

We were intrigued by the way an emphasis on principals' developing an
intellectually sound basis for their professional actions appeared side by side
in the literature of the fifties with the recommendations that principals
oversee "coffee and chat sessions[s]" (Jameson, 1957, p. 58); the management of filmstrips that include "How To Be a Good Patrol Boy" (Graves,
1956, p. 146) and "We Eat in the Cafeteria" (Fenske, 1956, p. 155); and
the format for a farewell party given by "the low-sixth-grade pupils . . .
[for] the graduating group" (Kyte, 1952, p. 248). We sought for ways to
reconcile these seemingly inconsistent approaches. Certainly one possible
explanation is that the interest in the 1930s in principals' involvement with
the trivial details of school management (Callahan, 1962; Cooper, 1933;
Messinger, 1939; Newlon, 1934, Payne, 1931) waned during the war and
immediate post-war period only to resurface during the relatively calm
Eisenhower years. Another explanation, though, is that during this decade
principals are seeking to face the demands of a profession that must deal
with the complexity of a "changing mode of life" (Hugget, 1950, p. 1);
"unparalleled . . . opportunity for professional growth" (Howard, 1958,
p. 1); "recent studies of child development and learning . . . [leading to]
newer approaches to teaching, learning, and developmental guidance"
(Zirbes, 1952, p. 28); and the knowledge that the future for which schools

prepare children is both "unknown and unpredictable" (Bain, 1952, p. 16). It is possible that principals, facing all of these challenges and finding their roles and practices increasingly analyzed and often directed by government officials and university theorists, seek to maintain some sense of normalcy by focusing on small details that give them a sense of stability in a decade whose "most dramatic characteristic . . . is the rapidity with which changes are taking place" (Howard, 1958, p. 3). A third explanation is that the authors are beginning to pick up some of the changes embedded in the incipient theory movement, if only superficially. While they are able to employ the grand principles of a discipline-based approach to school leadership, they are unable to show clearly how administrative practice might look different. Thus they are content simply to include the ideology of the emerging theory movement within the prescriptions of an earlier era, even when the two areas make strange bedfellows. This phenomenon may represent the root of the theory–practice gap that has characterized educational administration for the last 40 years.

DOMINANT TONES OF THE METAPHORS

Choosing words to describe the tone of the metaphors of the 1950s posed a challenge for us, since the expectations about the role and work of principals in this decade actually drive the profession in different directions. On the one hand, principals are beginning to be viewed as professional administrators who lead their schools according to data and theories emanating from universities and research centers. On the other hand, they are simultaneously pictured as overseers of minute details of school management. We finally decided to use four words to describe the tone of the metaphors in this decade—"objective," "academic," "detailed," and "specific." The first two adjectives describe one dimension of the tone of the fifties, for many of the writers (e.g., Griffiths, 1959; Huggett, 1950; Hunt & Pierce, 1958; Zirbes, 1952) emphasize that principals who lead their schools according to concepts from the academic world will be making decisions from an objective, impersonal vantage point. The other two adjectives reflect the fact that many of the concerns of the principals are with very small details of administering schools—the practice dimension of the role.

The Objective, Academic Tone

Both the language and the content found in Griffiths's seminal *Administrative Theory* (1959) demonstrate the objective, academic tone of this decade. In his preface, for example, the author writes:

The study of administration is now in its most fruitful period to date and this is particularly true in educational administration. Observers have commented that the content of educational administration has in the past been comprised of folklore, testimonials of reputedly successful administrations, and the speculations of college professors. Heretofore, it has been impossible to characterize the field of educational administration as being concerned with explanatory theory, with the creation of testable hypotheses, or with research-based conclusions. Changes in this diagnosis are still not general, but the prognosis is now good. . . . Whereas educational administration was once a laggard in the theoretical sense, it is now leading the way as all of education seeks a theoretical basis for its activities. (p. *v*)

Griffiths first offers a conceptual framework for understanding theories in general. He then presents his theory that decision making is at the heart of administration and that "the specific function of administration is to regulate the decision-making process in the most effective manner possible" (p. 73). The tone of Griffiths' writing reveals much about commonly held views of administration and administrators during the 1950s. He writes about the work of administration in an objective, impersonal, and analytical manner, carefully defining terms such as *theory*, *decision making*, and *organization* and using ideas of Homans (1950), Simon (1950), and others to break down administrative decision making into mathematical formulas.

Academic metaphors can also be found in Snyder's (1957) chapter on "Leadership in Staff Relationships" in the Thirty-Sixth Yearbook of the Department of Elementary School Principals, where he describes the principal as "the key person from whom all phases of a school program logically develop" (p. 53). Snyder then discusses the professional training and the qualities needed by principals, using "scientific" terminology taken from the theories of Anderson and Davies (1956) and McClure (1956). Furthermore, he recommends that principals demonstrate to the teaching staff, the Board of Education, and the public that they are administering their school from "a tested position . . . [which will involve] continuous evaluation and planning" (p. 55).

Another example of the academic tone of the language of this decade can be found in the work of Hanley and Schiesser (1953). These authors, writing specifically about the role of the principal in the school's science program, emphasize that educational leaders must think "scientifically" (p. 18) and must promote such thinking in their schools. Hanley and Schiesser equate thinking scientifically with thinking "clearly" (p. 18) and "sound[ly]" (p. 18). They state, "It is vital that a scientific attitude pervade all instruction in all subjects if we are to train thinking citizens who will be a credit to a democracy" (p. 18), and they imply that such an attitude must begin with school leaders who open themselves to learning from research conducted by academicians.

Zirbes's (1952) work also shows the academic/scientific tone of the images associated with the principalship during this decade. In her view, good school leaders remain abreast of and use the newest discoveries and insights from social science in their administration.

> Leadership in a given school should not wait for attack and then proceed defensively. . . . In an undefensive, uncontroversial approach, . . . evidence [i.e., the findings of social science] should be cited and discussed with parent [and other] groups. Principals can be expected to do this more objectively than classroom teachers. (p. 30)

Throughout her article, Zirbes emphasizes the importance of principals' being scientific in their leadership, contrasting a scientific, objective approach with an emotional, defensive one. In her view, the former approach is the only one adequate to meet the challenges facing educators and education in the fifties. She writes, "Principals and classroom teachers who are working together to clarify and demonstrate values of modern practice will . . . proceed . . . analytically and objectively" (p. 32), and she stresses that evaluative studies that produce data comparing the results of various teaching and organization methodologies must be conducted by those taking this analytical approach.

The Practice of School Administration (Hunt & Pierce, 1958) also contains a number of statements that demonstrate that principals of this decade are expected to administer their schools according to the tenets of social science and to use the methods of science in analyzing and solving problems. Hunt and Pierce open their work with these words:

> If the school administrator is to achieve success in guiding the growth of children in the current American social and education setting, he must be an individual who is not content to work in conventional, expedient, or naive ways. He must, on the contrary, be a student of and work consistently through basic educational and administrative principles. He must furthermore utilize his leadership in inculcating in his staff the same professional ideals and practice.
>
> Administrators too frequently depend on experience, descriptions of practices, or the following of particular patterns for solving problems that develop suddenly or difficulties that they encounter in the course of their work. They should strive to sense problems in advance and through the

use of principles develop and carry through appropriate procedures for their solution. These principles should be discovered through analysis and interpretation of functional relations. . . .

By thus utilizing his training in the same way that case data are used for developing principles to guide practice in medicine and law, the superintendent or principal acquires true administrative orientation. He uses the ways of science to achieve systematic, successful administration. (p. 15)

Citing various examples of research, these authors explore ways principals can, in fact, apply academically sound, scientific procedures to their administrative efforts.

The Detailed, Specific Tone

As noted earlier, the academic metaphors of this decade tend to occur alongside language stressing very ordinary, mundane conceptions of the principalship. The Thirty-First Yearbook of the Department of Elementary School Principals contains a number of examples of this. The yearbook opens with articles by Bain (1952), Story (1952), and Harding (1952) that discuss the philosophical and theoretical foundations for effective school leadership. Bain's article, for example, presents a number of principles of modern school management that are based on "the scientific findings on child growth and development" (p. 17), and Story reflects on research done by Raths that delineates eight "needs of children" (p. 19) which schools must strive to meet.

The next section of this yearbook deals with the principal's role in leading according to the latest "scientific findings" (p. 17) and theories. The authors writing in this section (e.g., Dunn, LeBaron, & Young, 1952; Henderson, 1952; Hunt, 1952; Scott, 1952; Zirbes, 1952) frequently use very commonplace images and examples in their discussion of the ideal principal. For instance, Dunn, LeBaron, and Young (1952) suggest that an effective principal will be "a capable administrator and supervisor" (p. 42) and an exemplar of "democratic fellowship" (p. 43). They then offer rather specific suggestions for ways a principal might fulfill these roles. These include focusing on the custodial staff and finding time "to serve a few groups like the Boy Scouts, Girl Scouts, 4–H clubs, Red Cross, church organizations, and service clubs" (pp. 43–44).

Hunt (1952) concentrates on ways administrators can help to develop a "spirit of happiness and friendliness" (p. 52) in schools. Like Dunn and his colleagues, she describes very specific actions that the principal should take, including such things as having an "office door . . . always open to both teacher and child" (p. 55) and conducting "frequent group meetings" (p. 54) in which the principal often "abdicates his position as leader" (p. 54). Scott (1952) also becomes quite detailed in his discussion of the principal's "leadership in studying behavior problems" (p. 56). He offers three specific techniques to help the principal lead teachers in this area: the use of a "motion picture presenting the problem" (p. 57) of some child in the school; the playing of records and tape recordings that audibly portray "the turmoil" (p. 58) that might occur if a teacher is not completely in control of a class; and the use of "role playing" in which "teachers [re-enact a] . . . classroom situation" (p. 59) in an effort to better understand all perspectives and to discover new ways of dealing with problems.

Yeager (1954) also offers discussions that take on a rather mundane tone at times. For instance, in a chapter concerned with communication between principals and teachers, he goes into great detail about administrative bulletins, even discussing colors of paper that might be used. He describes—in detail—things that principals might need to know regarding teachers' health status.

> The principal defects . . . are (1) heart conditions, (2) glandular condition, (3) overweight, (4) tuberculosis, and (5) genital-urinary disease. About one teacher in three uses eyeglasses part or all of the time. This should not be classed as a disorder, but undoubtedly is an occupational hazard. Teachers generally give attention to the condition of their teeth. (p. 329)

Maintaining that principals should work to promote health, he suggests ways leaders might respond to these varied physical ailments in faculty members.

Perhaps the clearest example of the expectation that principals should be concerned with minute and specific issues can be found in Kyte's *The Principal at Work* (1952), which is replete with very detailed discussions of how principals should conduct their work. One especially revealing passage is the section devoted to the organization and furnishing of the principal's office.

> The principal's office should contain a flat topped desk, swivel chair, several other chairs, table, bookcase, and wastebasket. If the desk does not contain a drawer usable for filing purposes, the principal should have a personal file. On or near his desk should be a telephone, a calendar, and a map of the school district or community. Desk pad, blotter, two letter trays, daily calendar pad, ink or pen stand, dictionary, and directories are needed desk equipment. (p. 188)

DOMINANT VALUES

The dominant educational values of the 1950s are clearly related to the widely held belief that the academic study of educational administration can supply insights to guide principals toward excellence in their work. These values include

1. Faith that social scientists, by engaging in deductive research, can discover "confirmed empirical laws" (Culbertson, 1988, p. 22) about teaching methods and educational administration and a strong belief in the value of theories to generate hypotheses and to explain research conclusions
2. Commitment to objective thought as that most able to guide the work of principals effectively
3. Belief that university-based preparation programs are needed to help principals understand social science processes and learn to think objectively

Faith in Scientifically Based Theories

Griffiths' (1959) work underscores the fact that this decade witnessed an increasing amount of faith that social science could discover sound administrative theories through deductive research. He states that textbooks by Hagman and Schwartz (1955), Griffiths (1956), Sargent and Belisle (1955), and Campbell and Gregg (1957) are all "characterized by a search for the substance of administration and for the theory which binds this substance together" (p. 2), a search that is especially evident in educational administration after 1950. Boyan (1963), Griffiths (1959), Gregg (1960, 1969), Moore (1964), Farquhar (1977), and Goldhammer (1983) all discuss a number of events that, in their view, help to turn the interest of scholars and practitioners to the science of education during the 1950s. These include the work of the National Conference of Professors of Educational Administration (NCPEA), founded in 1947; the development of the Cooperative Program in Educational Administration (CPEA) under the sponsorship of the W. K. Kellogg Foundation in 1950; the foundation of the Committee for the Advancement of School Administration (CASA) in 1955; and the formation of the University Council of Educational Administration in 1956.

In a 1982 paper, Griffiths offers a more personal statement on factors that influenced his own thinking in the 1950s, emphasizing the value placed during this decade on the scientific study of administration.

I taught physical science from a historical case approach at Colgate, was thoroughly disgusted with what passed for research and serious thought in educational administration, and was influenced by a number of social scientists trained in the logical positivist mode. . . . It seemed to me that the logical positivist approach was the proper antidote for self-serving testimonials, the pseudotheories . . . and the plain nonsense that constituted the field of educational administration. (pp. 3–4)

In an article entitled "A Century's Quest for a Knowledge Base" (1988), Culbertson also notes that the decade of the fifties saw a "leap toward an administrative science" (p. 14) in education. He cites works by several scholars (e.g., Getzels, 1952; Griffiths, 1959; Halpin, 1957) as being especially influential in promoting the values of theory making and scientific study in education. For example, he quotes Getzels (1952) as follows:

Systematic research requires the mediation of theory—theory that will give meaning and order to observations already made and that will specify areas where observations still need to be made. It is here that we would place the root of the difficulty in administration: there is a dearth of theory-making. (p. 235, cited in Culbertson, 1988, p. 15)

Culbertson notes that this emphasis "stimulated much inquiry as it made its way into classrooms, conference textbooks, and dissertations" (p. 15).

Culbertson also identifies several key ideas "at the heart of the theory movement" (p. 16).

[1.] Effective research had its origins in theory and [was] guided by theory. . . . Only by developing and using theory in research could the field move beyond its state of poverty;
[2.] Hypothetico-deductive systems [were] the best exemplars of theory . . .;
[3.] The social sciences [were] essential to theory development and training. . . . Social science theories [could] and should be used to develop in administrators needed understandings of organizations and society. (pp. 16–17)

Commitment to Objective Thought

The emphasis on the value of objective, rational thought in school administration is clearly related to one of the premises of social science in the 1950s, that is, that objectivity should characterize the research strategies, the decision-making methods, and the language of educational administration. For example, Campbell and his fellow authors (1987) comment on the focus of educational science following World War II, noting a resurgence of interest in Weber's study of organizations as rational bureaucracies. They state that, beginning in the late forties, many of the scholars approached their study with the assumption that "equality and justice for all would be preserved, at least in public institutions, by bureaucratic officials who would act objectively in discharging their duties. Bureaucratic rules . . . would ensure . . . impersonal social behavior" (p. 71). Campbell and colleagues further state that even those scholars who did not fully accept Weber's premises still approached the study of administration rationally, "viewing [Weber's] model in light of changing contextual factors, . . . seeking greater clarification and refinement of his ideas, and . . . searching for exceptions to the rules of administrative conduct he defined" (p. 72).

Griffiths' (1959) discussion of his theory of administrative decision making also exemplifies the emphasis on rationality and objectivity of this decade. As noted earlier, he offers a set of rational propositions about the decision-making process. He breaks the process down into six clearly defined steps and, using the work of Tannenbaum (1950), objectively lists "six limits on decision-making . . . : definition of purpose, criterion of rationality, conditions of employment, lines of formal authority, relevant information provided, and time limits" (p. 109). Griffiths' approach, especially his choice of words (e.g., "criterion of rationality, . . . lines of formal authority" [p. 109], "testable propositions . . . which can be derived from the assumptions and concepts of theory" [p. 88], and "structure . . . which makes possible the prediction of future interaction as regards the decision" [p. 108]), testifies to the value placed on objectivity in this decade and supports Culbertson's (1964) claim that "the core values of the [theory] movement were scientific" (p. 308).

Articles by Blough (1953) and Webb (1953) also show the high value placed on objective, rational thought in educational administration in the 1950s. Blough describes the importance of a well-developed science program in schools, stating that an important goal of such a program is

> to help pupils grow in what we commonly call a scientific attitude . . .
> [and to ensure that students] will be much more likely to be open-minded,
> to hold conclusions tentative until there is convincing proof; [to] be more
> inclined to challenge sources of information, more likely to act intelli-
> gently on the basis of available evidence, less superstitious and prejudiced,
> and more observing and curious. (p. 4)

Blough explicitly states that the attainment of these goals "depends largely on the will, the way, and the willingness of elementary school principals"

(p. 10). Webb (1953) reinforces Blough's statements, noting that principals should support the teaching of science in schools in order "to guide emotional responses [of teachers and students] away from the highly subjective and toward the objective—as background for future sensible attitudes and desirable behavior" (p. 22). Furthermore, Culbertson (1988), discussing the importance placed on objectivity during the 1950s, states that this decade witnessed the separation of the "'is' from the 'ought,' clos[ing] the door, in theory at least, upon a 75-year history of advocacy practiced by Payne, Harris, Cubberley, Strayer, Moehlman, and many others" (p. 16).

Belief in Academic Preparation Programs

A final value evident in the literature of the fifties is faith that scientifically developed academic programs can teach principals most of the skills needed for scientific administration of schools. Hunt and Pierce (1958), for example, emphasize the importance of training to prepare principals for effective leadership.

> If the school administrator is to achieve success in guiding the growth of children in the current American social and education setting he must . . . be a student of and work consistently through basic educational and administrative principles. . . .
>
> Administrators too frequently depend on experience, descriptions or practices, or the following of particular patterns for solving problems that develop suddenly or difficulties that they encounter in the course of their work. They should strive to sense problems in advance and through the use of principles develop and carry through appropriate procedures for their solution. These principles should be discovered through analysis and interpretation of functional relations. New problems will occur that have no counterpart in previous experiences; whether they will be met with guesses or intuitions or with procedures indicated by principles is a mark of the professional training and effectiveness of the school administrator.
>
> By thus utilizing his training in the same way that some case data are used for developing principles to guide practice in medicine and law, the superintendent or principal acquires true administrative orientation. He uses the ways of science to achieve systematic successful administration orientation. (p. 15)

A 1961 volume published by the Department of Elementary School Principals also emphasizes the academic training of principals. The contributors to this volume report on the results of regional and national meetings sponsored by the Department in the 1950s to "discover and improve procedures for finding and preparing those who will provide the kind of educational leadership so urgently needed" (p. 7). Those involved in these meetings, although they decried the condition of most preparation programs, did not deny the importance of administrative training. Indeed, they expressed great faith in the potential of programs to promote

> deliberate recruitment of able and interested men and women, . . . experimentation to develop improved preservice preparation for principals in colleges and universities, [and] . . . continuous inservice development of principals in school systems, colleges and universities. (p. 10)

Culbertson (1988) also notes the high value placed on the development of professional preparation programs that emphasize "theory development and . . . the building of a 'science of administration'" (p. 16). He refers specifically to the results of a 1954 meeting of the National Conference of Professors of Educational Administration and a 1957 seminar sponsored by the University of Chicago and the University Council for Educational Administration, noting that scholars attending both meetings (e.g., Griffiths, Halpin, and Thompson) called for university-based research and preparation programs that stressed "precisely defined concepts of science, . . . quantitative emphases, and . . . a theoretical orientation" (p. 17).

THE PRINCIPAL'S RELATIONSHIP TO OTHERS

The metaphors of the fifties reveal that school leaders are expected to function both as scholars and as managers responsible for detailed processes and interactions within schools and school systems. An analysis of the credentials of the various authors of this period and of the number of pages they devote to theoretical and practical concerns suggests two facts. First, the emphasis on scientific scholarship; objective, rational thought; and theory-driven leadership emanate, for the most part, from university settings. When practitioners discuss the principalship they frequently pay lip service to theories in brief portions of their works and then turn their attention to the small, specific details of school management. Second, despite calls issued by Anderson and Lonsdale (1957), Campbell (1957), Gregg (1957), Griffiths (1957, 1959), Halpin (1957), Norton (1957), and others for a theoretical approach to administration, in reality, the day-to-day details of schools are the chief concern of principals of the fifties. The dichotomy between conceptions of leadership espoused by theoreticians and those embedded in the activities of practitioners can be seen clearly in discussions of the principals' relationships with superintendents and other administrators, teachers, and nonprofessional staff members.

To Superintendents

In explicit discussions of principals' relationships with superintendents and boards, writers such as Kyte (1952), Hunt and Pierce (1958), and Shields (1955) often speak of principals, superintendents, and board members as being equal in status but different in their spheres of responsibility, implying that these administrators are colleagues in the task of school management. This view of the nonhierarchical relationships between principals and superintendents is, however, at times contradicted by authors (e.g., NEA, 1958; Rich, 1954) who write of strategies by which principals might convince their superiors of needs within their schools, thus implying that principals are answerable to and dependent on superintendents.

The belief that principals and superintendents differ only in their sphere of responsibility and that they relate as equals and colleagues can be seen in Kyte's (1952) discussions of the roles of these school leaders. He uses the same words—"responsible expert head, . . . chief executive, supervisor, co-ordinator, and educational appraiser" (p. 9)—to describe both the principal and the superintendent. He distinguishes only between their spheres of responsibility, with superintendents heading "the whole school system" and principals, "the school" (p. 9), stressing the fact that the work of both sets of professionals demands an awareness of "the interrelationships of each with the other" (p. 8). Hunt and Pierce (1958) also remark that principals and superintendents are expected to work together as colleagues in the administration of schools. They recommend that schools be administered "cooperative[ly]" (p. 29) by a council whose permanent members might include "the General Superintendent of Schools, Assistant Superintendents, university consultants, principals . . . , the director of instructional materials, and the director of curriculum development" (p. 35). This council could work to determine the philosophies and goals of schools and the curriculum and personnel assignments that would allow the goals to be reached and the philosophies to be maintained.

In an article describing a model reading program in Stockton, California, Shields (1955) also writes about cooperative, collegial relationships between principals and superintendents. She states that administrators in Stockton discovered a pattern of "more efficient organization" (p. 227) that complements "better educational practice [and] . . . more effective use of time" (p. 227). This effective organizational pattern involves a cooperative relationship between principals and system-level administrators who work together to discover and implement more effective methods of teaching reading. Shields emphasizes that, in terms of status and authority, all administrators are equal but that they differ in their spheres of influence and activities, with "the principal [assuming] leadership for the project at the faculty level with the central staff available on a consultative basis" (p. 228). In Shields' view, the impressive results of this cooperative effort—"city-wide improvement in reading skills" (p. 234), "evidence of improved professional attitudes toward the teaching of reading" (p. 234), and an increase in parental "understanding of the reading program and . . . confidence in the schools" (p. 234)—support the concept that cooperative administrative relationships are beneficial for children and the adults charged with their education.

Statements offered by other writers of the decade, however, suggest that equal, cooperative relationships within educational bureaucracies may, in reality, not have been commonplace. Several authors write of strategies that principals can use to convince superintendents and boards of needs in schools, implying that school-level administrators are still subservient to and dependent on central office officials. For example, Rich (1954), writing on "Clerical Help for Principals," addresses principals facing the challenges of "handling office mail, computing monthly attendance reports, counting money, entering data on permanent records, and the like" (p. 33). She offers a number of suggestions for convincing school boards that hiring a good clerical staff is "a wise investment . . . [because] business cannot be carried on successfully without clerical workers" (p. 35). Words from the Department of Elementary School Principals' publication *So Now You're a Principal* (1958) also support the idea that superintendents are still above principals in the educational hierarchy. Focusing on the principal's accountability to the superintendent, the authors of this volume write:

> It must be recognized that in many cases, the procedures for handling situations have been decided by a superintendent, or a board of education, and represent policy to be implemented by the principal. . . . Above all, he [the principal] must acquaint himself with existing policies! Whether he is in agreement with existing policies or not, it is his job to implement them. Later he can work toward getting changes made in some of the policies. (p. 11)

This contradictory picture of principals' relationships with other administrators can be explained in a number of ways. It is possible that those who write of cooperative, collegial relationships are writing within what Bolman and Deal (1989) would call the "symbolic frame," in the sense that they are speaking of ideal relationships that would be consistent with the popular concept of democratic, educational leadership (see Chapter 3). Those who stress the hierarchical nature of administrative relationships may, on the other hand, view these relationships from structural or political frameworks (Bolman & Deal, 1989). They certainly seem to be suggesting strategies by which principals can gain more power within an educational system that is inevitably hierarchical regardless of its rhetoric of equality and cooperation. To an extent, the complex picture painted above represents a shift occurring in the relationship between principals and superintendents—from more collegial and democratic structures to more bureaucratic and organizationally grounded arrangements. The shift in turn represents a change in the role of the principal in school districts—from partner to middle manager—as school districts begin to increase in size and centralization of functions (see Norton, 1957) and to rely more heavily on principles of bureaucracy developed by Weber (see Campbell et al., 1987).

To Teachers

Discussions of principals' relationships to teachers reveal yet another dimension of the tension between theory and practice in this decade. Authors write of principals as persons who communicate pedagogical theories to faculty members and support teachers as they implement these theories. They thus suggest a view of principals as democratic and supportive leaders concerned with concepts of instructional excellence. However, they also write of very specific techniques and curricula that principals should actually use, recommend, or oversee. In this decade, educators become quite concerned with excellence in instructional techniques (e.g., Bain, 1952; Hone, 1953; Witty, 1955; Zirbes, 1952). Principals are expected to lead and support teachers as they study and implement effective teaching methods. Dunn, LeBaron, and Young (1952) use the metaphor of a "pacesetter" (p. 37) to describe the principal's relationship to teachers. They clarify the meaning of this image by writing:

> Such a principal must have the ability to perform a variety of functions, he must understand and practice democratic leadership, he must want a well-adjusted school, he must be a capable administrator and supervisor, and he must exemplify the spirit of democratic fellowship. (p. 39)

In short, these authors think of an ideal principal as one who, in a highly supportive and democratic fashion, leads a team of faculty members toward excellence in teaching.

Hunt (1952) also emphasizes the importance of the principal's exercising democratic, supportive leadership with teachers. Noting that relationships among adults in the school affect the instructional climate, she states that "good relationships begin in the principal's office" (p. 52), and that "a feeling of mutual trust and confidence must exist between teacher and administrator" (p. 53). In Hunt's view, the responsibility for creating these positive, supportive relationships lies with the principal, who "should be accessible to classroom teachers . . . [and] so budget his time that he can give help and encouragement when it is needed" (p. 55).

Yeager (1954) agrees that the ideal relationship between administrators and teachers is a supportive one: "Wise educational leadership develops interest and creative endeavor in others. It commands their respect. It reduces friction, removes barriers, alleviates emotional tensions, inspires confidence, and seeks unselfish ends" (p. 524). Yeager's entire work is devoted specifically to exploring ways in which administrators can exercise this kind of educational leadership to aid teachers in working for "the welfare of the youth of the nation, and in consequence, . . . the nation itself" (p. 18).

Kopp (1958) offers still another statement emphasizing that principals should be supportive leaders of teachers. He cites a 1948 statement by Otto.

> The future role of the elementary school principal will not be that merely of a line officer responsible for the entire program and all the individuals in his school. The future role of the principal will be primarily that of co-ordinator, consultant, and staff education leader. (p. 213)

Kopp notes that "many of the points mentioned by Dr. Otto have become accepted procedure" (p. 213). This statement is especially revealing of changes since the thirties and forties. As noted in Chapters 2 and 3, military imagery is often used in these decades to speak about the principalship. Kopp denies the value of this kind of image and offers several alternatives that describe the supportive educational role of principals.

Consistent with the supportive nature of the ideal principal's interaction with teachers, the literature of the fifties continues to emphasize the expectation that principals lead democratically, sharing decision-making power with their staffs. Nultan (1954), for example, writes that "administration is sharing" (p. 29) and states that this sharing especially involves sharing of authority with teachers. Hunt (1952) also notes that

> The term "leadership" in itself carries the implication of group action. A leader, in the truest sense of the word, never stoops to the tactics of the dictator. Democratic leadership encourages each member of the group to make his best contribution, and utilizes the resources of all. (p. 53)

Similarly, Kyte (1952) describes the ideal principal as "a democratic worker" (p. 13) who involves teachers in the administrative process. He writes that

> Teacher participation in policy making and the resultant activities of a democratically operated school lead to (1) unity of aim and purpose of

instruction, (2) acceptance of understood duties and responsibilities, (3) provision for enlightened co-operation, and (4) a feeling of wholesome, professional security. (p. 13)

These references paint a picture of a principal whose relationship with teachers is governed and shaped by theories, ideals, concepts, and principles, and certainly the metaphor of the supportive academician represents a part of the conception of the principalship in the 1950s. Another part, though, can be seen in other sections of the literature from which the metaphor of the principal as manager emerges and in which principals are described as overseeing classroom activities in great detail. For example, Starkey (1952) offers suggestions to school leaders for working with "borderline children." She suggests they find such "jobs" for these students as

collecting and mounting pictures for a unit entitled "Power-Man's Substitute for Muscles," . . . developing a unit on how changing seasons affect us, . . . [and] working as a committee on . . . [a] unit, "In and Out of Our Solar System." (p. 219)

Focusing on another area—principals' involvement in the instructional arena—Habern (1956) offers suggestions regarding ways that administrators can enhance students' experience by taking photographs of different activities. Describing the principal as "the office photographer . . . subject to call at any time the teacher or children discovered an opportunity for a good picture of some particular phase of the unit in progress" (p. 151), he notes that these photos can greatly enhance the experiences of both students and teachers.

Other writers focus on ways administrators can help in the teaching of reading and math. Schott (1956) suggests that principals recommend and oversee the use of "the Numberaid abacus and its subsequent development, the Numberfun Counting Frame" (p. 86). Postel (1955) recommends that principals develop special reading programs "that make the most of children's needs and interests. They are: (a) the individual reading units, (b) the current events papers, and (c) the class newspapers [named, in his school, *The Comet, The Flash,* and *The Courier*]" (p. 135). Postell further recommends such varied topics for these class newspapers as "'A Trip to the Fire Station,' 'How To Color Easter Eggs,' 'What I Saw at Yellowstone Park,' [and] 'My Parakeet'" (p. 136) for the primary grades and, for seventh- and eighth-grade students, articles on "what the important points in making a book report are, enumerating the duties of a boy on the safety patrol, and why boys may benefit from taking cooking and sewing as well as girls" (p. 138). These and numerous other authors (e.g., Cooper, 1953; Hone,

1953; Phillips, 1952) clearly view the principal as someone responsible for day-to-day educational events unfolding within specific schools and classrooms.

To Nonprofessional Staff

In the fifties, a number of educational writers also devote considerable attention to the relationships between principals and nonprofessional staff members, especially custodians and clerical workers. Once again, apparently contradictory messages appear in the literature. Quite a few pieces (e.g., Dugan, 1954; Hunt & Pierce, 1958; Kopp, 1958; Kyte, 1952; Rich, 1954) state that principals are expected both to delegate many tasks to various staff members in order to free the principals' time for supervision and instructional leadership and to treat nonprofessional staff with dignity and respect, including them in activities with teachers and other school personnel. Many other statements (e.g., Arndt, 1959; Hanft & Sutton, 1952; Kopp, 1958; Kyte, 1952; McQuade, 1959; NEA Research Division, 1958a, 1958b), though, suggest a different view of principals' relationship with nonprofessional staff, calling for principals to closely supervise the clerical and custodial tasks that they delegate.

The belief that effective principals should delegate tasks and responsibilities to staff members is evident in Rich's (1954) article, "Clerical Help for Principals." Rich stresses that principals' chief responsibilities

> include school management, organizational problems, instructional improvement, curriculum building, orientation of teachers new to the staff, guidance, school–community relations, self-improvement, discovering the untapped resources among the staff, knowing the culture in which the children spend their out-of-school time, guiding parent and teacher study groups, arranging materials for publication, maintaining a sense of humor and a continuing personal vigor and vitality. (p. 33)

Rich suggests that the only way principals can ever approach being able to handle all of these tasks is to have help who can handle "time consuming clerical details" (p. 33). At least ideally, principals should delegate many responsibilities to trustworthy secretaries.

Kopp (1958) notes that, in the late 1950s, principals are beginning to view delegation as a dimension of good administration and therefore to delegate more of their routine work to clerical help than did their predecessors. He suggests, however, that "additional clerical help [is still needed to] make possible a richer educational program for children" (p. 203), guided by principals who can devote their attention to supervising and helping teachers. Like Rich (1954), Kopp recognizes the importance of relationships between principals and nonprofessional staff that can free principals from routine administrative duties, but he acknowledges that such relationships are still more of an ideal than a reality in the 1950s.

Kyte (1952) also addresses the issue of principals' relationships to clerical staff. His recommendations clearly indicate that, in a model situation, principals would delegate much responsibility to the secretarial staff.

> In planning for the most effective use of the school secretary's time, the principal should keep in mind the following points:
>
> 1. The secretary is employed to carry on the clerical work of the school.
> 2. The principal is responsible for delegating this work to the secretary and for supervising her.
> 3. The secretary's functions are classifiable under two heads: (a) the work of the school office, and (b) the responsibility of a secretary to the head of the school.
> 4. The assignment of clerical and secretarial responsibilities to the trained office worker is an effective means for releasing all other persons in the school from any responsibility for most of the clerical work.
> 5. Duties and responsibilities which are instructional or administrative in nature are professional functions never to be assigned to the secretary. (p. 473)

Kyte also devotes an entire chapter of *The Principal at Work* to "The Principal's Direction of the Custodian," where we read:

> In assisting the custodian to plan work schedules and to develop efficient methods of working, the principal should keep in mind the following significant points: Generally the janitor is on duty during a long working day. His work is varied, complex, energy-consuming, and often emotionally taxing. . . . The principal, as well as the janitor, should know what constitutes reasonable standards of quality and quantity of workmanship. The former should recognize that the latter's accomplishment is governed by his understanding as acquired primarily through his experiences. Need for improvement in his skill is a supervisory challenge to his principal. (p. 208)

Hunt and Pierce (1958) also view the sharing of responsibilities between principals and custodians as an effective administrative practice. They suggest that "opportunities should be seized to enlist the custodial personnel to work with principals and teachers at the local level and on committees at district and central-office levels on the educational program, the common concern of all (p. 262). Dugan (1954) writes that principals should seek to delegate responsibility to custodians and to include them in decision making when possible. She notes that "all staff members need to recognize their responsibility for the success of the educational enterprise" (p. 24).

The vision of the principal as a person who delegates duties and shares responsibilities with custodians, secretaries, and other staff members obviously has a place in the thinking of educational writers of the fifties, but it does not convey a complete picture of the principal's relationship with nonprofessional staff during this decade. Many authors suggest that delegation and shared responsibility are often not realities in principals' lives in the 1950s. Kyte (1952), for instance, who conceptually embraces these two concepts, indicates, by his detailed lists of principals' tasks, that he really does not conceive of school leaders as letting go of clerical and custodial duties. In his discussion of the opening day of school, for instance, he states that the principal should "inspect building and grounds; . . . check enrollment data; . . . observe cafeteria service; assist checker, if necessary; . . . confer with traffic officers about their squads; . . . check enrollment report; [and] check cafeteria report" (p. 113). Surely a principal who has truly delegated tasks and responsibilities would not need to oversee the carrying out of all these activities.

Hanft and Sutton (1952) offer another picture of the principal as the person responsible for seeing that clerical tasks are effectively carried out. They write about one leader's efforts to encourage the sale of milk in the lunchroom and to convince the community that the school-operated supply store was not hurting the town's businesses. This model principal led a group that "circulated questionnaires, interviewed . . . children, distributed bulletins [and] made promotional posters" (p. 116). He oversaw the writing and duplication of all distributed material, tabulated the results of the questionnaire, and essentially assumed responsibility for everything related to the issue of concern.

Articles in *The Elementary School Principalship* (NEA Research Division, 1958a, 1958b) also support the contention that principals of the fifties generally engage in many detailed clerical and custodial activities. In "School Resources Available to the Principal" the NEA Research Division notes a paucity of personnel available to assume tasks that otherwise fall to the principal: "One common observation of the principals is that there is not enough resource help" (p. 63). In another article, the Research Division reports that many principals are not able to focus on instructional leadership because of clerical tasks and states that—between 1928 and 1958—"there is evidence of only a small shift in the relationship of time for performing major functions of the principalship" (p. 99). It further states that most principals wish to devote more time to work with teachers and students but that "lack of clerical help is the main impediment" (p. 100).

Articles by McQuade (1959) and Arndt (1959) in a yearbook published by the Department of Elementary School Principals underscore the fact that, despite the rhetoric about shared responsibility, principals, and not custodians, are responsible for development and maintenance of the school plant. McQuade advises building-level administrators to oversee the school plant's adaptation to snow, heat, rain, and other climatic conditions. He advises principals: "If your site already has good trees on it, make sure that every possible one is saved" (p. 107). "No matter where you live, you'll probably end up with a large portion of your school grounds in grass. In the Southwest, you'll have to irrigate" (p. 108). "Avoid annual or perennial flower beds. They're too small in scale to amount to anything, too fragile to survive the children, and very troublesome to keep up" (p. 109). Arndt writes:

> The custodian of a school will ordinarily take care of some minor maintenance jobs. But his other duties will prevent him from doing very much repair work while school is in session. Also the custodian may not be capable of performing jobs requiring specialized skills. (p. 165)

He advises principals to be aware of numerous maintenance needs, including those related to carpentry, plumbing and heating, painting, the electrical system, and roofs and floors, in order to ensure that "school plants be properly maintained" (p. 169).

To Parents

Writers in the fifties continue to stress the importance of principals involving parents in the educational enterprise. Here, too, the influence of the theory movement can be seen. The discussions of principal–parent relationships suggest both a continuation and a variation of a theme evident in the literature of the 1940s. Writers in both decades stress parental involvement in school activities whenever possible. In the forties, the basis for encouraging such involvement was primarily ideological. Educational authors wrote of the importance of democratic leadership in schools and saw involving parents as part of this type of leadership. In the fifties, on the other hand, the emphasis on parental involvement is grounded in social science theories that claim that involving parents will serve the best interests of the children in the schools (e.g., Alexander & Dinkel, 1952; Department of Elementary School Principals, 1958; Hunt & Pierce, 1958; Kyte, 1952; Pearson, 1952).

The 1957 Yearbook of the NEA's Department of Elementary School Principals is devoted to the topic of parental involvement in the schools and provides many excellent examples of the ways educators of the fifties conceive of the relationships between principals and parents. A statement offered by Street (1957) in the opening section of the yearbook reflects the attitude prevalent throughout this volume: "To be secure in the leadership role, the principal must be convinced of the essential goodness of lay participation" (p. 12). Street goes on to describe a model program in Oak Park, Michigan, which involves two levels of parental participation.

> The most common is that in which parents become familiar with the school program in specific ways such as with field trips, with cooking classes, with stamp programs, and with parent-teacher association room coffees. . . . [The other method is one] in which the parents and staff cooperatively make decisions regarding the policies and curriculum of the school. (p. 16)

Street argues that achieving effective participation at both of these levels depends primarily on the principal. He writes, "It is the principal's duty to help parents and staff develop and support the school program with intelligence and courage" (p. 20).

Snyder's (1957) work in the same NEA volume stresses the influence of research and theory on conceptions of principal–parent relationships. Citing theories of Anderson and Davies (1956) and McClure (1956), he argues that excellent leadership will seek to involve a number of people, including parents, in making administrative decisions. He notes that "a sound program of teacher–parent and parent–teacher relationships must be developed jointly by the principal, the teachers, and the parents" (p. 55). Walter (1957) expresses similar ideas.

> The most important contribution any school can make to good parent–school relationships is a friendly attitude toward parents. . . . The principal must set the example for the staff. Most staff members will consciously or unconsciously follow the pattern he creates.
>
> Closely related to this friendly attitude is a receptiveness for parent cooperation. . . . The principal can do much to encourage this receptiveness by his staff.
>
> Another responsibility of the school is to find constructive outlets for parental energy. . . . It is up to the principal and the teachers to identify such areas and ask for help with them. (p. 119)

Dunn (1952) also emphasizes the importance of parental involvement in schools and the role of the principal in encouraging such involvement. She states that parents who take an active interest in schools can help to ensure "the maintenance of high educational standards" (p. 112), and she notes that "to be worthy of his position the principal . . . should be a leader" (p. 112) in promoting parental involvement. Zirbes (1952) similarly notes that principals can support and encourage lay involvement in education by keeping parents informed of the rationale behind school practices.

To Students

In this decade, writers also stresses the importance of principals cultivating personal, friendly relationships with students. A section of *Bases for Effective Learning* is devoted to exploring ways principals can help children achieve emotional stability (Reiffel, 1952), with special emphasis on helping those who might be outsiders (Miller, 1952) or isolates (Roberts, 1952). In discussing the principal's role in "social control and discipline," Kyte (1952) says that effective administrators will attempt to understand students, approaching "school control from the standpoint of the many circumstances and conditions which have contributed to the development of each child's personality" (pp. 404–405)—a clear sign of the influence of the social sciences on educational administration. Kyte further states that disciplinary actions "should be exercised with sympathy and kindness . . . [leading to] obedience [which] may be conceived as enthusiastic acceptance of a democratically authoritative plan of action" (p. 406).

In a similar vein, Hunt and Pierce (1958) emphasize that principals must seek to be personally involved with students.

> Principals and teachers, utilizing the resources of the central office, should assist individual pupils in meeting personal and instructional problems both in and out of the classroom. The principal shares in the process by organizing his office and the school program so that supplementary services actually improve teaching and learning. (p. 279)

These authors stress that all children must be treated as individuals and that principals should give special attention to helping "deviate children" (p. 286), including mentally and physically retarded, emotionally maladjusted, and gifted students.

Maxwell (1954) also writes of the importance of the personal involvement of principals with the pupils in their schools. He offers 10 metaphors to describe roles that a principal should assume in this area: "observer," "contributor," "inventor," "discoverer," "coach," "referee," "challenger," "friend," "example," and "counselor" (pp. 25–29). Maxwell notes that, in fulfilling these various roles, a principal will become "acquainted with a child . . . through casual conversation" (p. 25), make "a child feel well accepted" (p. 28), and take an active, supervisory role in extracurricular programs.

To the Academic Community

Thus, in the 1950s, we see the emergence of a dual expectation of the principalship: On the one hand, principals were expected to be scholars and theorists; on the other, they were expected to continue to be managers of details. The source of this apparent contradiction may be the fact that, as we have noted, educational administration as a scholarly discipline began to emerge only in the late 1940s. Writers in the fifties, apparently influenced by strides in the profession, frequently note that, in addition to relating to persons within their school systems, principals should relate to the academic community, learning from scholarship, applying research insights and principles, and testing theories and hypotheses in their schools.

Much of the literature of this decade suggests that academicians play the role of contributing insights to aid practitioners and that principals should order their work in accordance with theories and insights from research. The expectation that scholars should contribute to practice is clearly stated by Norton (1957).

> A grand design for a profession of educational administration . . . needs to be drawn and put into operation. This should include a program for the recruitment of talent of appropriate physical, intellectual, emotional, and spiritual capacity. There should be much more effective facilities for preservice professional education and continuing in-service development of those who serve in this calling. . . . The resources and quality of graduate schools for the professional preparation of educational executives should be vastly improved. The responsibility . . . for bringing these things about should be recognized and acted upon. (pp. 79–80)

Griffiths strongly echoes Norton's belief that theorists can and should supply information useful to practitioners. In "Toward a Theory of Administrative Behavior" (1957) Griffiths discusses the types of theories that would result in useful principles for administrators and concludes that "improved understanding of administrative behavior depends upon the progress which can be made in the development of *theory*" (p. 388). He expresses great optimism that theory, properly developed, will greatly improve the practice of school leadership.

> A theory of administrative behavior will make it possible to relate what now appear to be discrete acts to one another so as to make a unified

concept. The great task of science has been to impose an order upon the universe. . . . Within a set of principles, yet to be formulated, it will be possible to recognize interrelationships among apparently discrete acts, it will be possible to predict the behavior of individuals within the organizational framework, and it will be possible to make decisions that will result in a more efficient and effective enterprise. (p. 388)

Implicit in the writings of Norton (1957), Griffiths (1957), and other leaders in the educational theory movement is the belief that principals should respond to academic insights by studying and implementing discovered principles and by gathering data in their schools that could aid in formulating additional principles. This view is explicitly stated by other writers, such as Miller (1957): "Theory needs testing and such testing eventually must be accomplished with the cooperation of, and through the acts of, practicing administrators. Any sound theory developed will require understanding and acceptance by practicing administrators if it is to yield the improvement for which it is designed" (p. 523).

Contributors to *So Now You're a Principal* (Department of Elementary School Principals, 1958) similarly state that an effective principal "makes concrete provision both for keeping aware and contributing to the advancement of human knowledge in his own and related fields" (p. 4). Hunt and Pierce (1958) repeatedly stress that principals should study all aspects of school life, including individual student needs, effective teaching methods, and organizational strategies. Kyte (1952) emphasizes the principal's interactions with the research community, noting that, while principals can use class records to evaluate teaching methods,

research in the school should not be confined to the classroom only. Principals can spend considerable time with professional profit to themselves and to the children by applying research techniques to their own work. . . . Principals are in strategic positions to make the investigations and to facilitate the research of other persons. (p. 369)

STANDARDS FOR EVALUATION

As we have analyzed the metaphorical language of educational writers in the decades between 1920 and 1960, we have sought for evidence of standards by which the work of principals could be evaluated. We have thus far found little to indicate overt, explicit measures of effectiveness. Virtually all the works we have reviewed seem to assume that principals whose work demonstrates congruence with the values of their respective cultures are doing well, and, by extension, those whose work fails to show such congruence are not as effective. In many ways, the literature of the 1950s continues in this pattern. Despite a widely held belief in the relationship between certain behaviors and measurable, objective outcomes, most writers do not suggest that these measurable outcomes be used to evaluate principals' on-the-job performances in any substantive or comprehensive way. A few do note that measures can be developed to judge the effectiveness of instructional techniques, but these authors relate such outcome measures only indirectly to the work of principals (see, for example, on measuring the effectiveness of science education efforts, Blough, 1953; on evaluating reading programs, Smith, 1955; Witty, 1955; and Durell, 1955).

Writers of this decade, although apparently loathe to suggest evaluative measures for practicing principals, do call for standards to assess the readiness of candidates for the principalship. As Culbertson (1988) notes, one of the chief concerns of the 1954 meeting of the NCPEA and the 1957 seminar sponsored by the University of Chicago and the University Council for Educational Administration (UCEA) was that persons entering the principalship successfully complete a university-based preparation program that emphasized a scientific approach to administration. Davies (1952) underscores the belief that principals should successfully complete a thorough preparation program before entering the profession, when he argues that a principal must be "skilled in human relationships and communication techniques . . . [and] a statesman in his grasp of international, national, and local philosophy, values, goals, and political action" (p. 128). He notes that these abilities can be attained only by participation in a program focusing on "the humanities, arts, and social sciences" (p. 128).

Fisk (1957) distinguishes between two types of training for the principalship. He contrasts a "man-on-the-job approach" (p. 202), where administrators learn effective approaches by actually encountering situations in the school, with an academic preparation program. Fisk believes that principals who have successfully completed an official training program are more likely to be able to meet the challenges of school leadership. A similar view is also offered by Anderson and Lonsdale (1957), who write that effective principals should complete programs that stress "concepts and theory in educational administration . . . [and] the development of skills in human relations and group processes" (p. 438). Hall and McIntyre (1957), Wynn (1957), and Miller (1957) also call for educational administrators to exercise their "professional responsibility" (Miller, p. 519) to set high standards—which would involve participation in training programs—for entry into the principalship.

Two aspects of the approach to evaluation advocated by authors in the fifties are noteworthy. First, these writers tend to focus on assessment of candidates for the principalship rather than on practicing principals. This may be due to the fact that most of these writers are professors of educational administration. They thus would naturally write about issues with which they were familiar and advocate changes in parts of the educational system over which they had some control. Many also seem to have such faith in administrative science that they believe that successful completion of programs in this area can actually ensure principals' success (Griffiths, 1957). This focus on evaluating persons prior to their entry into the field may also reflect the fact that it is easier to talk about evaluation than actually do it. Most of the authors who write from this perspective voice their ideas in terms of what *should* be done, not in terms of what *has been* or *will be* done to determine whether principals are really administering effectively.

A second noteworthy aspect of principal evaluation in the fifties is that this is the first decade when scholars suggest any kind of general objective criteria against which principals can be judged. Writers of the fifties stress that performance in university-based, academic programs can serve as a gauge to assess principals' abilities to lead. In the decades that follow, other evaluation plans will emerge, plans proposed by a variety of different persons and groups to answer such questions as, Should principals be evaluated? If so, when? By whom? By what standards? What should happen if a principal does not measure up?

CONCLUSION

The 1950s are clearly years of great change for principals in the United States. During this time, forces from both academic and political spheres begin to permeate the boundaries between schools and the outside world. Principals have to reckon with demands for restructured school systems following the 1954 *Brown* v. *Board of Education* decision, just as they have to contend with expanding forces in universities calling for the scientific administration of schools. The educational literature of this decade suggests that the principal of this decade is viewed as having two distinct roles in the educational processes within the school. On the one hand, she or he is considered to be the person responsible for knowing and applying the highly objective laws and principles that organizational and administrative science are discovering. Thus, one foot is firmly planted in the emerging science of organizations (see Boyan, 1963). In this role, the principal is viewed as being under the authority of this "objective" body of knowledge. On the other hand, the principal is also frequently viewed as the person responsible for planning school activities down to even the smallest details and as the person ultimately responsible for the implementation of these plans. Thus, a second foot is firmly grounded in the minute details of educational practice. These two role expectations, while not entirely contradictory, do present a rather odd picture of this decade's understanding of the role and function of educational leadership. For, even as scholars argue that principals are leaders, not managers (Hunt & Pierce, 1958), and that delegation of responsibility and time management are critical for effective administration (Yeager, 1954), they seem to be suggesting that principals should be actively involved with overseeing the small details related to virtually all the school's activities.

Thus, in the 1950s, the principalship is in what might be called a transitional phase in terms of role definitions. Women and men in positions of school leadership are receiving messages concerning their roles and functions from a number of quarters, and they seem to be wavering between taking highly theoretical perspectives on their work and dwelling on mundane issues of practice. In retrospect, it is clear that uncertainty about leadership issues on the part of principals, and, indeed, on the part of those who write about them presages the conflict that permeates the literature of the next two decades.

CHAPTER FIVE

The 1960s

> The decade of the sixties changed our lives—changed every-
> thing. It was such a revolutionary period that anyone who
> lived through it remembers it as an immediately identifiable
> span of time. . . .
> I was lucky to be an assistant managing editor and then
> the managing editor of LIFE during that incredible decade. It
> was not always pleasant—many frightful events occurred dur-
> ing the sixties—but it was always exciting. Coming to work
> each morning, I never knew what striking photographic
> image, in black-and-white or color, would cross my desk and
> appear in the pages of LIFE.
> To mention only a few:
> The tragic assassinations of John F. Kennedy, Robert F.
> Kennedy, and Martin Luther King Jr. The Vietnam war. The civil
> rights movement, from the Selma march to the riots in Watts,
> Newark and Detroit. The Beatles, followed by the Rolling
> Stones and Janis Joplin and everybody else, and then fol-
> lowed by long hair and mod clothes. Neil Armstrong and Buzz
> Aldrin walking on the moon—that "giant leap for mankind."
> The rock concert. The tiny miniskirt. Public nudity. Oil spills. The
> environmental movement and the "discovery" of the wild
> world. Sexual freedom. The first heart transplant. Marijuana
> and LSD. The generation gap.
> It added up to a whole new American way of life. . . .
> (Ralph Graves, 1989, preface)

These words, opening a special anniversary publication of *Life* Magazine during the 1960s, clearly reflect the social and political turbulence that,
in many ways, characterizes life in America during this decade. Schools, like
most institutions, are certainly affected by the events and the mood of the

sixties. Indeed, education and its leaders are, at times, in the very center of what Campbell and his colleagues (1987) call the "social revolution" (p. 83) that occurred during these years. As we examined literature on the principalship written during these years, we were struck by the efforts made by principals and academicians to maintain stability and a sense of normalcy in schools. As we note in Figure 5.1, these metaphors suggest that conceptions of schools as rational, goal-driven systems dominated thought and practice. Principals are viewed as inhabitants of a specific role, differentiated by training, duties, and responsibilities, within these systems.

DOMINANT METAPHORICAL THEMES

Specific themes that emerge from the metaphors of this decade include the following:

1. The principal of the sixties is viewed as a member of a well-developed educational bureaucracy with clearly defined bases of power and responsibility.
2. The principal is expected to function as a protector of the bureaucratic system. This involves guarding the various distributions of power within the hierarchy and exercising astute political judgments in handling those who challenge the system.
3. Categorical, quantitative, empirical terms increasingly dominate discussions of the principal's work, suggesting that she or he is expected to use increasingly sophisticated, scientific strategies for planning and measuring.
4. Faith that "correct" technique and modern technology will produce expected outcomes results in the belief that the principal is to be held accountable for her or his decisions and activities.
5. Accountability pressures and political demands leave the principal feeling vulnerable and confused about role expectations.

Principal as Bureaucrat

The entrenchment of a bureaucratic conception of the principalship during the 1960s is noted by Campbell and his colleagues (1987). Titling their chapter overviewing this period "Rationalism Rediscovered: Bureaucracy and the Study of Administration" (p. 63), these authors report that an interest in Max Weber's concept of organizations as rational bureaucracies experienced a resurrection in administrative circles after World War II. By

FIGURE 5.1 Analysis of the Metaphors of the 1960s

Dominant Metaphorical Themes

The principal of the sixties is viewed as a member of a well-developed educational bureaucracy.

The principal is expected to function as protector of the bureaucracy, guarding the various distributions of power.

Categorical, quantitative, empirical terms increasingly dominate discussions of the principal's work, suggesting that he or she is expected to use increasingly sophisticated scientific strategies.

Faith that "correct" technique and modern technology will produce expected outcomes results in the belief that the principal can be held accountable for her or his decisions and activities.

The pressures of this accountability and the political demands on school leaders leave the principal feeling vulnerable and confused about role expectations.

Dominant Tone

Technical and mechanistic

Dominant Values

Uniformity and standardization in preparation programs, administrative and instructional techniques, and evaluative strategies

Relationship to Others

To state level policy makers and district level superintendents—
  Subordinate
  Lieutenant responsible for carrying out directives
To teachers—
  Builder of morale
  Dispenser of pedagogical knowledge
To students—
  Instructional and disciplinary influence through teachers
To parents and community members—
  Builder of harmonious, supportive relationships

Standards for Evaluation

Principals are evaluated on the performance or quality of the "pupil product" as measured by standardized tests

Evaluation is both formative and summative. It tends to focus on discovering problems and working to correct them the sixties, the belief that this type of governance structure was appropriate for schools became widespread, and both scholars and practitioners began to highlight bureaucratic images in their treatments of the principalship.

Many contributors to Carver and Sergiovanni's (1969) edited volume, *Organizations and Human Behavior: Focus on Schools*, for example, utilize Weberian concepts and language in their discussions of schools and their leaders. In the preface, the editors emphasize the similarities between schools and other bureaucracies.

> Research to date has revealed that human behavior, as a result of organizational life, manifests remarkable similarities as one moves from hospital, to school, to retail store, to welfare agency, and to military unit. Teachers and nurses, for example, react similarly to dysfunctional effects of status hierarchies within their respective organizations. Accountants, middle managers in business and industry, and teachers report remarkably similar orientations to satisfying and dissatisfying factors in their work. Military officers, medical chiefs of staff, hotel managers, police commissioners, school superintendents, and vice-presidents have similar problems and concerns with respect to subordinates who possess more—and often exclusive—technical and professional ability than they. Conflict between line and staff officers occurs in schools in the same manner and probably with the same regularity as it does in military, business, and industrial organizations. Thus, while the school administrator is particularly concerned with one kind of formal organization, his vision may very well be improved by studying organizations in general. (p. *ix*)

These scholars and other contributors to this volume do not accept Weberian concepts in an uncritical fashion. They do, however, use them as touchstones in their analyses. Indeed, they often select bureaucratic images to describe schools and principals even as they argue that this kind of model is not totally appropriate for education. The very titles of the following articles reflect the dominance of Weberian assumptions during this decade:

> "The Nature and Types of Formal Organizations" (Blau & Scott)
> "Hierarchy, Specialization, and Organizational Conflict" (Thompson)
> "Hierarchical Impediments to Innovation in Educational Organizations" (Abbott)
> "Functions and Pathology of Status Systems in Formal Organizations" (Barnard)
> "Dysfunctions in Organizations" (March & Simon)
> "Formality versus Flexibility in Complex Organizations" (Bell)
> "Models of Bureaucracy Which Permit Conflict" (Litwak)

"Relation of Bureaucratization to Sense of Power among Teachers" (Moeller & Charters)

Abbott's comments are particularly indicative of a hierarchical view of educational leadership.

> The American schools have been particularly receptive to the bureaucratic ideology, albeit perhaps unwittingly. Bureaucratic principles have been incorporated into the organizational practices of the educational enterprise in at least the following respects:
>
> First, the school organization has clearly been influenced by the need for specialization and factoring of task. . . .
>
> Second, the school organization has developed a clearly defined and rigid hierarchy of authority. . . .
>
> Third, the school organization has leaned heavily upon the use of general rules to control the behavior of members of the organization and to develop standards which would assure reasonable uniformity in the performance of tasks. . . .
>
> Fourth, despite frequent proclamations regarding togetherness and democracy, the school organization has made extensive application of Weber's principles of impersonality in organizational relationships. . . .
>
> Fifth, employment in the educational organization has been based upon technical competence and has constituted for most members a professional career. (pp. 44–45)

Although Abbott writes disparagingly of the bureaucratic structure of schools, he expresses doubts about the possibility of change.

> In essence, I have argued that it is unreasonable to expect any radical departure from traditional educational practices as long as we insist on placing undue emphasis upon hierarchical status. If we are to break out of the strait jacket in which we now find ourselves, we must examine our ideology with rigor and candor. We must be willing to admit that we do not necessarily live in the best of all possible organizational worlds. And we must display creativity in devising some type of organizational arrangement which will serve more adequately the types of institutions in which we work.
>
> I must admit that I do not now visualize very clearly what type of organization that will be. (pp. 49)

The thoughts of Jones, Salisbury, and Spencer (1969) also reveal a belief that schools are rational organizations that function most effectively when administrators operate under principles consonant with the tenets of bureaucracy. In one section, they suggest that principals might look to the military bureaucracy for leadership models.

> Certain fundamentals are customarily followed by successful military leaders in making decisions and taking action. The fundamentals used for the proper exercise of command are known as leadership principles.
>
> Perhaps no one would suggest that a secondary school be operated or administered in the same manner as the Army of the United States; however, many of the principles of leadership enumerated here as being essential for effective military leadership have some application to secondary school administration. (p. 125)

Jones and colleagues emphasize two other aspects of school leadership that are quite consistent with Weber's conceptions of ideal bureaucratic leadership. They write of the importance of principals possessing "professional competencies" related to the "technical aspects of educational administration" (p. 176), an emphasis in line with the Weberian view that "employment in a bureaucracy is based upon technical competence" (Abbott, 1969, p. 45). Additionally, they stress the need for principals to order their work to achieve rationally developed goals and objectives. Indeed, they note that "poorly defined goals and responsibilities" could cause "much harm or delay" (Jones et al., 1969, p. 150) in the school's operation. Labeling a lack of clarity in this area as "a type of professional sin that cannot be long tolerated" (p. 150), they suggest that principals who operate rationally within and through hierarchical structures possess a kind of moral righteousness.

In her work on the role of junior high administrators, Noar (1961) indicates that she also views the principal as a mid-level bureaucrat. She argues that the principal has the "responsibility for directing faculty discussion, study, and action" (p. 105) and that "the principal faces the task of creating and administering a series of parent–pupil–teacher meetings" (p. 112). To be sure, Noar notes the importance of "a permissive, democratic climate characterized by friendliness, seriousness of purpose, sincerity, and industry" (p. 111), but she consistently portrays principals as the members of the educational hierarchy with the authority and responsibility to cultivate such a climate. Indeed, she places the onus for "creating" a democratic atmosphere squarely on the principal (p. 111).

The comments of Douglass (1963), like Noar's, indicate that, regardless of rhetoric about shared decision making, the principal is considered to be the ultimate authority, responsible for and in control of the development of democratic governance. For example, he describes the principal's selecting "appropriate lay persons" or "having the organization appoint appropriate people" to assist in decision making (p. 9). Douglass further notes that at times the principal might "have to step in and assume responsibility ordinarily belonging to a department head, teacher, or student officer in order to prevent things from 'going to pot'" (p. 17). In general, the scholars of this decade, while praising the idea of democratic leadership, write of principals as leaders who, because of their hierarchical position, clearly have the last word on decisions and activities affecting governance, teaching, and student activities.

Principal as Protector of Bureaucracy

Noar (1961) and Douglass (1963) also reveal a second metaphorical theme from this decade—principals are supposed to support the educational bureaucracy. They are expected to protect their own authority, to respect the position of superiors, and to guard against injudicious appropriation of power by teachers. Fulfilling this expectation requires shrewdness and political acumen.

Boyan, in "The Emergent Role of the Teacher in the Authority Structure of the School" (1969), offers a clear example of this emphasis. Describing a central administrative challenge, he writes that

> the aspirations of teachers as professionals in public bureaucracies and the militant behavior of teachers as members of extra-school organizations have brought them into sharp confrontation with the traditional [i.e., administrator-based] authority structure of the school. (p. 201)

Drawing on a diverse body of scholarship (e.g., Blau & Scott, 1962; Etzioni, 1964, 1965; Katz & Kahn, 1966), Boyan proposes that teachers, because of their professional competence, are demanding a voice in school governance. In his view, this voice is appropriate only when decisions concern the educational program. When the issues under scrutiny are administrative in nature, the decisions should be made by principals and superintendents (see also Griffiths, 1969). Boyan argues that principals have the responsibility for guarding their rights to make decisions in "the administrative authority structure" and for seeing that teachers have a part in "the supervisory advisory structure" (p. 210).

Austin, French, and Hull (1962), in their *American High School Administration: Policy and Practice*, portray the principal as

> the final authority in the school . . . [one who] is willing to bear responsibility, and like General Eisenhower before the Normandy invasion, to be prepared to accept the full responsibility for failure if one expects, in case of success, to be accorded his share in the glory. (p. 128)

Douglass (1963), writing in a similar vein, argues that principals in the sixties need to recognize the "increased complexity of modern high-school administration" (p. 24) and that they need to learn to wield their power effectively and appropriately. Offering frank advice regarding the best way to deal with superordinates, he cautions that "the superintendent of schools has the full authority to set aside decisions of the high school principal, to veto, to revoke, to supplement, and to change procedures at any time" (p. 27). Because superintendents hold this power, Douglass recommends:

> The principal should have his contacts with the board of education entirely through the superintendent. . . . The principal and the superintendent should work closely together, be frank with one another, and cooperate as fully as possible. The principal should recognize that appeals can be made from his decisions by teachers of pupils in his school. (p. 27)

In addition to suggesting ways principals should work with superiors in the educational system, Douglass explores methods that effective leaders can employ to develop general political acumen. He argues that these skills are important if principals are to deal successfully with threats to the established system. Again, offering clear recommendations, Douglass concludes that

> administrators must remember that, since the schools are open to all the children of all the people and are supported by all taxpayers, an important factor in establishing professional leadership is the character and nature of the religious, business, fraternal, and social affiliations made in the new community. . . .
>
> It is not suggested that the schoolman must be servile or allow himself to be victimized in his business dealings, but it is a mark of the possession of diplomatic qualities to be able to carry on one's business relations in a small community in such a way as not to arouse antagonisms which are strong enough to alienate support of the principal and his educational program. . . .
>
> Independence in political affairs has become so general among men of learning that except for those who have political ambitions, party regularity and political partisanship, particularly of an active sort, involve many dangers and promise few benefits. . . .
>
> The study of the community should be made to reveal as accurately as possible the key men and women and the key organizations. In every community there are men, women, and organizations that are outstandingly influential in determining community attitudes and actions. The principal must not neglect to know these people and to gain their confidence and good will. (pp. 556–557)

Jones and colleagues (1969) offer additional evidence of the view that effective principals are those who employ power and influence networks to protect and support the bureaucracy. They describe networks existing within both the school and the community. Stressing that successful principals maximize the strengths of personnel resources, they note, "One measure of a successful principal is his ability to work with others and to lead them to accomplish their mutually developed objectives" (p. 168). Jones and his colleagues also discuss the importance of principals operating shrewdly within the larger community. Noting that "the principal . . . should be able to adjust his knowledge and thinking to situation patterns" (p. 169), they recommend specific ways school leaders can understand, use, and influence the thinking of influential community members.

Principal as User of Scientific Strategies

Also explicit in this decade is the assumption that principals will use scientifically proven strategies to achieve measurable educational goals. Indeed, the interest in theory and theory-driven research, which only superficially manifested itself in the fifties, is much more noticeable in the literature on the principalship in the sixties. This is evident in the categorical, quantitative, empirical metaphors that often found their way into descriptions of practice. Glass (1986b), discussing a factor possibly related to this emphasis, notes:

> A burgeoning technology was working alongside societal changes in producing a school system of increased complexity which necessitated a management system extending beyond repeated applications of taxonomies of "school management principles." The evolving complex society called for management and conceptual tools designed to lead large groups of students and staff in a task of formal socialization to a changing technological world. (pp. 93–94)

Glass (1986c) also reports that, beginning in the late 1950s, "the struggle for the development and acceptance of administrative theory [and] application of social/behavioral science research and tools" (p. 132) are two of the dominant themes of administrative texts. Campbell and coauthors (1987) express similar views about the multitude of empirical images and especially note the peaking of faith in science as a problem-solving discipline— "the bloom was on the rose and social science knowledge was expected to lead to administrative progress" (p. 186).

Glass (1986b) states that a dominant interest is providing practitioners as well as researchers the tools of scientific inquiry" (p. 95). He notes that this involves providing "to administrators a tool by which to describe, explain, and predict phenomena associated with the management of the educational enterprise" (p. 95). Articles in research reports published by the Educational Records Bureau also offer numerous examples of the scientific, empirical language that pervaded educational scholarship in the 1960s. Cook (1962), in the report *Improving the Efficiency and Quality of Learning*, focuses primarily on the ways "the enterprise of programmed instruction opens up an arena for a technology of education" (p. 21). His views are especially revealing of the high level of interest in developing a "technological framework" (p. 21) for educative activities.

> A genuine technology is more than a codification of effective practice and a checklist of current wisdom. It is more because a framework is provided which permits and encourages a genuine cumulation of results in relation to specific practice. By providing a common market in which theories can price and sell their wares, technology brings a leavening effect to such theories, drawing them out of the parochial bound of a special vocabulary, a favorite experiment, or an isolated preoccupation. And where ways of thinking can be so harnessed to scientific evaluation, the practical effects will cumulate, refine, and build upon themselves, free from the pendulum of fads and counterfads, short-term emphases and slow correctives. (p. 21)

Stoddard (1963) discusses "sources of excitement in contemporary education" (p. 13) and expresses his faith in the efficacy and usefulness of programmed instruction that has been tried and tested in experimental studies.

> Machine (programmed) instruction is largely devoted to the spinal cord of learning and retention. It can be used to stimulate the student in the collection of facts, formulae, and the true-or-false of the familiar dichotomy. It is an aid to numerical computation, vocabulary, and grammar. . . . To the extent that machine instruction will do a vast amount of academic dishwashing for students and teachers, I am for it. The greater the proper use of machines, the greater the assurance that the needs of the lower brain centers are being met. (p. 15)

Research-related metaphors appear in virtually all of the articles in the Educational Records Bureau volume. Trump (1962) writes of the importance of assessing "standards" to ensure that their "research base is related to the quality of education" (p. 38). He argues for "qualitative judgments [that] involve . . . both the collection of quantitative data and professional interpretation of the data" (p. 38). Taylor (1962) calls on colleges and universities to become "new experimental institutions" (p. 53) that lead the way in meeting educational needs. Others, focusing on developments in specific disciplines, discuss the "reappraisal of the English curriculum" (Rosenblatt, 1963, p. 63), "experimentation with three methods of instruction in high school mathematics" (Rushton, 1963, p. 74), "better interpretation of [standardized] test results" (Ohlsen, Anderson, Sides, Roose, & Litterick, 1963, p. 84), and "experiments with an augmented alphabet for beginning readers" (Downing, 1963, p. 99). Noar's (1961) choice of words in her discussion of the junior high principalship also suggests that conceptions of school leadership were affected by the experimental, technological ethos of this period. She, for example, praises "principals and others [who] have accepted the challenge to create the school of tomorrow, today, and have studied, planned, experimented, and evaluated to that end" (p. 105).

Rock and Hemphill's (1966) *Report of the Junior High-School Principalship* similarly reveals a belief that this role can be understood if subjected to the proper kind of research. The authors, after gathering extensive data about junior high principals, and analyzing and interpreting results, present definitive answers to a number of administrative questions, including

> Should education on the junior high level be heavily elective, or should it be characterized by many required subjects? Should high level classes include a block of time as opposed to being completely departmentalized, or should there be a gradual increase in departmentalization with grade level? What grades should be included in the junior high schools? Should the name be changed to "middle school" and the program altered quite basically? What are the attitudes and opinions of junior high school administrators on general education issues and policies? (p. 3)

Striking in Rock and Hemphill's presentation is their certainty. After conducting a survey of "a representative group of principals" (p. 3) in a systematic fashion, these authors "project a national profile of the junior high school principal . . . [that includes] information on access to the principalship, duties and responsibilities, professional attitudes, and other valuable data" (Ellsworth Tompkins, National Association of Secondary School Principals [NASSP], quoted in Rock & Hemphill, p. *v*).

Hemphill, Richards, and Peterson's (1965) "technical report" (preface) is another work that discusses the principalship as a role, comprehensible to scholars who can carefully dissect it and categorize its key dimensions. After attempting to survey every senior high principal in the United States, these researchers analyze data within four categories.

Background of the Principalship
Educational Issues as Seen by Principals

Duties and Compensations of the Principalship
Civic and Professional Activities of Principals (p. 15)

Hemphill and colleagues compile results into tables that, in total, present "a comprehensive, reliable, and up-to-date picture of the American senior high school principalship" (p. 3). Again, what is noteworthy is the sense of surety of the scholars conducting this research. They apparently are quite confident that their research has, in fact, captured the essence of the principal's role and work. This confidence is clearly shared by the NASSP, their sponsoring organization, and is buttressed by the measures the researchers took (i.e., mailing a questionnaire to every principal in the United States, piloting the initial instrument and revising it to eliminate ambiguity, and statistically analyzing characteristics of late responders in order to paint a picture of nonresponders) to increase reliability and validity.

The results of the National Principalship Study conducted by scholars from Harvard University's Graduate School of Education are, in a similar way, discussed in quantitative, empirical language. Gross and Herriot (1964), in *The Professional Leadership of Elementary School Principals: Final Report No. 1*, focus "on the effects and determinants of the professional leadership exhibited by principals as the executives of their schools" (p. *iii*). Gross and Trask (1964), in *Men and Women as Elementary School Principals: Final Report No. 2*, discuss "the part of the study that examined the backgrounds, careers, and performance of women and men as elementary school principals and the relationship of the sex of principals to the functioning of their schools" (p. *iii*). In the third monograph, *The Role Behavior of School Principals: Final Report No. 3*, Dreeben and Gross (1965) review findings on "effects and determinants of three aspects of the principals' role behavior: closeness of supervision, support of innovation, and involvement of parents in school affairs" (p. *iii*). And Dodd (1965) in the final volume, *Role Conflicts of School Principals: Final Report No. 4*, describes "the Role Conflict instrument" (p. 1/3) and reports outcomes of testing "a set of hypotheses about the determinants and effects of role conflict" (p. 1/3).

Principal as Accountable Leader

The belief that certain acts or attributes are causally linked with particular educational outcomes apparently contributes to the expectation that principals can and should be held accountable for events within their schools, an expectation conveyed in both the content and the metaphors of works from this decade. In the final section of this chapter, we examine in detail the messages concerning standards for evaluating principals; therefore, we limit our discussion here to a single set of references that focuses on the expectation that principals account for educational results within their schools. We explore, in greater detail, the language that suggests that this accountability caused many school leaders to feel a sense of confusion and vulnerability.

The report of the Twenty-Fifth Conference of the Educational Records Bureau and the American Council on Education, *Measurement and Research in Today's Schools* (Traxler, 1961), contains a number of papers that implicitly highlight the expectation that school leaders are accountable for students' progress. Articles by Noll (1961) and Brown (1961) on preparing teachers to administer and interpret measures of student achievement, and Drews' (1961) work on evaluating "approaches to the identification of gifted students" (p. 109), point to the burgeoning belief that educators' actions have measurable effects. Fenollosa, Kendrick, Lennon, North, Seashore, Spencer, and Turnbull (1961) in turn discuss ways in which schools and their administrators might mitigate some of the negative effects of this problem by engaging in "systematic thinking about the purposes for testing in relation to the management of testing" (p. 54).

Principal as Inhabitant of a Role in Conflict

Dodd (1965) offers a number of propositions that suggest that principals experience considerable role conflict due, in part, to the wide array of groups to which administrators are accountable. He notes that school-level administrators are responsible for four internal processes.

(1) Management of the instruction program; . . .
(2) Dealing with students; . . .
(3) Housekeeping functions; . . .
(4) Dealing with teachers. (pp. 3/9–3/10)

Principals, according to Dodd, are expected to account for their handling of these functions to the general public and to superordinates in the educational hierarchy. The expectation that they handle many tasks effectively and keep others both informed and satisfied causes considerable stress for principals, stress further compounded by the many demands from teachers for demonstrations of effective administrative leadership.

Austin, French, and Hull (1962) also discuss the stress caused by conflicting expectations from various stakeholders.

[The principal] must accept the responsibility for everything that happens in the school, his burden is heavy and always present, and he is often tempted to lighten it by limiting his activities.

Instead of meeting his responsibilities in full, he may be tempted to operate the school in such a way as to evade them. The standards of achievement may be raised so that slow learners or troublesome students are eliminated. The afterschool use of the school building may be curtailed so that school property is more easily protected. The social program may be limited so that the school can deny responsibility for excesses and indiscretions committed by youth in the social programs they build for themselves away from the school. (pp. 150–151)

These authors devote much of their text to exploring ways administrators might effectively face the demands on them so they survive professionally and personally and effectively lead their schools toward achieving "the legitimate goals of a sound and consistent program of education for youth" (p. 150).

Jones and colleagues (1969) devote much of their *Secondary School Administration* to discussing "one of the stern realities facing the principal and his secondary school, [the fact] that many demands are made on his time and attention" (p. 66). Many "demands to meet pressing social and economic needs" (p. 73) are issued from the worlds of higher education, business, and government. These authors provide numerous recommendations to help principals cope with these challenges. Jones and his colleagues call on administrators to utilize insights culled from research on leadership and on instructional techniques to guide teachers to high levels of pedagogical effectiveness.

Interestingly, there is a startling absence of metaphors in the literature of the 1960s conveying the belief that theorists and practitioners were seriously reckoning with the challenges accompanying moves to desegregate schools. Also missing is language suggesting that poverty-related educational problems and social unrest were being given thoughtful consideration by school leaders. The lack of attention to these issues in literature from this decade becomes especially interesting when juxtaposed with assessments by Campbell and colleagues (1987), Ravitch (1974), and others, who conclude that these socio-cultural concerns dramatically affected expectations for and the work of principals. In the following sections, we offer additional insights on this phenomenon and, in the final section, discuss causes and implications of this discrepancy.

DOMINANT TONE OF THE METAPHORS: TECHNICAL

During the 1960s, the tone of the metaphorical language in education changed in some rather dramatic ways. Prior to the mid-1950s, as we have noted, the images utilized by educational writers suggested that the principalship had important spiritual, intellectual, civic, and patriotic dimensions. However, even when authors praise the noble purposes of schooling, scientific management, and theory-driven leadership, the metaphors reveal a great deal of concern with mundane, highly practical issues. The language of these earlier decades contains an interesting admixture of lofty and trivial metaphors. In the sixties, the metaphors used in discussions of the principal's role and work, drawn largely from the factory and the laboratory, take on a technical, mechanistic tone. These images convey implicitly what many authors were beginning to claim explicitly: If the proper parts were in place and functioning, principals could and should function with the effectiveness of well-oiled machines.

Austin, French, and Hull (1962), for example, employ mechanistic images in their discussions of organizational problems.

> It is very difficult, if not well-nigh impossible for even the best of administration to overcome serious defects in organization by trying to better the administration of the enterprise. If a machine is poorly designed to accomplish a certain operation, one cannot greatly improve the situation by paying more for a better operator. What is needed is a better-designed machine. In like manner, a poorly organized institution cannot be brought to maximum effectiveness by providing it with an extremely competent administrator unless he is given full authority to restructure its organization so that the good administration he is capable of providing will have a chance to succeed. (p. 15)

This mechanistic understanding of leadership prompted scholars to attempt to comprehend various administrative roles by dissecting them and analyzing the various component parts. Again, Austin and colleagues (1962) demonstrate this view when they observe that

> Gulick's functions . . . are part of a body of knowledge about administration which suggests that a science of administration is possible. Universal qualities which are identifiable throughout most, if not all, of the work of administrators can be examined as one would study specimens of geological or biological interest. The determination of classifications of functions, for instance, is part of the collection of evidence that good administration is not a haphazard practice based upon hunches and superstition. (p. 17)

Jones and his colleagues (1969) also employ images with a technical tone and, like Austin and colleagues (1962), tend to equate the principalship with the sum of its various parts. In their preface, they outline their approach and beliefs.

> Leadership is treated as furnishing the conceptual tools for better role performance. . . . The principal is envisioned as the one who knows about all phases of administering the school and establishes procedures and a working environment that make it possible for others to carry out the work of the school. (p. *v*)

This kind of attitude led logically to the assumption that principals with proper training and the right tools could manage effectively. The mechanistic, technical metaphors certainly fit beautifully with this belief. Again, Jones and colleagues offer an excellent example of this view.

> There is great need today . . . for school administrators who are equipped to face new problems. It is not possible today to give all the answers to all of tomorrow's problems. But it is possible to assist people to develop competency in applying theory, research, and experimental methods to the school and community setting. Persons with the proper professional training and with the requisite personal qualifications can guide, tutor, lead, manage, and maneuver the human, physical, and social resources of the community toward the solution of problems. (p. 1)

Glass (1986b) selects some of the same images in his analysis of the views of administration conveyed in texts of this period. He describes these works as focusing on leaders "who managed human and fiscal resources in the institution known as the school" (p. 94). He also concludes that a dominant concern of this decade was proper administrative "use of social and behavioral science tools, models, techniques, methodologies, and theory" (p. 102). In her treatment of the effective junior high principal, Noar (1961) also uses technical metaphors. Discussing ways to plan an effective daily schedule, a "task [that] is usually the principal's responsibility" (p. 116), she systematically explores several factors influencing its accomplishment. Again, the language is mechanistic and technical.

> The organizational structures of junior high schools vary in accordance with all the variable factors that have to be taken into consideration—size of building, number of teachers in relation to number of rooms, the amount of time to be given to each learning area, the subject areas to be included in the core of common learnings, and the time to be devoted to it, the grades to be included in the reorganized program, the number of practical and fine arts rooms, and the capacity of the gymnasium. The plan used may be as simple as blocking time, subjects, and pupils on a departmentalized basis. (p. 116)

The technical tone of metaphors is also conveyed by the format of administrative reports issued during the sixties. The reports on the senior and junior high school principalship by Hemphill, Richards, and Peterson (1965) and Rock and Hemphill (1966) contain a series of discrete tables that purport to describe school leaders. The four-volume report of the National Principalship Study (Gross & Herriot, 1964; Gross & Trask, 1964; Dreeben & Gross, 1965; Dodd, 1965) uses a similar format in that the authors separate issues related to this role and present them as easily distinguishable entities. Phrases used by Gross and Trask in their discussion of data analysis strategies are especially revealing of this perspective. Their statement that "a principal components factor analysis was undertaken" (1964, p. 1/17) reveals that these scholars believe that an understanding of the principalship can be reached through an analysis of its separate functions.

DOMINANT VALUES: UNIFORMITY AND STANDARDIZATION

The metaphors chosen by authors of the 1960s reveal the high premium placed on standardization. Indeed, many scholars of this era call for uniform, standardized methods and measures in preparation programs, leadership and pedagogical techniques, and evaluative strategies. When considered in light of the prevailing assumption that schools are bureaucracies that function effectively when persons in clearly differentiated roles utilize proven techniques and technologies to effectively fulfill assigned tasks, this emphasis on standardization is not surprising.

Powell, Cohen, and Farrar (1985) maintain that this infatuation with uniformity and standardization represents misdirected attempts to process, with minimum effort, large numbers of students through this country's schools (see also Goodlad, 1984; Sizer, 1984). They claim that increases in numbers, especially of minority students, presented new challenges to administrators in the 1960s, but that principals in various schools attempted to meet these challenges "in the same fashion" (p. 296). This typically involved leaders devising "routine response[s]" that "diluted" (p. 294) programs so that they were palatable to virtually all students. Oakes (1985) offers a similar assessment. Specifically focusing on the virtually universal practice of "dividing students into instructional groups on the criterion of assumed similarity in ability or attainment" (p. *ix*) and offering standard types of instruction to these various groups, Oakes paints a vivid picture of life in schools when uniformity is valued.

> The events of junior and senior high school . . . [appear as] a complex but well-choreographed series of much-practiced and often-repeated steps. Each student performs a set routine, nearly if not completely identical to

that of his school mates. Even the stumblings, bumpings, and confusions seem so predictable and occur with such regularity that chance alone cannot explain them. . . .

So it goes, year after year. School counselors, only semivisible most of the time, emerge periodically to sort through the maze of classes and students until somehow everyone has a class arranged for every hour for the following year. And so the dance continues with only slight variations on the dominant theme of sameness. (pp. 1–2)

Oakes and Powell and his colleagues agree that this valuing of uniformity and standardization developed as administrators—beginning in the late fifties and continuing through the sixties—sought simple solutions to complex problems related to diversity, equity, and quality.

Another factor that apparently contributed to the valuing of "packaged" educative responses was the unbridled faith that science could uncover universally effective technologies for managing schools and teaching children. Austin, French, and Hull's (1962) contention that "a science of administration is possible" (p. 17) was noted earlier. Other phrases from these authors bear witness to the fact that standardization and uniformity are important values of this decade. They call for "the determination of classifications of [administrative] functions, . . . analysis and synthesis, . . . [and] the establishment of cause-and-effect relationships" (p. 17). Austin and colleagues contend that these activities should enable theorists, practicing principals, and policy makers to develop policies and programs applicable and useful for great numbers of diverse schools. The major recommendation of these authors, a recommendation clearly expressive of the premium they place on standardization and uniformity, is centralization of school governance at the state level.

> [The] responsibility [for education] is adequately discharged only when the state through its educational office takes the positive, active, and forward-looking part that enables—and requires where necessary—each local school to do its full share toward meeting the state's need. Since it is unlikely that at any time the standards set by the state represent the ultimate of what can or should be attained, the state authority should be continually at work to improve or raise standards. (p. 48)

Hemphill, Richards, and Peterson (1965) provide further evidence of the value placed on uniform standards. They report that their extensive survey of senior high principals reveals "most principals believed there is a need for greater uniformity in secondary school certification standards throughout the country" (p. 7).

The authors of *Professional Administrators for America's Schools: Thirty-Eighth Yearbook of the American Association of School Administrators* (1960) express similar sentiments. They criticize a misdirected commitment to and understanding of democratic leadership, noting that many principals—in their efforts to share responsibility—neglect "certain principles of group action . . . [and] certain basic rules of organization and administration" (p. 136). These authors recommend the development of standards in programs of principal preparation as an antidote to professional and organizational inadequacies. Campbell and his colleagues (1987) note that others, including Miller (1963), Goldhammer (1963), and the University Council for Educational Administration, also supported approaches to preparation that stressed, among other things, the acquisition of a core, "generic" (Campbell et al., 1987, p. 189) body of knowledge.

Authors of this decade also apparently value standardized instructional approaches. Hemphill and colleagues (1965) and Rock and Hemphill (1966) argue that pedagogical leadership is an area where some measure of standardization is valued. Both groups of scholars indicate that structured, "programmed" (Hemphill et al., 1965, p. 8) instructional strategies were of interest to virtually all survey respondents and that many principals were seeking ways to use these strategies in their schools. The interest in standardized, packaged teaching techniques is also evident in several of the reports of the conferences sponsored by the Educational Records Bureau and the American Council on Education. The very titles—*Measurement and Research in Today's Schools* (Traxler, 1961), *Improving the Efficiency and Quality of Learning* (Traxler, 1962), *Innovation and Experiment in Modern Education* (Traxler, 1965), and *Modern Educational Developments* (Davis, 1966)—hint at the high value placed on discovering the "best" approaches to teaching certain subjects. The words of Douglass (1963) reveal a similar perspective on administrative values. He calls on principals to learn "fundamental [and, by extension, universal] principles of textbook selection" (p. 147) and to utilize the "very important and well-subsidized studies [that] have been conducted on the content of secondary-school courses in mathematics, science, and foreign languages" (p. 151) to guide them in recognizing effective instructional approaches.

THE PRINCIPAL'S RELATIONSHIP TO OTHERS

The belief that schools are Weberian bureaucracies has clear implications for expectations about principals' relationships with state-level policy makers, superintendents, teachers, students, parents, and the larger community. In general, the metaphors embedded in discussions of these relationships underscore the belief that principals are expected to relate to superintendents, teachers, and students in ways consistent with a defined chain of command and hierarchy of status. Policy makers, insofar as their decisions affect school-level events, are represented as top-level members of this hierarchy. Principals are expected to operate under the authority of their superiors and to attempt to influence the thinking of various officials as necessary. Parents and community members are generally considered to be outside of the command structure of the hierarchy. They are, however, viewed as having indirect influence on the thinking and morale of educators. For this reason, principals are expected to work to keep these groups apprised of the school's accomplishments and needs, and to attempt to satisfy the interests of outside groups.

Campbell and his coauthors (1987) argue that the sixties witnessed a kind of clash between an open systems concept of schooling and a tightly defined bureaucratic view. They conclude that principals who had been accustomed to a "closed and top-down concept of organizations" (p. 198) were, during this decade, forced to grapple with complex demands emanating from forces outside education. Our analysis suggests that, under this pressure, most principals clung to the belief that schools were rational hierarchies and that their various relationships should be consistent with this assumption.

To State Policy Makers

Austin and his colleagues (1962) believe that local administrators should order their work to carry out state-level directives. When these directives are inadequate or inappropriate, principals are expected to work within established channels to urge changes.

> The really professional competent school executive, by reason of the completeness of his education in organization and administration ought to be able to keep his sense of direction in the midst of present relationships because he clearly recognized [the following] points: . . .
>
> The federal Constitution by indirection makes education a function of these States; we therefore have fifty state systems of education. . . .
> Since we do have fifty legally constituted state systems of education, local schools are subordinate parts of these systems and not independent units. . . .
> Local school executives charged with the education of youth have a particularly heavy responsibility to explain to colleagues and laymen in general the need for rapid improvement in federal, state, and local relations in education. (pp. 56–57)

Normative statements couched in categorical language help to feature a commitment to the view that administrators should carry out state-level policies.

> Since local schools are parts of a state system of schools, they cannot properly be a phase of local, city, or county general government. . . .
> Local control, home rule, and local initiative, however, are not unqualified virtues of which we can never have too much. . . .
> By the same token, centralization at the federal and state levels is not an unqualified evil. (p. 56)

To Superintendents

Other scholars and practitioners from this era focus their discussions on relations between school- and district-level administrators. Douglass (1963) especially stresses the principal's responsibility to serve as "the lieutenant of the superintendent of schools" (p. 26).

> While [the principal] should have much authority and responsibility within his individual school, it should always be recognized that his authority has been delegated to him by the superintendent of schools. . . .
> The superintendent of schools has the full authority to set aside decisions of the high school principal, to veto, to revoke, to supplement, and to change procedures at any time. (p. 27)

To be sure, Douglass maintains that "the relationship between the principal and superintendent should be one of co-operation and discussion" (p. 27). These activities are, however, to be carried on with a clear understanding of the established chain of command. Indeed, immediately after discussing the ideal of collegial relationships, Douglass argues, "The principal should have his contacts with the board of education entirely through the superintendent" (p. 27).

Gross and Herriot's (1964) comments on superintendent–principal interactions highlight the fact that authors in this decade view these roles as possessing distinct spheres of authority—with the superintendent clearly in a controlling position. They, for example, contrast the role of "many principals . . . [and] their administrative superiors" (p. 98). They further note that principals are in the "lowest levels of management in public education" (p. 96) and that they are answerable to superintendents, "the officials responsible for the overall management of vital sectors or functions of school systems" (p. 96). In a similar manner, Jones and colleagues (1969), even while writing of the virtues of democratic relationships among principals, superintendents, and boards, focus on the fact that these relation-ships occur because high members of the school hierarchy authorize them. "Superintendents must delegate the necessary authority and responsibility for principals to use their leadership effectively" (p. 178).

To Teachers

The bureaucratic framework that influences superintendent–principal interactions also has an impact on conceptions of principals' relationships with teachers. Indeed, writers in this decade argue that principals are re-sponsible for their teachers' morale and performance and are expected to act in ways promoting both. With regard to teacher morale, authors frequently discuss the importance of democratic leadership and shared decision making (e.g., Austin et al., 1962; Gross & Herriot, 1964; Jones et al., 1969; Keller, 1963). Interestingly, though, many suggest that principals should create a sense of democracy within schools but should carefully control and limit expressions of teacher autonomy. Austin and his colleagues (1962) provide examples of this perspective. In one section, they write of the importance of "teachers . . . participat[ing] in administration" (p. 179) in order to "im-prove the morale of the teaching staff" (p. 180). They believe, however, that principals should monitor and control the limits of teacher participa-tion. In another section, they write stingingly of a concept of democratic leadership that assumes that "the principal has no more responsibility for the school than any other member of its staff" (p. 127). Indeed, they emphasize that, within schools, principals possess the greatest amount of responsibility and authority.

> The principal will find it necessary to assign tasks and delegate authority, but he will still bear the ultimate responsibility. In making some decisions, he may choose to accede to pressure from without or within the school, but he will not escape responsibility. The pressure groups which impor-tuned him will not hold him blameless if the outcomes of their requests, to which he has yielded, are unsatisfactory. They are not responsible. He is. (p. 127)

Gross and Herriot (1964), in their discussions of effective leadership styles, claim that principals can actually use democratic leadership to rein-force their own authority. Indeed, their study confirms "that a principal can reduce the reluctance of his teachers to accept his professional leadership by inviting them to help him in arriving at decisions" (p. 625). In a similar vein, Jones, Salisbury, and Spencer (1969) argue that "it is the job of the principal to develop and maintain high morale among his faculty members"

(p. 179). In doing this, they stress that schools must be treated as "work-shop[s] of democracy" (p. 178), and they emphasize that principals play an important role in supporting this idea.

> The person who heads the secondary school makes it largely what it is. If the principal does not know how to use the faculty and to stimulate their thinking, the school will never achieve its potential. A well-qualified principal, on the other hand, may make it possible for an individual school and its faculty to overcome many obstacles and to produce an efficient school that gets the job done. (p. 179)

Again, what is noteworthy is the portrayal of a principal as a controlling, almost Machiavellian, person who can "use" others.

Not only do scholars of this decade focus on ways principals might promote faculty morale; they also believe that a central administrative task is helping teachers achieve instructional excellence. Again, statements on this topic suggest that principals are often viewed as surpassing teachers in pedagogical knowledge, and the expectation is that they seek various ways to impart this knowledge to faculty. Noar's (1961) words, for example, stress that the principal is expected "to create a school in which the students will continue to develop their mental and manual skills" (p. 104) by "help-ing his staff to acquire the necessary teaching skills" (p. 107). Her language implies that this basically involves unilateral action on the part of the school leader. She writes of principals accepting "responsibility for directing faculty discussion, study, and action" (p. 105), "recognizing the gap [in teaching] which exists between knowing what to do and how to do it" (p. 107), seeking "enterprises which will enlist teachers in study and activity" (p. 109), and "continuously interpret[ing] the process [teachers] are using in terms of classroom work with children" (p. 111).

For many authors of this decade, fulfilling these responsibilities requires that principals provide education, especially in pedagogy, for teachers. Doug-lass (1963) writes, at some length, of techniques for "stimulating in-service growth of teachers" (p. 101). Hemphill, Richards, and Peterson (1965) note that senior high principals consider supplying "education leadership in . . . interaction with teachers" (p. 6) to be a central administrative task. And Rock and Hemphill (1966), writing about junior high principals, call for these leaders to take an active role in evaluating curricular innovations and making recommendations to teachers. Jones and his colleagues (1969), emphasizing that "the principal is held responsible for improving the in-structional program in his school" (p. 179), devote numerous pages to discussing procedures that principals might use to improve teaching meth-ods. They also write at length about very specific curricular issues and suggest that the principal be involved actively in program development. This, in their view, involves specifying units to be covered in every subject.

Discussing ways to promote excellent teaching, Austin and his coauthors (1962) feature the importance of principals evaluating teachers' classroom performances and providing useful feedback to faculty members. Describing evaluation as "a constant feature of the work of a school staff and an integral part of planning and replanning of all activities in the school" (p. 193), these authors seem quite comfortable with principals conducting very critical assessments. They quote the following statement as one accurately describing the proper principal–teacher relationship:

> The relation of the principal to his teachers should be the most intimate of all. If a teacher fails, the principal fails; if the teacher succeeds, the principal succeeds. To sum up what the principal's job is, I should call him a referee—the captain of the ship—the boss of the firm—a juvenile court judge before whose tribunal come not only the culprits but also the adults who frequently contribute to the pupils' shortcomings. (Stuart, 1923, quoted in Austin et al., 1962, p. 134)

In their discussion of principal behavior that promotes "teacher effort," Dreeben and Gross (1965, p. 4/16) emphasize the importance of close and frequent supervision. Indeed, they present empirical evidence to support the idea that "the closer the supervision a principal exercises over staff members, the greater their effort to be of maximum service to their pupils" (p. 4/19). Again, they claim that this scrutiny is primarily intended to uncover pedagogical problems. They choose the word "surveillance" as a synonym for supervision and note that this involves checking to see whether teachers

> Waste a lot of time in their classroom activities. . . .
> Do "textbook teaching" only. . . .
> Usually "drag their feet" when new ideas are introduced into the school
>   program. (p. 4/19)

Furthermore, they imply that rewards and punishments should be meted out according to findings of the principal. "A principal who supervises closely is in effect auditing the performance of his staff and communicating that maximum effort to serve pupils will be rewarded and minimum effort will expose them to negative sanctions" (p. 4/18).

To Students

Consistent with the notion that principals should work through a chain of command in interacting with others, the literature of the sixties has little to say about direct interactions between principals and students. Dreeben and Gross (1965) clearly convey this in their analysis of principal–teacher and teacher–student relationships.

> The position of the teacher is analogous to that of principal in the sense that occupants of both positions have obligations to immediate superiors for carrying out school-wide and system-wide policies. In addition, teachers and principals serve individuals whose interests differ at a number of points from those of their superiors. (p. 2/18)

Further statements by these authors underscore their belief that principals deal with teachers, and teachers with students. Indeed, they never write of principal–student relationships, stressing instead that principals, because they are dealing with "hired employee[s]" (p. 2/19) have an easier time than teachers, who "must cope with both a class . . . , an aggregation of pupils as a social unit, and with these same pupils individually" (p. 2/20).

Douglass (1963) expresses the same view of principal–pupil relationships. He does, however, acknowledge that in some situations, "an elaborate organization for guidance [to prevent principal–student interactions] is often not possible" (p. 306). He notes that this could cause difficulties in that "it is difficult for him [the principal] to assume the double role of 'terror' to evildoers and 'friend' of the sinners" (p. 306). This author suggests that, even in the case of direct interactions with students, principals should include counselors, teachers, or others as often as possible.

Jones and colleagues (1969) portray principals' relationships with students as consisting chiefly of evaluations of grades. They write that "the administration of the modern secondary school must assume keen interest in grading" (p. 219), and they suggest that principals use student scores as "an instrument of instructional improvement" (p. 219). Again, the emphasis is clearly on working within the bureaucracy. If students' grades suggest deficiencies, principals are to remedy the situation by working with teachers.

To Parents and Community

Parents and community members are considered to be outside the school hierarchy by writers in the 1960s. However, because they influence schools, principal–parent–community member relationships do receive some attention in the literature. In general, principals are expected to engage in "public relations [that seek] to bring about a harmony of understanding between any group and the public it serves and upon whose good will it depends" (American Association of School Administrators, 1950, p. 12, quoted in Jones et al., 1969, p. 387). Most thinkers of this era agree that this requires principals to study the community to which they must relate (Douglass, 1963), defending schools by offering hard data to critics (Hemphill et al., 1965; Jones et al., 1969; Noar, 1961), cultivating "relations with key community organizations" (Douglass, 1963, p. 558; see also Austin et al., 1962), and involving "parents as planners" (Austin et al., 1962, p. 554) in key school matters.

STANDARDS FOR EVALUATION

One assumption inherent in a bureaucratic notion of organizations is that decisions and actions on each level in the hierarchy directly affect work done on the level immediately below. A logical corollary of this belief is that the performance of persons on each plane reflects on that of those above them. These ideas clearly influence authors who discuss evaluative strategies in the sixties. It is also important to note that this is the first period when authors write at length about evaluating the practice of administrators.

Several articles in Carver and Sergiovanni's *Organizations and Human Behavior* (1969) underscore the assumption that performance of subordinates reflects on that of their superiors. March and Simon (1969), for example, discuss the work of Merton, Sleznick, Gouldner, and Litwak and note ways organizational performance could be used to evaluate and guide the actions of leaders. Their work, replete with charts outlining chains of responsibility and feedback patterns, clearly conveys the assumption that the effectiveness of those in authority can be assessed by examining the output of those below them. March and Simon's emphasis is on the ways assessments can be used in formative evaluations to guide—changing if necessary—administrative actions. Noar (1961), in a similar manner, maintains that principals can, indeed, be evaluated by the accomplishments of students and teachers. Like March and Simon, she accentuates the formative nature of these assessments, writing that "the evaluation program of a school . . . includes[s] research into the effectiveness of the total program in accomplishing the goals that faculty, pupils, and community set up. In order to achieve the outcomes for which they are intended the evaluation activities must be continuous, cooperative and constructive" (p. 345).

Others emphasize the ways evaluations can be used to make summative judgments about administrator effectiveness. Austin, French, and Hull (1962) choose language that clearly suggests that principals can and should be judged by the performance of teachers and students. Douglass (1963) writes of evaluation as a means to formally assess principals' effectiveness. Like others, he stresses the appropriateness of judging leaders by "the pupil product" (p. 613) they produce. Unlike most other writers, Douglass actually specifies who should do this evaluating. In his view, "outside agencies and individuals, . . . state departments of education, . . . local supervisors and administrators, . . . [and] teachers" (pp. 609–610) have the right and the duty to assess principals' performance. Furthermore, Douglass outlines ways evaluative data should be used by focusing on the ability of state-level agencies to give or withhold accreditation on the basis of this information. Douglass specifically discusses the school as the recipient of rewards or punishments as a result of this assessment. Because in other sections he clearly links the school and principal, it would seem that, in a very real sense, any evaluation of school performance is also an assessment of the administrator.

As noted earlier, principals of this decade experienced a fair amount of inner conflict and stress. Dodd (1965) suggests that this conception of judging the principal by the "product" (p. 3/4) is one source of such stress for the principal and, citing Lortie (1961), notes that teachers experience a similar kind of stress. He also reports that principals experience "strain" (p. 3/11) because of the many persons evaluating them. The standards and emphases of "students, teachers, administrators, and parents" (p. 3/12) are frequently different; yet all of these groups are in a position to judge the principal. The results of the National Principalship Study (reported by Dodd) indicate that principals experience "conflicting expectations and role conflict" (p. 3/4) because of these multiple evaluators.

CONCLUSION

The metaphorical language of the 1960s suggests that this decade was, to borrow from Cuban (1984), one of "constancy and change." The constancy lies in the continued faith in rational thought, planning, social science, and technology as phenomena capable of providing school leaders with answers to pressing questions. The prevalence of bureaucratic, techni-cal, categorical language and the tendency to discuss the principalship in terms of clearly defined responsibility and authority bear witness to the impact of this faith on conceptions of the principalship. The change lies in the fact that some of the not-so-sanguine logical conclusions of this faith in rationality and science—as they affected the principalship—were explicitly acknowledged for the first time. The seeds of discontent had been planted.

Missing in this decade is the lofty language that dominated the litera-ture of the twenties, thirties, and forties. The principalship is viewed as a job that can be learned. Principals act in accord with directives from their immediate superiors, not some spiritual ideal or patriotic belief. Theory is to be tested and used by administrators, and its usefulness and their effectiveness are to be judged according to the kinds of products produced.

Significantly absent are frank discussions of problems related to desegregation, poverty, and the general social unrest that pervaded our culture during this decade. It seems that, as complex social problems expanded, the emphasis on the proper application of bureaucratic and scientific principles and the confidence that this focus would solve any educational problem also increased. In many ways, it seems as if principals and those who wrote about them spent much time and energy denying the reality of these complex problems. Along with this denial, a strong commitment to rationally motivated activity appears to have mushroomed. Administration in the sixties is portrayed as a highly impersonal activity. Feelings and beliefs are not discussed; concrete ways to improve the quality and level of production are.

CHAPTER SIX

The 1970s

In their analysis of educational trends, Campbell and his coauthors (1987) describe the 1970s as years in which "external factors" (p. 93) exert a heavy influence on administrative thought and practice. They specifically credit increased federal involvement in local schools and the rise of numerous, often vocal, special interest groups with altering many tasks of educational leaders. Our analysis of the metaphors of this decade, summarized in Figure 6.1, suggests that conceptions of the principalship are, indeed, affected by what might be called the "opening of schools" to outside scrutiny and governance.

DOMINANT METAPHORICAL THEMES

Specifically, the following themes emerge from the literature of this era:

1. The principal is expected to lead not only teachers and students, but also persons within the larger community.
2. Additionally, he or she is charged with imparting "meaning" to educational efforts.
3. The principal is expected to relate well to persons and to facilitate positive interactions among and between students and teachers.
4. During this decade, the principal is expected to skillfully juggle a number of roles, even if those roles require very different traits or abilities.

Principal as Community Leader

Burden and Whitt (1973), in the very title of their book, *The Community School Principal*, underscore the concern of this decade that principals relate not only to those within schools, but also to persons in the commu-

FIGURE 6.1 Analysis of Metaphors of the 1970s

Dominant Metaphorical Themes
The principal is expected to lead, not only teachers, but also persons within the
    larger community.
Additionally, he or she is charged with imparting "meaning" to educational
    efforts.
The principal is expected to relate well to persons and to facilitate positive
    interactions among and between students and teachers.
The principal is expected to juggle skillfully a number of roles, even if those
    roles require very different traits or abilities.

Dominant Tones
Humanistic
Socially Relevant

Dominant Values
Self-actualization
Cultivation of an emotionally supportive climate
Societal transformation

Relationship to Others
To superintendents and boards of education—
    An influential persuader
To teachers—
    Partners in a nonbureaucratic system
To students—
    Facilitator of development
    Protector of rights
To the community—
    An educator
    A volunteer coordinator

Standards for Evaluation
Objective Evaluative Mechanisms
Trait Approach

nity. Arguing that changing social situations force principals to extend the
scope of leadership activities, they write:

> Community power is a coming reality. The previous view that the local
> school could remain aloof and isolated from those it was purported to
> serve is no longer a viable one. The changing concept of democracy that
> means all people are to be involved, not just those in power, places new
> responsibilities on the building administrator. (p. *xiii*)

For these authors, building community alliances is a strategic activity engaged in by the shrewd principal who recognizes that her or his continued professional success hinges on the support of persons outside schools. Noting that "it is incumbent on the principal of a school to build into his leadership style a method of community involvement" (p. 177), Burden and Whitt offer a number of tactical suggestions—many drawn from observations of practice—in an effort to help principals accomplish this task. They note, for example, the words used in a brochure published by the Flint, Michigan, School Board (no cite given). This brochure, aimed at administrators, details "Four I's [which] Assure Successful Community Participation." These are

> IN—Get the people of the community into the school, primarily by means of recreation and education.
>
> INTERESTED—Get them interested. Explain the problems and help the community to solve them. Get the staff and administration interested in community problems.
>
> INVOLVED—Ask people to help. They are willing and able when given the opportunity.
>
> INFORMED—The informed person is the responsible citizen concerned with improvement. (cited in Burden & Whitt, 1973, pp. 178–179)

The principal is portrayed as the person responsible for ensuring that schools and communities connect in meaningful ways. "This [community] participation cannot come about unless the principal provides for an open system as opposed to the traditional closed system" (p. 179). This means that principals must avoid the tendency to separate their schools and themselves "sociologically and even psychologically from [their] constituents" (p. 179).

Sergiovanni and Carver (1973) agree that principals must consider themselves integral members of communities and that civic leadership is obligatory for school officers. Indeed, they assert that the principal's role as a public leader/servant is, perhaps, the most important one. "School executives are first and foremost guardians of the public interest" (p. 17). To be sure, they acknowledge that on-site management of the school as an organization and as a center of learning is an important way principals can guard this interest, but they are quick to caution that these activities cannot and should not be undertaken by principals who are not committed to and linked with larger communities. For Sergiovanni and Carver, this means assuming social and leadership roles with those operating outside the schools.

The literature of the 1970s also encourages principals to have their schools undertake an additional form of involvement—the education of members of the community. For example, a brochure by the Center for Community Education (1971) calls leaders to engage in "Community Education [which is defined as] the process of bringing a community together under one umbrella" (quoted in Burden & Whitt, 1973, p. 182). According to this document's authors, exercising this kind of leadership requires a return to a traditional understanding of the school's place in the community.

> Basically, it is a return to the concept of the "little red schoolhouse." The "little red schoolhouse" was, first of all, a meeting place for all social, recreational, and governmental activities. It was a place identified with by all ages and groups. (quoted in Burden & Whitt, 1973, p. 182)

Another set of suggestions for ways to establish this school–community link can be found in a report on one successful enterprise (Drake–Des Moines Institute, 1971). The structure discussed, labeled the Charrette model, details a number of options principals might consider. These include establishing a school–community linkage by using a liaison or ombudsman, providing transportation to school events for large groups of citizens, opening gymnasiums and other athletic facilities for outside use, and working closely with social agencies and organizations such as the police force, the United Way, and the state employment service. The Charrette model also advocates that principals create and lead discussion groups containing school personnel and community members.

Burden and Whitt (1973) discuss other strategies found in the literature of this period to help the principal become "an involved person" (p. 188) and community leader. For example, they describe the work of James Solberg, "a junior high school principal in Seaside, California, [who] has long been an advocate of reaching out and becoming a partner in the community, thus becoming personally involved and (in the end) . . . requir-[ing] people to become involved in the school" (p. 188). Solberg's practices of dropping "in, unannounced, at students' homes, just to chat," intervening "in the abrupt eviction of a poor family," and participating "on a committee that is instrumental in developing a local legal aid service for the poor" (Solberg, 1968, p. 38) are praised as effective activities. Other examples of community leadership are offered by John Worden (1971). His leadership tasks include

1. Cultivating an awareness of the community
2. Actually exploring (using a variety of mechanisms) some areas of concern
3. Discussing with other leaders ways alliances might be built

4. Planning joint activities with community residents and school personnel
5. Formally establishing some link between the school and its environs
6. Acting on that linkage
7. Evaluating the actions and arrangements

By identifying these as "leadership" activities, Worden emphasizes that they fall within the principal's purview.

Principal as Imparter of Meaning

In the seventies, the belief that schools should offer meaningful experiences—to students, teachers, staff, and community members—receives a great deal of attention in administrative literature. Much of this writing suggests that principals are expected to see that educational experiences are, in fact, "meaningful" ones. This emphasis is vividly illustrated in *Schools in Search of Meaning* (Macdonald & Zaret, 1975), a yearbook published by the Association for Supervision and Curriculum Development. Opening this volume are words that express the concerns motivating this quest for meaningfulness.

> "Schools in Search of Meaning," was the general topic assigned for the Yearbook of 1975. . . . We recognized that implicit in our charge were three fundamental problems:
>
> 1. That schools no longer appear to mean what most of us hoped that they would mean in American society;
> 2. That the development of relevant personal meanings in schools is a precarious and doubtful endeavor; and
> 3. That the search for meaning in our professional lives and activity should be a function of all educators. (pp. 1–2)

Having identified these as problems, the contributors to this volume explore the idea of meaning as it applies to various issues and/or special interest groups. In some of the articles, clear statements are offered regarding the principal's actual or ideal role in the search for meaning.

One of the more dramatic examinations of issues of meaning as they relate to school leadership is an article by William Burton entitled "Schools and Sex (A Tragedy in Two Parts)" (1975). In this piece, written as poetry, Burton looks critically at the ways principals have handled such issues as youthful sexuality. In one passage he suggests that administrators have allied themselves with various authority figures such as "dad, teacher, principal, dean, boss, judge, governor, president" (p. 74) to act in meaningless and repressive ways. Indeed, he claims that "all school people and parents are sadists who are neurotically compelled to oppress young people" (p. 73). He further notes that, for those in "The system of AUTHORITY," the concept of "Respect . . . always seems to apply only up" (p. 73). If Burton's work had appeared in some other volume, it might be considered an expression of the anti-establishment culture of this period. What is interesting is its inclusion in the ASCD Yearbook, a volume supported by a prominent professional organization whose readers are primarily administrators and teachers with some decision-making power. The presence of this indictment of school leaders in this work carries a powerful implicit message that principals should act in ways that ensure that schooling is meaningful, especially for those with little or no official authority. Additionally, Burton's focus on sexuality as a topic that should concern principals hints at a point we discuss more fully in the next section. That is, schools find their meaning by involvement in nonacademic, social issues as well as those more typically linked to education.

Principal and teacher Dwayne Huebner (1975) offers words suggesting that principals who act as protectors and cultivators of genuinely meaningful educational experiences will find themselves facing conflict. Indeed, he argues that a commitment to meaning will require principals, at times, to upset the order and stability of schools and their governance structures.

> The tension between educating the individual and maintaining an orderly classroom and school resides not in the school as a bureaucratic institution with defined expectancies and roles. Behind the roles and the expectancies, behind the bureaucracy and the orderliness, are the interests of people. People have invested their lives and their meanings in the school, its maintenance, and its supporting mechanisms and ideologies. The tension made manifest in the conflict between the possible education of the individual and the maintenance of the school is the tension between those who have an interest in a future emerging in the lives of the children and young people, and those who have a future which now exists in their everyday-ness—the structures, orderliness, and meanings attached to the school and school related pursuits. (pp. 28–29)

The view that meaningful leadership may require administrators to abandon a commitment to bureaucratic principles can be found in the statements of Berman (1977b). Arguing that principals must act and react as *persons* rather than as inhabitants of a hierarchical position, she challenges administrators to develop flexible structures that "accommodate to the persons within [them] and not vice versa" and to discover "means of formal and informal communication that stress meaningful dialogue among parts of the whole" (p. 276). In her view, this is the only type of leadership for schools where each individual's "ideas are . . . respected, honored, and given the opportunity to develop and mature" (p. 275).

Berman's linking of meaningful leadership with an emphasis on the human side of schooling can be found in other works from this period. William Hitt, for instance, in an impassioned book entitled *Education as a Human Enterprise* (1973), argues that schooling finds its meaning in its ability to contribute to the development of persons and that "inspired leadership and dedicated teachers" (p. 152) must recognize and support this goal. He specifically calls on educators to link "a rational and systematic approach to educational planning [with] the human dimensions, involving the active participation of the education community in the change process" (p. 152). Sergiovanni and Starratt (1971) similarly link meaningful leadership with a greater commitment to "the human school" (p. 2). These authors specifically explore ways principals might understand and undertake supervision as "a process [that offers] a . . . meaningful mode of analysis" (p. 10) of educational activities. In their view, principals holding "human perspectives" (p. *v*) and practicing "enlightened supervision" (p. 2) will be able to help teachers and students enjoy meaningful, satisfying school experiences.

Principal as Facilitator of Positive Relationships

The idea that principals are to foster a sense that education is a meaningful experience is closely linked to the expectation that good leaders will engage in and encourage positive, supportive interpersonal relationships. Indeed, in this decade education's meaning often is linked to three related beliefs: that schools and their leaders should encourage the holistic development of persons; that fulfilling this goal entails working to ensure that students and teachers have positive emotional experiences; and that experiences of this type depend, in large measure, on participation in positive, supportive, nonconflictual relationships. These beliefs, it seems, converge to shape the assumption that good principals participate in and encourage such relationships.

One of the boldest expressions of this expectation can be found in Jordan's essay, "Love in Administration," contained in Bradfield and Kraft's text, *The Elementary School Principal* (1970). In this piece, Jordan argues that successful principals will exhibit love in their personal and professional interactions. Indeed, he purports that "optimum results can be accomplished through love . . . [a word that] means, here, sympathetic understanding, empathetic feeling, strong liking, fondness, good will, friendliness, brotherhood, compassion" (p. 3). Furthermore, Jordan suggests that this quality, if pervasive in schools, has the potential to virtually eliminate conflict.

> It may be . . . that conflict can be avoided altogether if the dynamic mix of people, organizational procedures and goals, and situational features engenders a vigorous, viable, friendly, sustaining kind of administrative action. (p. 8)

If read in isolation, Jordan's rather dramatic claims might run the risk as being dismissed as naive or utopian. Other authors, though, express similar sentiments. Burden and Whitt (1973), for example, write:

> In simple terms, it means that a principal must be able to convey the true meaning of LOVE to the staff. This is the beginning of developing a cooperative environment that leads to a consensual educational leadership model. Ashley Montagu writes:
> Love, social behavior, cooperation, and security mean very much the same thing. Without love, the other three cannot exist. To love thy neighbor as thyself is not simply good text material for Sunday morning sermons, but perfectly sound biology. Men who do not love one another are sick—sick not from any disease arising within themselves, but from a disease which has been enculturated within them by false values of their societies. Principals who fail to give recognition to teachers for the good things they accomplish are sick because it indicates an absence of love. (Burden & Whitt, 1973, p. 23, quoting Montagu, 1955, p. 247)

Other authors, using slightly less dramatic language, also express the belief that good school leaders will concentrate on positive interpersonal interactions. Sergiovanni and Carver (1973), citing the work of Raymond Miles (1965), call on principals to adopt a human resource model of administration. At the center of this framework is the assumption that effective leaders will acknowledge and respond to a range of needs, including the "common needs for belonging and respect" (p. 40). Principals within this framework will not neglect goals related to individual and organizational performance. They will, however, recognize the link between pleasant and satisfying relationships and performance goals. Sergiovanni and Carver go so far as to address the question of what happens when persons "do not or cannot operate in accordance with [this model]" (p. 48). They suggest that leaders, using communication and coordination, should seek "to build and support people so that they are, as Maslow puts it, 'converted'" (p. 48). This suggestion underscores that heavy emphasis is placed on working effectively with people, for these authors view positive interactions as the desirable ends of administrative action and as the preferred means by which all can be encouraged to achieve these ends. Sergiovanni and Carver's use of Maslow's term "converted" is also worthy of note. Its religious connotation suggests that the establishment of an environment where "everyone can enjoy good team work, friendship, good group spirit, good group harmony, good belongingness, and group love" (Maslow, 1965, quoted in Sergiovanni & Carver, 1973, p. 46) is a goal leaders might pursue with almost religious fanaticism.

Cecil Patterson (1977) joins with Sergiovanni and Carver in asserting that principals must emphasize and practice positive interpersonal relations. He suggests that "education must become concerned with the development of individuals not as disembodied intellects, nor even as citizens of a single nation, but as persons, as members of a world community, as members of the human race" (p. 164). Patterson argues that leaders need to seek three relational qualities in order to reach this ideal: "empathic understanding . . . respect . . . [and] facilitative genuineness" (pp. 165–166). The first of these is defined as "knowing of another being which is achieved from putting oneself in the place of another" (p. 165). Respect, Patterson defines as

> an acceptance of [another] as a person of worth, without judgment or condemnation. It is unconditional, not dependent on his behaving as we would like him to or agreeing with us. It is a caring and valuing of him as a person, a human being, with a deep concern for him. (p. 165)

In regard to facilitative genuineness, Patterson notes:

> Being genuine is being real, honest, open, sincere, as contrasted with being deceptive, maintaining a facade or playing a role. There is no incongruence between what one is thinking and feeling and what one says. Authenticity and transparency refer to the same thing. Genuineness is not to be confused with so-called "brutal honesty or frankness." It does not require that one express all of one's negative feelings, momentary irritations, and hostilities as some encounter leaders advocate. These feelings are often more related to one's own hang-ups than to the behavior of the other person and are not facilitative in relationships with others. (p. 166)

Berman (1977b) also calls on administrators to facilitate positive relationships and to equip persons to function both "as individuals [and] as members of larger communities" (p. 275). In her view, setting an example of interacting positively is a valuable strategy for principals who wish to facilitate emotionally sound schools. "The range of behaviors necessary to living a full life is frequently taught through example as well as through opportunities for planned experiences" (p. 277). Burden and Whitt (1973) agree, noting:

> The major challenge facing the administrator in the larger school is that of providing an atmosphere wherein the entire administrative staff functions as a team. The delineation of areas of authority and responsibility, the adoption of comprehensive lines of communication, and the establishment of effective working relationships within the administrative team is of primary importance. No segment of the school group can be neglected in the drive to establish positive staff interaction. (p. 96)

Principal as Juggler of Multiple Roles

A common thread runs through the themes we have discussed thus far. Principals are expected to engage in and support emotionally positive relationships—within and outside their institutions—in order to contribute to the meaningfulness of a schooling experience. Writers of this era do not portray fulfilling these expectations as an easy or a simple task. Indeed, they suggest that satisfactory functioning requires that the principal embrace a number of seemingly unrelated roles.

The words of Mintzberg (1973) illustrate these multiple role conceptions. He offers 13 metaphors to describe principals—metaphors organized under three broad headings: "interpersonal facilitator, . . . information manager, . . . [and] decision maker" (p. 56). He claims that the principal as an interpersonal facilitator functions as "figurehead, leader, [and] liaison"; as information manager, she or he is "monitor, disseminator, spokesman"; and as decision maker the principal is an "entrepreneur, disturbance handler, resource allocator, [and] negotiator" (p. 59). Taking a similar view, Small (1974) offers a number of metaphors to describe the principal. These include

initiator
stimulator
reactor
implementor
conduit
orchestrator
mediator
persuader
dissuader
advocate
ombudsman (p. 21, 22).

Commenting on the complexity and number of expectations, Roe and Drake (1974) suggest that these cause considerable conflict for principals. Indeed, they describe the school leader as

> a professional person being torn apart on the one hand by his intense interest and desire to lead in instruction and learning and on the other hand by his responsibility to "keep school" through the proper administration and management of people and things as expected by the central administration. (p. 10)

These authors note that the managerial role, alone, demands that principals keep records, make reports, develop budgets, handle scheduling, supervise the building, administer supplies, monitor all school programs, and manage student activities. These responsibilities, they emphasize, do not in any way include the expectations that principals function as instructional leaders. Indeed, these authors suggest that the concept of principal as instructional leader is more a dream than a reality. They write, "Under present circumstances it is expected that the principal be primarily an administrator and manager. The instructional leadership talk is often lip service paid to create a greater self-respect within the professional group itself" (p. 10).

Inbar (1977) concurs with Roe and Drake's contention and notes that "school principals are victims of multiple discrepancies in role perceptions" (p. 80). Brennan (1973) also agrees and suggests that differences in expectations extend beyond principals' current views of their roles and encompass beliefs about ways these roles may evolve over time. Rhetorically he asks, "What may the next step be: scholarly educational leader, business manager, educational statesman in a democratic school or educational realist?" (p. 177).

These multiple expectations may exist, in part, because of diverse views regarding the principal's place in the educational bureaucracy. On the one hand, some literature calls on school leaders to operate outside the hierarchical framework. On the other hand, quite a few scholars discuss principals as consummate members of traditional governance structures. The first perspective is evident in *Schools in Search of Meaning* (Macdonald & Zaret, 1975). Contributors here tend to take a critical view of existing structures and call on concerned administrators to work against them. Words from the "Introduction" are illustrative.

> Education is the activity of liberation (a la Nietzsche): liberation from ignorance, fear, want, disease, and alienation from oppression and liberation from the role of unwitting oppressor. . . .
> The present . . . endeavors that pass for education are not neutral [and] have actually resulted in the acceptance of broader moral values that

destroy the development of personal meaning and are representative of a form of oppressive social meaning. (pp. 4-5)

One contributor, Burton, bitterly condemns "the system of AUTHORITY" (p. 73) in schools as one that perpetuates "repression [which is] to have by controlling [and] seduction [which is] to control by having" (p. 72). Brennan (1973), writing less prescriptively, states that research on leadership roles demonstrates "that principals are not bureaucrats" (p. 175).

The contrasting view is expressed by Roe and Drake (1974), who argue that "the principal of the local elementary, middle or secondary school finds himself in the middle of this developing administrative bureaucracy" (p. 34). Sergiovanni and Carver (1973), while noting some "dysfunctional effects of bureaucratic organization" (p. 137), also imply that a certain type of hierarchy is both useful and inevitable. Their choice of "the school executive" (p. 135) as the metaphor for the principal is revealing, as are their words.

> When an individual is appointed to the school organization (the social system) he assumes a positional identity: superintendent, principal, teacher, student. These are all identities which, in the relatively formally-created social system of the school, carry with them certain generally agreed-upon images. (pp. 177-178)

Overall, we see both continuity and change in the dominant metaphorical themes of the 1970s. Like her or his counterpart in the 1960s, the principal of the 1970s is subject to multiple role expectations, which emanate from persons within school systems and from those without. There are, however, important changes. The major revision is a shift in metaphors from the principal as "bureaucrat" and as "protector of the system" to the principal as "facilitator of meaning construction" and as "initiator of emotionally sound relationships." At the core of the change is a reorientation of the principal's work away from a structural stance toward a human perspective. The language also reveals a reorientation from an administrative focus on the educational system to a concern with the larger school community.

DOMINANT TONES OF THE METAPHORS

We have chosen the phrases "humanist" and "socially relevant" to describe the tone of the metaphors from this decade. In our view, these words capture certain emphases characteristic of beliefs about the role and tasks of principals. They also point out some interesting differences between the expectations of the seventies and conceptions and beliefs from earlier periods.

The Humanistic Tone

Our claim that the figurative expressions of the 1970s possess a humanistic tone is based, in large measure, on the many references to the administrator's role in facilitating holistic human development. William Hitt's *Education as a Human Enterprise* (1973) contains numerous revealing examples. In his opening chapter, Hitt identifies three models of educational leadership: "traditional, . . . technological, . . . and human" (p. 1). He strongly condemns the first model but suggests some merit can be found in the technological and human perspectives. Hitt argues that "humanism" (p. 21) provides "a unified philosophy of education" (p. 20) capable of relating "educational theory and educational practice in a form that is useful to the practicing educator . . . [and of providing] guidance for the formulation of educational goals as well as for selecting the means for achieving the goals" (p. 20). Two passages vividly describe the humanistic educational leader.

> The humanist is a scientist-advocate who promotes the idea of man achieving his full potentiality. He is grounded in science as he endeavors to understand man, but, in addition, he advocates that this knowledge be applied to help many become more fully human. (p. 21)

> Our model of the effective [educator] is a person who has a stable self-concept, a sense of personal identity. His thoughts, feelings, words, and actions are unified and consistent. He is open to correction. He is able to generate his own ideas and make his own decisions. He is accountable to himself and to others for his actions. He is an effective problem solver. He has an active concern for the welfare of other people. He has a zest for life. (p. 55)

Weinberg (1971) also stresses the practical and philosophical importance of principals seeking to develop "humanistic school[s] . . . concerned with knowledge, interpersonal relations, human potentialities, and social problems" (p. 16). He suggests that the first of these concerns, knowledge, is typically considered to be within the bailiwick of the educational leader and implies that, in the past, others have been neglected. Weinberg argues that a concern with relationships and human potential should receive administrative attention and that such concern will, in fact, characterize humanistic principals and schools. "The humanistic school is one in which the latent outcomes of activities which appear to show little in the way of production will be evaluated in terms of maturation in the area of inter-personal relations" (p. 17).

Sergiovanni and Starratt (1971) also offer a number of phrases that exemplify a humanist tone. For example, in their preface, these authors explain their purposes with these words:

> *Emerging Patterns of Supervision: Human Perspectives* has as its primary goal the humanizing of American education. . . . We believe that humanizing education with its focus on self-actualization of youngsters, can be achieved only in a humanizing organization which focuses on self-actualization of teachers and other educational professionals. (p. *v*)

These authors discuss, in some detail, the actions and philosophies of humanistic or "enlightened" (p. 17) administrators. They stress that such leaders will concentrate on three major tasks: "planning, communicating, and changing and facilitating group supervision" (p. *vi*) and that they will continually seek to involve "teachers and other employees" (p. 16) in these activities. Going beyond a discussion of observable behaviors, Sergiovanni and Starratt also write of beliefs principals with a human perspective will hold. Specifically, they argue that "good" school leaders will hold a "democratic philosophy" (p. 5) that emphasizes respect, acceptance, and cooperation. And they suggest that these principals will conceive of their role in terms of "leadership" rather than "authority" (p. 5).

A final example of the humanistic tone of metaphors from the 1970s can be found in Burden and Whitt's (1973) discussions of the principalship. They write of the need for "responsive and responsible leadership at the individual building level . . . [to allow] for the possibility of rediscovery of . . . qualities of humanness" (p. 5). Such leadership, they argue, will be "participative" (p. 8) and "collegial" (p. 15) and will stress "commitment" (p. 13), "diversity and flexibility . . . [and] growth" (p. 14).

The Socially Relevant Tone

In addition to stressing the importance of humanistic leadership, scholars of the seventies call on principals to consider the social impact of their actions and decisions and to act in ways that have relevance to key problems. Diane Ravitch (1983), writing about this decade, offers some observations that may explain this emphasis. She points out that the mid- to late 1960s were a time of great social turmoil and that "violence against blacks and civil rights workers in the South; the assassination of President Kennedy; the rediscovery of poverty; [and] the beginning of American involvement in Vietnam" (p. 233) represented "transcending demands . . .

[which] overshadowed" (p. 233) traditional academic concerns. Ravitch suggests that these demands prompted educational leaders to search for "'relevant' curricula" (p. 234) and new organizational strategies "to change society and to turn it against war and racism" (p. 238).

Weinberg's (1971) writing reflects this concern for social relevance. He argues that schools will never "be free to pursue academic ends" (p. *xiv*) until educators recognize that "the school [is] an agency of ameliorative action in the solution of social problems, problems arising out of marginal urban living and out of the social and psychological consequences of minority group membership and economic deprivation" (p. *xvi*). Weinberg devotes his book to analyzing a host of these problems and to discussing their implications for superintendents, principals, and teachers.

Dodson (1974), writing in the same vein, explores socially relevant organizational strategies. Because leaders in the seventies "are now coping with a society which . . . is held together more by force rather than consensus" (p. 101), a society peopled by those who feel a strong sense of alienation from one another, he suggests that "the educational establishment must be brought in line with the changing nature of society" (p. 108) and that, at the very least, this will involve an organizational structure that seeks "decisions collectively arrived at by a participatory set of actors who have an equity in the issues" (p. 107).

The words of Zaret (1975), Burton (1975), and Macdonald (1975) also reveal an administrative concern with relevance to pressing social issues. Focusing on "women's new consciousness" (p. 38) and its impact on schools, Zaret calls on educational leaders, especially female leaders, to "disclose contradictions in schooling and society, then move toward critical reflection and cooperative action in the immediate context" (p. 49). These activities, in her view, will assist the school in becoming "a liberating educational force, an appropriate beginning in women's search for meaning" (p. 50). Burton, as noted earlier, condemns principals for failing to deal responsibly and responsively with youthful sexuality issues. In so doing, he implies that good and effective leaders will, in fact, seek ways to support young people in this area. Macdonald, in turn, condemns schools and their leaders for supporting existing power structures and ideologies and calls on educators to literally "re-form" (p. 94) their organizations in order to reform and transform the cultures in which they are found.

Macdonald's admonitions are quite typical of writings from this decade and demonstrate a difference between the seventies and earlier periods. In preceding decades, principals and academicians who wrote about them expressed concern over social issues and human development. They, however, seemed to believe that traditional administrative strategies were adequate for addressing these concerns. In the seventies, scholars and practitioners discuss the role and tasks of the principal in terms that suggest a disillusionment with earlier role conceptions. The metaphors used in this period reveal an awareness of the increasing complexity of school leadership and a belief that principals must radically change the ways they think and act.

DOMINANT VALUES

During the 1970s, the language used by educational writers suggests a special concern with three values.

1. The "self-actualization" of each person in the school setting
2. The cultivation of an emotionally supportive school climate
3. Societal transformation

Although these are discussed as distinct phenomena, many writers link them, suggesting that the realization of one will contribute to the others and that, in fact, one will not occur in a substantive way unless the others also are present.

Self-Actualization

The repeated references to self-actualization reflect the influence of Abraham Maslow on scholarship of this decade. Words from Sergiovanni and Carver (1973) are typical.

> We propose a philosophy of administration—partly based on faith, ethics, and humanistic concerns and partly based on theoretical and empirical foundations—as a basis for an applied science of educational administration. This basis is generated from a contemporary movement in psychology which seeks a humanistic alternative to Freudian psychology and to psychological behaviorists. The movement is sometimes referred to as "Third Force" psychology and Abraham Maslow is considered to be its preeminent spokesman. (p. 45)

The philosophy offered by these authors places "intellectual, social, and emotional self-actualization for youngsters" (p. 49) as a central goal of administrative activity. It, however, assumes that this goal can be reached only if adult educators are themselves "self-motivated, responsible, dedicated professionals, requiring little or no supervision or regulation" (p. 63).

According to Sergiovanni and Carver, evidence of these qualities suggests that teachers and administrators have reached a desired state, moving "from esteem to autonomy to self-actualization" (p. 63).

Similarly, Hitt (1973) also suggests that self-actualization of students and teachers should be a central administrative goal. He recommends "the study of self actualizing individuals" and of "the work of Maslow and other humanistic psychologists . . . [to] provide a rationale for the formulation of educational goals" (p. 9). Similarly, Patterson (1977), writing of appropriate goals, suggests that they will include the development "of what Rogers (1961) calls the fully functioning person, a person who is open to and aware of his feelings, who is able to relate to others, and who is developing and utilizing his potentials" (p. 164). He expands on this idea, noting that "other terms referring to [this] same concept are self-realization, self-enhancement, and self-actualization. The last, self-actualization, is becoming generally accepted. Combs (1972) states that it is the primary goal of humanistic education" (p. 165).

The Cultivation of an Emotionally Supportive Climate

Numerous other scholars, at times using slightly different terminology, also indicate the high value placed on the experience of self-actualization and suggest that enabling teachers and students to have such an experience should be a central goal of principals. Many argue that this involves leading so as to create or cultivate a certain climate in schools—one wherein feelings are expressed, acknowledged, and respected. Clarence Newell (1978) writes at length of the importance of administrators developing "a wholesome climate" (p. 185). For Newell, this means a climate in which feelings are valued and expressed. He writes, "It is the feeling system in which individuals are involved which constitutes the group or organizational climate which they are currently experiencing" (p. 183). Newell argues that a positive climate or system is one characterized by "interpersonal relationships based upon mutual trust and respect" (p. 184). Recognizing that teachers are the adults interacting most frequently with students, Newell charges the principal to lead so that teachers "feel joyous and energetic" (p. 185). Using research from the previous decade suggesting links between leadership styles and school climate (e.g., Hemphill, Griffiths, & Frederickson, 1962; House, 1968; Murdy, 1962; Sykes, 1962; Wilhelms, 1963), Newell concludes "important relationships were found to exist between an administrator's personality and administrative practices, communications patterns in the school, and the school's emotional atmosphere" (p. 178). In one passage, rich with figurative language, he states:

The primary figure in the feeling system of a school is the administrator, and the surest way to change a feeling system in a school is through a change in the behavior of the principal. In addition to delegated authority, a principal symbolizes a parent figure to many children and staff, and thus has the power to affect the school which goes far far beyond delegated legal authority. (p. 185)

In Newell's view, good principals are those who value positive and supportive interpersonal relationships in which individuals can grow. Burden and Whitt (1973) agree. Using an array of theoretical and empirical research, they suggest that principals fostering such relationships will act in emotionally supportive ways. Citing Nash (1970), they call for principals to recognize "that sharing, intimacy, and closeness are aspects of life that are essential to survival" (p. 11) and to promote "the kind of group atmosphere that . . . motivates people to learn and create . . . in which there is much real listening, openness, trust, constructive feedback, and free speculation" (Nash, 1970, p. 21, quoted in Burden & Whitt, p. 11).

The value attached to school climates supportive of "affective" dimensions of life, characterized by "pure pleasure, delight, or feeling . . . [and] maturing, growing, and becoming" (Berman & Roderick, 1977, p. 3), is quite evident in the 1977 yearbook of the Association for Supervision and Curriculum Development. In this volume, Roderick (1977) suggests:

Schools can provide settings designed to evoke feelings—settings in which persons can experience pleasure, passion, delight, and spontaneity. Schools can provide settings in which provision is made for valuing— settings in which interests, judgment, intention, decision, and reflection are necessary components of a person's repertoire of behaviors if the potentials within the settings are to be realized. Schools can provide settings designed for the art of growing—settings in which extending ideas, commitment, striving, revising, transforming, and developing wholeness are evident. In other words, schools can provide for development of the affective. (p. 201)

Implicit in Roderick's discussion is the belief that schools not only can, but also should foster individuals' emotional growth and development and that principals should be leaders in this process.

Hedges and Martinello (1977) agree. Writing that a goal of education is "to free people to be themselves" (p. 231), these authors argue that this includes helping people learn to feel "without apology and with understanding of the noncognitive dimension of being" (p. 231). Hedges and Martinello present a number of recommendations for practice that underscore the value placed on the affective health of students and teachers. For example, they admonish educators to consider ways learning experiences might contribute to "the development of thinking and feeling processes" (p. 232). Specifically focusing on administrator–teacher relationships, these scholars advocate that principals engage in supportive "formative . . . evaluation [which] concentrates on growth from benchline data rather than on idiographic comparison" (p. 232). Thus, they can support a climate where "each person must be valued for himself with his uniqueness recognized and respected" (p. 232).

Others emphasizing the high value placed on the affective dimensions of school leadership are Berman (1977b) and Hitt (1973). Berman addresses her remarks especially to administrators, and her use of personification is revealing. She consistently describes "the school" as possessing human traits and emotions and both implicitly and explicitly encourages administrators to recognize this dimension of their organizations. She, for instance, notes that "the school cherishes persons" (p. 275) and that "the school must possess a sense of wholeness . . . [and] a means of formal and informal communication that stresses meaningful dialogue among the parts of the whole" (p. 276). Berman admonishes principals to recognize these phenomena and to give "attention to the development of feeling, valuing human beings" (p. 277). Hitt (1973) is yet another author who calls on principals to acknowledge the emotions of teachers, students, and parents. Indeed, he argues that those who take a rational approach "without considering human feelings, desires, and values could do more harm than good" (p. 120).

The Transformation of Society

Yet another value of this decade, the transformation of society by educational efforts, is, in the writings of many, linked to self-actualization and the creation of emotionally supportive schools. Humanistic educational scholars apparently believe that persons who have moved through Maslow's hierarchy will be able to accept and express feelings. In all likelihood, such persons can do much to remedy social problems. Della-Dora and House (1974b) express this view. Praising an "open society," one free of "racism, sexism, social class barriers, concentration of economic power, and the whole concept of a hierarchy of human worth" (p. 4), these authors suggest that educational leaders play a major role in the achievement of such a culture. Answering the question, "How do we move toward an open society?" these scholars write:

> Most of all, however, we need to rediscover that educational systems are not neutral in the movements that determine what the U.S.A. will look like in the future. . . .

An open society is more likely to come into being if teachers and administrators want it to and also if we work for it. Those who believe that the schools are not to be involved in social change and that educators must keep out of the arena of social action are really arguing that education and educators should preserve all oppressive forces which currently exist. (p. 7)

Dodson (1974) agrees and asserts that increasing societal conflict in this decade mandates changes in traditional understandings of authority and power. He suggests that education runs the risk of losing "legitimacy in a growing segment of American society" (p. 108) and advocates "alternate models of organization" (p. 108) in which administrators share power with teachers, students, parents, and community members. Sizemore (1974) writes of educators' role in developing "a healthy black community" (p. 109), noting societal changes that seem linked to school desegregation and calling for stronger leadership in this area. Wolfe (1974) takes a similar approach in her discussion of education and women. She states that educational and political movements "have not only recognized woman power, but have dictated affirmative action in providing for the full utilization of the skills and talents of all women" (p. 180). In her view, this represents only a beginning. Addressing administrators and teachers, she asserts, "Education has a unique responsibility in this change of image, since in our society we believe that the public school is the means by which and through which we perpetuate the American dream" (p. 186).

Burden and Whitt (1973) also believe education can and should play a role in the creation of a healthy society and specifically write of the school-based administrator's role in this process. Like Dodson (1974), they believe this involves an organizational structure in which power, authority, and responsibility are shared so that "the people . . . become full partners in building a true community school" (p. 184). These authors describe several schools where principals have "give[n] up power" (p. 184) and suggest that both those schools and their communities come closer to being true democracies. They, however, like others cited in this section, also admonish principals to go further in responding to the "mandate to work with the community, educate the community, and provide support to the citizens" (p. 204).

THE PRINCIPAL'S RELATIONSHIP TO OTHERS

The language of the 1970s suggests that an interesting shift is occurring in expectations about principals' relationships. In contrast to previous decades, the principal of the 1970s is not typically portrayed as a bureaucrat with a clear base of authority. Nor is she or he pictured as an "expert" in either managerial or educational techniques. Instead, principals' relationships tend to be described as ones where influence depends on interpersonal skills. Principals are expected to lead by suggestion and persuasion rather than by mandate. Cunningham and Gephardt (1971) nicely sum up this expectation. Clarifying terminology in *Leadership: The Science and the Art Today*, they write:

> The emphasis is on individuals—human beings and their behavior in leadership roles. As a result the leadership model inherent in [this volume] took on a characteristic of direct interpersonal interaction—the face-to-face contacts by which individuals are influenced to behave in particular ways. (p. *xv*)

In this section, we discuss ways this understanding of leadership influenced principals' interactions with others.

To Superintendents and Boards of Education

In this decade, authors do not write, at length, of principals' relationships with superordinates in the school system. This is most likely related to the general dissatisfaction with a hierarchical leadership model and to the concomitant change in the role conception of principal from protector of the bureaucracy to initiator of emotionally healthy relationships. When interactions between school-based and district administrators are discussed, the emphasis is on the principal's role in influencing or persuading others, thus gaining approval for proposed activities. Newell's (1978) words nicely illustrate these expectations. He reports that principals wishing to initiate an organizational change such as "participatory policy making" need the support of "superiors in the organizational hierarchy, for such policy making fares best when the administrative superior is willing for it to succeed" (p. 242). Noteworthy in his language is a lack of emphasis on the necessity of principals' securing agreement before acting. Indeed, one could argue that there is a marked difference between seeking the support of superintendents and boards and seeking their permission. Newell continues to discuss principals' relationships with superiors in terms that underscore the absence of traditional, hierarchical relationships. For instance, in language rich with qualifiers, he suggests that principals will want "*at least implicit* assurance that higher administration *will not be strongly opposed to*" (p. 23; emphasis added) some action or decision.

Newell stresses another point about administrative relationships. That is, principals most likely to persuade superintendents and boards are those able to relate and communicate well. He describes effective interactions with these words:

> Because of differences in viewpoint and personality, there is not one best way to proceed. When a school principal wants to obtain administrative support, he may approach his superior directly, may discuss the general idea with him over a period of time before making a specific proposal, may try to link the proposal to some motive or purpose of the superior, may make a point of giving the superior official credit for any ideas which he has contributed, may try to help the superior to grow in his knowledge and understanding, or may insist upon the right to go ahead regardless of the skepticism of higher-level administration. (p. 243)

Arnold Finch (1974), a superintendent in Fresno, California, during the 1970s, offers a similar perspective on the principal's relationship with her or his superordinates. Specifically discussing the implementation of a new inservice program, he notes that principals "should have unreserved approval and commitment of the board of education before moving ahead" (p. 105). Again his choice of words is informative. The use of "should" rather than "must" implies that board support, while important, is not a requirement for one's activity. Similarly, "approval and commitment" suggest that the relationships between school site and district administrators tend to be guided less by hierarchical positions and procedures (as in the 1960s) and more by less formal, more personal, norms. He also emphasizes that principals who possess a particular quality—a "deep professional commitment" (p. 105)—and who communicate clearly with board members will, in all likelihood, receive support for their actions.

With only a few exceptions (e.g., Lipham & Hoeh, 1974), writers of this decade do not dwell on principals' relationships with higher-level administrators. In many ways, this absence reveals as much as the metaphors discussed above. In previous chapters, we have noted that interactions between these two groups receive a fair amount of attention. This suggests that superintendents and boards were perceived as possessing a certain amount of authority or control over the activities of building-level leaders. The focus is on the organizational aspects of the principal's work. In the seventies, it appears that this formal control has diminished and that an emphasis on negotiating, bargaining, and persuading has moved to the forefront. This focus is now on the personal and political dimensions of the role.

To Teachers

Consistent with the diminishing of traditional, bureaucratic assumptions and the growing importance of the human relations and political perspectives, principals of the seventies are often portrayed as relating to teachers as partners rather than subordinates. At times, this portrait seems to reflect a real flattening of the educational hierarchy; at other times, the language used to describe these "equal" relationships suggests that principals continue to retain the final word on decisions even though their roles and interactions are described in egalitarian terms.

The expectation that principals relate to teachers as partners is evident in Davis' (1974) chapter on team teaching programs. Addressing administrators, he hails team teaching as "an organizational pattern within which the school can greatly improve the quality of its instructional program" (p. 149). After noting that "reform [in this direction] must be instituted by administrators . . . [and that] more principals should provide the necessary leadership" (p. 166), Davis cautions:

> An over-anxious administrator cannot launch a successful program through administrative fiat. Success comes about through changes in teachers' attitudes and through a growth in understanding, not through duress. . . . Invariably, team teaching succeeds on a voluntary basis but fails when imposed. (p. 167)

Stevens' (1974) discussion of ways principals might deal with "problems caused by school personnel" (p. 632) also suggests a belief that administrators and teachers should interact as professional colleagues rather than as managers and underlings. He offers four scenarios in which a teacher has done something to elicit parental complaints and discusses possible administrative responses. In each instance, the preferred option is one in which the principal utilizes her or his discretion and relational ability to enlist the teacher's help and cooperation. He, for instance, suggests that an "imperious teacher" (p. 633) should be wooed by "encouragement or praise, sincerity and understanding" (p. 633). In discussing "the bearded teacher" (p. 634), Stevens advises leaders to talk with the educator in question and to remember that "making demands or challenges to the teachers will very likely create even greater problems [because] most teachers react negatively to any restriction of personal rights" (p. 635). Even when discussing ways to approach a "teacher [who] makes many mistakes and consistently uses poor judgment," Stevens notes that "the principal must . . . *persuade* the teacher to exercise more caution" (p. 635; emphasis added).

Even Lipham and Hoeh (1974), who discuss principals' relationships in more traditional, bureaucratic terms, stress that administrators can and should relate to teachers as colleagues. Noting that "teachers today are better prepared than ever before" (p. 247), the authors intersperse sections suggesting that principals act in authoritarian ways with reminders that leaders should talk "frankly and openly with . . . teachers . . . [regarding] mutual expectations held for each other's roles" (p. 146) and admonishes that principals' motives should include being "of assistance" (p. 249) to teachers and "foster[ing] understanding and interaction" (p. 294).

To Students

Only occasionally do scholars of this decade discuss direct interactions between principals and students. More often, they focus on leadership activities that indirectly foster students' well-being. Of special interest are activities that facilitate individual development and those that stress protecting students' rights. Several terms appear frequently in discussions of the principal's relationships with students. These include "culture" (e.g., Sarason, 1971; Simpson, 1977, p. 186), "climate" (e.g., Newell, 1978, p. 195; Senate Select Committee on Equal Opportunity, 1970, p. 305), and "innovation" (e.g., Howard & Bardwell, 1974, p. 231; Weinberg, 1971, p. 56). Writers portray principals as persons responsible for developing a school culture and an organizational climate that promotes holistic development. This, in the view of many, will lead to the development and implementation of innovative instructional and organizational processes.

Simpson (1977) argues that schools must possess a culture where "individual development and societal goals are integrated into likenesses and commonalities shared by the members of the groups" (p. 186). Her special concern is student development, and she writes of ways adult educators— principals and teachers—might facilitate this. She suggests that leaders who would foster a developmental culture must be sensitive to the links between "environmental changes" (p. 197), educational processes, and "human needs" (p. 198). Armed with an awareness that these three are related and that schools are central to progress in both society and individual lives, educators "with heightened awareness [will] become part of an organized and dynamic effort to create a new reality, a desired whole" (p. 198).

Simpson describes this desired whole in terms of "culture" (p. 186). Newell (1978) uses the phrase "organizational climate" (p. 195) to describe the same phenomenon. He calls on each educator to cultivate a developmentally sound climate because it "affects every individual in an organization [and] it is particularly influential in the lives of children, who are still at an impressionable age" (p. 195). Newell especially admonishes principals to assume this responsibility. "The type of climate which develops in a school is induced to a considerable degree by the administrator, who typically wields more influence than any other single individual in a school" (p. 195). Like Simpson, Newell stresses that such climates occur when educators are sensitive to individual and societal needs. "To be effective, administrative leadership must encompass the relationships outside as well as within the school organization" (p. 195).

The Senate Select Committee on Equal Education Opportunity (1970) concurs. It concludes:

> In many ways the school principal is the most important and influential individual in any school. He is the person responsible for all of the activities that occur in and around the school building. It is his leadership that sets the tone of the school, the climate for learning, the level of professionalism and morale of teachers and the degree of concern for what students may or may not become. (p. 45)

Many writers note that fostering healthy climates or cultures requires innovative thinking on the part of principals. The Senate Select Committee, for example, suggests:

> If the school is a vibrant, innovative, child-centered place; if it has a reputation for excellence in teaching; if students are performing to the best of their ability one can almost always point to the principal's leadership. (p. 305)

Newell (1978) similarly links a positive school climate with "educational innovation" (p. 177). Acknowledging that structural changes are needed, he also charges administrators to consider changing "administrative practices [and] communication patterns" in order to affect "the school's emotional atmosphere" (p. 178).

Goldhammer, Becker, Withycombe, Doyel, Miller, Morgan, Delorretto, and Aldridge (1971) also suggest that good principals will strive to discover new, nontraditional organizational and instructional strategies in order to create excellent, student-centered schools. Contrasting two types of leaders and schools, they write:

> In the "beacons of brilliance" the principals are charismatic leaders, they seem to instill enthusiasm in their teachers. . . . Teachers and principals, along with parents, constantly appraise the effectiveness of the schools in an attempt to devise new programs and strategies to overcome deficiencies. Programs of study are adaptable and emphasis in the instructional program is placed on children's needs. . . . The "pot-holes of pestilence," on the other hand, result from weak leadership and official neglect. . . .

Instructional programs are traditional, ritualistic, and poorly related to student needs. (pp. 1–2)

Writing on the topic "How to Organize a Non-Graded School," Howard and Bardwell (1974) suggest that principals embrace innovative structures and techniques in order to "free students to learn and teachers to teach in different ways" (p. 197). They discuss the advantage of nongraded schools, arguing that such organizations are more nearly able to meet the goal of "individualizing instruction" (p. 231). Numerous expressions used by these authors underscore their view that a shift toward such schools represents a move away from tradition and toward innovation. For example, in describing traditional schools, they write:

The educational system is plagued with inflexibilities that would put most industries and businesses into instant bankruptcy. Too much of what passes for change in education consists merely of a kind of academic graveyard-moving—the moving of dead educational programs into new settings. Progress is being impeded by:

Rigid organization patterns
Rigid curricula
Rigid buildings and
Rigid people. (p. 197)

In contrast, Howard and Bardwell (1974) recommend nongraded-ness—a concept they equate with "organizational innovation" (p. 238). They stress that nongraded institutions will be "school[s] of the future" (p. 238) and that they will allow each principal to help her or his school "progress in its own unique way" (p. 235) toward the goals of

making the curriculum more meaningful, stimulating students to think critically and express themselves clearly, helping students master skills which are essential to semi-independent and later independent learning, and fostering an attitude of inquiry on the part of the students. (p. 231)

Educational authors in this decade also devote much attention to informing principals of the ways they might protect students' rights. Lipham and Hoeh (1974) offer a good example. In their chapter on "The Principal and the Students," these authors conclude that

The values of the larger society expressed in constitutional provisions, laws, court decisions, and administrative regulations all serve to delimit and define the relationship of the student to the school organization.

> Currently, several trends are altering considerably the legal status of the student. The changes having greatest implications for the principal student relationship relate to compulsory school attendance, discipline, freedom of expression, freedom from search and seizure, and due process; the principal should know and understand each of these areas. (p. 286)

Although they express concern that leaders understand these issues in order to protect students from liability, Lipham and Hoeh emphasize that the protection of "the basic rights of the student as an individual" (p. 295) should be the central administrative concern.

To the Community

As noted earlier, principals of the 1970s are expected to extend the sphere of their leadership activities, seeking to involve and inform community members. Two activities receive a great deal of attention. First, principals are expected to lead in educating the public, especially in regard to educational activities. Second, principals are expected to involve community members as volunteers in school activities. This involves recruiting, coordinating, and recognizing outside persons who, in some way, enter into the educative process. These two expectations, in the view of many scholars, represent a strategic response to increasing pressures from outside forces. In essence, authors tend to emphasize that educating and involving potential critics in some aspect of school life is an excellent way to avert major challenges, complaints, or litigation, for ideally this involvement will transform potential enemies to allies.

Burden and Whitt (1973) comment at length on the responsibility of the principal to improve the community by offering educational opportunities to its members. Citing concepts presented earlier by the National Society for the Study of Education (1953), Clapp (1939), and the United Community Services of Metropolitan Boston (1971), Burden and Whitt call on principals to concern themselves "with a totality of life within a given community" (p. 183). This, in their view, means viewing education

> as a method of attacking the complex problems of a society in a transition and thus providing the necessary resources in order that community members may find solutions through meaningful and real participation under the aegis of a familiar and generally accepted institution. (p. 184)

They go on to discuss, in great detail, ways leaders might fulfill the charge "to recognize needs and convey these to the community in such a way that people feel comfortable in accepting the leadership from the school" (p. 200).

Banks, James, Broadhead, Della-Dora, and House (1974) also discuss the principal as a community educator. They admonish administrators "to provide opportunities for educational experiences for all cultural, racial, or economic groups" (p. 194). In the view of these authors, this requires broadening the concept of education to include providing all persons with means to deal with "racism, poverty, poor physical and mental health, social class discrimination, and elitism" (p. 196).

Clifford (1975) and Weinberg (1971) are two others who suggest that principals have a responsibility for community education. Clifford does this by emphasizing the importance of "universal education" (p. 75). In her view, leaders committed to this concept will seek ways to reach especially the poor and disenfranchised. This will inevitably require that leaders engage in activities that educate and empower members of the larger community as well as the children in specific schools. Weinberg, as discussed earlier, argues that schools must address social concerns. He calls on educational leaders to accept the "responsibility not only to provide the knowledge and skills required to eliminate poverty but to bridge the gap between the family and the school, to show the way not only to where the opportunities are but how to use them" (p. 56). Weinberg cautions that this will require bold, innovative thinking and planning. "Sometimes it is necessary to stretch our imaginations to the bursting point" (p. 56) in order to discover ways to educate students and their family members.

Closely linked to the expectation that principals will educate persons in the community is the belief that educational leaders should oversee and encourage volunteer involvement. In some instances, authors write of these two activities as virtually inseparable, arguing that effectively overseeing a community involvement program will require educating those who participate. Others emphasize the service dimension of volunteerism. In any event, most who discuss this topic suggest that the principal is responsible for overseeing the effort.

Perkins (1974) is one who suggests that leadership in the area of community involvement requires varied strategies. At times, enlisting persons in volunteer positions will entail providing some educational opportunities. Writing on the topic, "Getting Better Results for Substitutes, Teacher Aides, and Volunteers" (p. 3), he notes that administrators may need to organize and perhaps lead "on-the-job training" (p. 34), perhaps in the form of "pre-service workshops" (p. 34). He also discusses a host of ways principals might enlist "local citizens to serve as unpaid volunteers to help extend and strengthen the education program" (p. 35). Burden and Whitt (1973) also discuss several ways principals might link schools and community members. Stressing that "the principal should be a catalyst" (p. 186), these authors recommend enlisting outsiders in educational decision making. They offer several examples of programs that model ways to encourage "the total community [to be] involved in the development of its school" (p. 202).

Lipham and Hoeh (1974) agree that an important competency for principals is the ability to explore "innovative programs and [to plan] for the cooperative utilization of the total resources of the community." Their focus is on "a wide variety of human and physical resources that should be tapped for the enrichment of the instructional program" (p. 345). They advise elementary principals to recruit "speakers with specific competencies, . . . policemen, firemen, merchants, professional people, and other citizens [to] help to develop in children a greater degree of career awareness and community understanding" (p. 344). For secondary principals, Lipham and Hoeh stress the importance of utilizing "on-the-job training stations in work-study programs, part-time employment, and volunteer work . . . to ensure for many students a smooth transition between school and the world of work" (p. 344). In the view of these authors, an important function of the administrator is arranging and coordinating community support for these programs.

STANDARDS FOR EVALUATION

The metaphors of the seventies suggest that the belief that principals can and should be evaluated objectively has become widespread. Some authors describe assessment strategies for accomplishing this task. In their view, objective, quantitative measurement is both important and possible. Others take a slightly more subjective approach, offering lists of desirable traits and suggesting that practicing and prospective principals might be evaluated according to their possession of these qualities.

Objective Evaluative Strategies

Immegart (1971) is one who writes of the need for objective evaluative tools to assess a person's readiness to enter the principalship and, once she or he is in practice, to continue the ongoing evaluation of competence. He suggests that empirical research on leadership provides a good base for developing measurement instruments. Citing Bass (1960), Immegart calls for a blending of

less objective methods . . . wisdom and introspection, case histories, choice (or reputational study), job placement (or position study rating), categorizations of observed behavior, situation tests, and projective sketches . . . [with] experimental as well as more objective stud[ies] of leadership. (p. 225)

He suggests that insights gleaned from these different modes of inquiry can assist in predicting the success of potential principals and in evaluating and guiding those already in the field.

Several contributors to Erickson's edited volume, *Educational Organization and Administration* (1977), also write of objective evaluative strategies. Coleman, Campbell, Hobson, McPartland, Mood, Weinfeld, and York (1977), for example, write of the "relation of school factors to achievement" (p. 131). When discussing "teacher variables" (e.g., "the teachers' family education level [a positive effect], the teachers' own education [a positive effect]," etc. [p. 144]), these authors imply that these can be used to evaluate principals' hiring practices. Hanushek's (1977) article suggests a similar conclusion. He offers an equation modeling the educational process. Some of the variables are outside the control of principals (e.g., "family inputs or education . . . peer influences . . . [and students'] innate endowment" (p. 151). However, another variable—"school inputs" (p. 151)—is, at least to some extent, dependent on administrative action. Hanushek suggests that his model provides a way to evaluate the outcomes of schooling and to identify the degree to which these outcomes relate to variables under the principal's control. Thus, his equation can be used to determine if principals are contributing positively or negatively to results of educational efforts. In the same vein, Lipham and Hoeh's *The Principalship: Foundations and Functions* (1974) concludes with "an examination of the conceptual, human, and technical competencies required of the principal, based on the theoretical foundations of the principalship" (p. 349). Arguing that "a competency-based approach . . . [provides] a systematic means for analyzing and synthesizing the . . . skills required for effective and efficient performance in the principal's role" (p. 351), these authors provide a detailed assessment instrument to be used in evaluating school leaders.

Trait Approach to Evaluation

Lipham and Hoeh (1974) suggest that administrative competencies can be assessed by looking for behavioral indicators. Others, writing about similar issues, focus on traits good principals will (or should) possess. Burlingame (1971) and Stodgill (1971) are among those discussing this approach. Like Immegart (1971), they suggest that research on leadership can provide a basis for evaluative measures. Burlingame discusses the strengths and limitations of "the great man viewpoint" (p. 49), a method that focuses on qualities possessed by persons historically judged to be good leaders. He identifies several qualities that seem to be present in these outstanding educators (e.g., "a sense of missionary zeal" [p. 52], an "ethic of work" [p. 53], and the possession of "some type of intellectual base" [p. 54]). Suggesting that these "virtues [appear] to be common in all types of educational leaders discussed in biography" (p. 56), Burlingame explores the possibility of evaluating principals on this basis. He ultimately questions the widespread usefulness of a checklist of traits as an evaluative strategy. However, his lengthy discussion and the inclusion of this article in Cunningham and Gephart's *Leadership: The Science and the Art Today* (1971) suggest that educators are concerned that leaders possess traits associated with greatness.

Stodgill (1971), using a conceptual framework derived from earlier "research on personality traits" (p. 83), reviews and synthesizes a number of works dealing with leadership traits. While acknowledging that trait research, as an evaluative mechanism, "is extremely difficult to put into effect" (p. 96), he nevertheless suggests that studies of "the personality of leaders" have important implications. For, he purports, "leaders do exhibit personality and personality is a factor in leader acceptance by a group" (p. 100). Stodgill ultimately calls for joining "the measurement of traits . . . with an analysis of situational requirements in order for measurement efforts to have any predictive value" (p. 101).

Writing in a philosophical vein, Hitt (1973) also suggests that an effective leader will possess the following characteristics, some of which could be called traits:

> His thoughts, feelings, words, and actions are unified and consistent. He is open to correction. He is able to generate his own ideas and make his own decisions. He is accountable to himself and to others for his actions. He is an effective communicator. He has the ability to think rationally. He is an effective problem solver. He has an active concern for the welfare of other people. He has a zest for life. (p. 55)

In Hitt's view, educational leaders must possess these traits if they wish to promote them in students. By extension, principals should be judged according to their possession of these qualities.

CONCLUSION

The metaphors of this decade indicate yet another shift in conceptions of the principalship. Persons inhabiting these roles are expected to exercise political and personal skills as they work to develop humane, affectively oriented schools. Additionally, they are challenged to view their work in the context of the larger culture as they strive to contribute, in countless ways, to their communities. To some extent these expectations appeared in earlier decades. In the 1920s, for instance, leaders were described in non-bureaucratic terms and were admonished to recognize that their work affects the larger society. A special concern of this decade is that the principal uphold the generally accepted moral and cultural values. Similar views appeared in the 1940s when principals were asked to serve as democratic leaders of schools that embodied—for the world—the benefits of the American way of life. In that era, the language was less lofty and spiritual and more patriotic. In the seventies, the locus of values defining the principalship shifts yet again. Leaders are to be guided by a concern for the overall well-being of individuals and their communities. In the concluding chapter, we examine this evolving understanding of the principal as a broker of some type of values. We look at changes in values and contrast this view of the leader with one holding that principals are, first and foremost, executives within a rational, clearly defined educational hierarchy.

CHAPTER SEVEN

The 1980s

In Chapter 6, we discussed a number of metaphors linking school leadership with community involvement and the principal with the task of ameliorating social problems. These support the contentions of Weick (1976), Campbell and colleagues (1987), and others, that the boundaries separating schools and the world outside them are becoming indistinct and permeable. In the preceding decade, we see principals responding to this reality by reaching out into the communities, involving and educating "nonstudents," and seeking to address not only academic issues, but also psychological, physical, and social concerns. In the eighties, the openness of schools continues to affect our understanding of the role of school leader. However, in this decade, the directional flow of influence shifts. In the seventies, the language paints a picture of principals reaching out to touch, in some way, the community. In the eighties, we see the community —politicians, businesspersons, academics in colleges and universities, and others—reaching into schools in an effort to guide and shape both the educational processes and those who lead in them (Murphy, 1990b). In Figure 7.1, we offer our analysis of metaphors that reflect writings on the principalship in the 1980s.

DOMINANT METAPHORICAL THEMES

The high level of interest in education and educational leadership in the 1980s resulted in an abundance of books and articles that discuss the principalship at length. After analyzing the abundant and rich metaphorical language of this decade, we propose that the following statements represent dominant themes:

1. The principal is expected to serve as an instructional leader, guiding teachers and students toward productive learning experiences.

FIGURE 7.1 Analysis of Metaphors of the 1980s

Dominant Metaphorical Themes

The principal is expected to serve as an instructional leader, guiding teachers and students toward productive learning experiences.

Central to the concept of instructional leadership is the idea that the principal is to solve problems and provide resources.

The principal of the eighties is frequently asked to be a visionary, developing and communicating a picture of the ideal school.

The principal is expected to go beyond painting a portrait of a good school and is charged with functioning as a change agent.

Dominant Tones

Urgent and demanding

Businesslike

Dominant Values

Effectiveness

Accountability

Relationship to Others

To superintendents, boards, and other governing bodies—
  Steward of available resources

To teachers—
  Facilitator of personal and professional development
  Monitor

To students—
  In prescriptive works, the standard setter
  In descriptive works, an involved person and educator

Standards for Evaluation

Principals are judged by student achievement outcomes as measured by elaborate assessment instruments

---

2. Central to the concept of instructional leadership is the idea that the principal is to solve problems and provide resources in order to facilitate the teaching/learning process.

3. The principal of the eighties is frequently asked to be a visionary— to develop and communicate to constituents a picture of the ideal school.

4. Additionally, a good principal is expected to go beyond painting a portrait of the good school. She or he is charged with leading schools toward realizing this vision. Almost invariably this requires changes in the educational operations. Thus, the successful principal of the 1980s is often described as a change agent.

Principal as Instructional Leader

In every decade, some attention has been paid to the principal's impact on teaching and learning processes. Often the assumption has been that principals can and should affect the instructional climate of schools rather indirectly—by holding up widely accepted values, by managing individual institutions effectively and efficiently, by promoting democracy, by running schools according to "proven" principles, by oiling the system's bureaucratic machinery, and by interacting positively with the larger society. A dominant assumption of the eighties, conveyed in the language of this period, is that the principal can and should become directly involved with the teaching/learning process. Most often, the metaphor used in discussions of this assumption is that of principal as instructional leader. Indeed, as Greenfield (1987) notes, this phrase is often used as a kind of "slogan guiding the efforts of reformists" (p. 75) of this decade.

The belief that improving technical core operations is a central leadership task is evident in the list of "traits of the effective principal" (Phi Delta Kappa, 1982, p. 2) that opens *The Role of the Principal*. Heading this list is the statement that successful leaders "devote time to the tasks of coordinating and controlling instruction" (p. 2). Numerous other traits (e.g., "understanding teaching styles and learning styles and the relationship between the two, . . . provid[ing] coherence to the school's instructional program, . . . [and acting as] an instructional manager" [p. 2]) further emphasize the importance of this role conception.

Leithwood and Montgomery's (1982) discussion of elementary school principals focuses specifically on ways leaders might enter into this role. They suggest that good principals will have a clear commitment to the goal of "promoting student cognitive growth" (p. 334). The importance placed on this commitment is underscored when these authors note that "effective principals are able to define priorities focused on the central mission of the school . . . [and] intervene directly and constantly to ensure that priorities are achieved" (p. 335). The strong, controlling verb "intervene" is especially revealing. It suggests that leading in the instructional arena allows and even mandates that principals become actively involved in classrooms (Murphy, Hallinger, Weil, & Mitman, 1983).

In their extensive analysis of the literature on instructionally effective schools, Clark and Lotto (1982) stress the centrality of the image of the principal as an instructional leader. They note that the largest set of variables linked to effective administration focuses on "program leadership and direction" (p. 4) and that the prevailing view is that good principals "emphasize student achievement as [the] primary outcome of schooling . . . and monitor and evaluate student progress" (p. 5). Ross and MacDonald (n.d.)

concur. They note that in successful schools, "the principal is a strong instructional leader, . . . reviews and approves teachers' lesson plans, . . . and has definite plans for attaining achievement gains" (p. 1).

The titles of Greenfield's edited volume, *Instructional Leadership: Concepts, Issues, and Controversies* (1987), and of Smith and Andrews' *Instructional Leadership: How Principals Make a Difference* (1989) are also revealing. In the former, scholars, representing a range of theoretical persuasions, reflect on the appropriateness and meaning of the instructional leadership metaphor. In the latter, practical suggestions for exercising such leadership are offered.

Hallinger and Murphy's "Instructional Leadership in the School Context" (1987) exemplifies an academic perspective on this understanding of the principalship (see also Murphy, 1988, 1990d). Noting that research on effective schools has led to the expectation that principals "play a more active instructional leadership role" (p. 180), these authors discuss the interplay between this understanding of the principalship and the social and organizational contexts of schools. After examining the influence of "the school's technology, the type of district support, the characteristics of the teaching staff, the school level, and the social context," Hallinger and Murphy suggest that good instructional leadership "is context-dependent rather than uniform in nature" (p. 199). Researchers and practitioners are urged to examine the "complex constellation of forces" (p. 199) that affect administrators' work in order to improve teaching and learning efforts.

Focusing on one such force, Peterson (1987) examines the interaction between "the system of administrative control used in a school district . . . [and] the instructional leadership of principals" (p. 139). Like Hallinger and Murphy (1985a, 1986, 1987), he suggests that no one system is always linked with effective administration of teaching and learning. Peterson calls on scholars to delve more deeply into "the combination of multiple, interlocking methods of influence" (p. 151), with the goal of better equipping principals "to be instructional leaders and to function in a role demanding discretionary actions, complex decisions, and comprehensive planning" (p. 151).

Little and Bird (1987) stress another quality of principals who are instructional leaders. These persons, they suggest, possess "a 'close to the classroom' orientation" (p. 120). Little and Bird argue that "administrators directly involved with teachers in classrooms" (p. 122) are those most able to create "an expanded structure of leadership and . . . mechanisms by which teachers can emerge as leaders with respect to teaching" (p. 121).

Others, agreeing on the fact that the principal should be an instructional leader, suggest that a certain craftsmanship or artistry on the part of leaders is needed. Blumberg (1987), for example, argues that metaphors from science and art are inadequate to describe the work of school-based administrators and suggests that the image of leadership as craft is useful. Comparing principals and potters, he notes that effectiveness in both fields requires an understanding of desired outcomes, knowledge of "the materials to be worked with" (p. 48), the possession of "appropriate skills and techniques" (p. 48), and the ability to use judgment and discretion.

Smith and Andrews (1989), writing for practicing principals, offer case studies of effective instructional leaders. Some are "articulate, skilled expert[s] in human relations" (p. 60); others are "aggressive, demanding, and data driven" (p. 60); all are successful. Based on these and other studies, Smith and Andrews suggest the legitimacy of "a variety of styles in instructional leadership" (p. 84; see also Dwyer, Lee, Rowan, & Bossert, 1983). They devote their work to exploring the many manifestations of effectiveness in this arena.

Principal as Problem Solver and Resource Provider

The belief that principals should be instructional leaders is, indeed, widespread in the literature of the 1980s. Many authors, however, concur with Greenfield's (1987) assessment that "instructional leadership is an elusive concept and offers little guidance about the actual nature of leadership in schools" (p. 75). In an effort to clarify and operationalize this concept, numerous scholars have identified behaviors of effective administrators (Hallinger & Murphy, 1985b; Hallinger, Murphy, Weil, Mesa, & Mitman, 1983; Leithwood & Montgomery, 1986; Murphy, 1990d; Murphy, Weil, Hallinger, & Mitman, 1982). Two receiving a good deal of attention are problem solving and providing needed resources to teachers. We discuss these two together because, in many instances, principals who solve problems are portrayed as those who are able to secure materials, money, time, or information for teachers.

Clark and Lotto's (1982) analysis of variables relating to effective instructional leadership supports our contention that principals are expected to know and address teachers' concerns and problems and that this often involves providing needed resources. In their discussion of "characteristics of school leaders," these authors note that the literature dealing with effective principals "portrays the principal as an administrator who is seeking solutions to school problems" (p. 9). Clark and Lotto examine specific ways in which principals exhibit these characteristics. Drawing upon literature and the comments of an expert panel, they offer the following statements as evidence that able leaders are skillful at obtaining resources:

Principals in IESs [instructionally effective schools] do a better job of acquiring funds and resources, especially project monies, and they use them to reinforce their best staff members. . . .

Effective principals are good money getters because money is power, the power to make things happen, get materials, provide staff training— even to get people's attention that achievement is of concern. (p. 18)

Deal (1987) similarly describes the good principal as a problem solver and resource provider. He uses several revealing metaphors in his discussion. For instance, he notes that the principal, functioning "as engineer or supervisor" spends time "resolving conflicts" (p. 239), devising plans and policies, and obtaining resources that address and ameliorate problems. Additionally, the effective leader operates "as power broker or statesperson" (p. 239)—roles that thrust her or him into the midst of conflict-filled situations and require the discovery or development of resources to deal with these situations. Deal writes:

The principal as power broker sees conflict as a natural by-product of collective activity. . . . The principal spends considerable time in the ring dealing with conflict—as a participant or as a referee.

The principal as statesperson works to build coalitions. He or she knows the special interest groups and tries to find common ideological grounds on which the groups can work together. . . . The principal rarely uses his or her power directly inside the school. But internal solidarity is used freely as a bargaining chip, as scarce resources are allocated to individual schools within the district. (p. 240)

Achilles (1987) also writes of the effective principal as one who addresses educational problems and seeks to provide teachers with all they need to function. At a very basic level, Achilles suggests that a good leader "fosters open communication, decision-making, and problem solving channels . . . [and] focuses faculty meetings on solving problems" (p. 27). As this principal moves toward higher levels of excellence, she or he shifts "from problem to program orientation" (p. 27) and seeks to acquire information and materials to assist teachers.

Blumberg and Greenfield (1980) and Hoyle, English, and Steffy (1985) also argue that the effective principal solves problems by providing needed resources. The first two identify "vision, initiative, and *resourcefulness* as three key elements associated with a principal's effectiveness" (Blumberg & Greenfield, cited in Greenfield, 1987, p. 59; emphasis added). In turn, Hoyle, English, and Steffy, in their 1985 volume *Skills for Successful School Leaders*, devote several chapters to strategies for managing conflicts and for cultivating and administering resources. They claim that effective leaders will use "group process, interpersonal communication, and motivation skills" (p. 35) to deal with problems. Additionally, they call on principals to develop skills in acquiring and managing money to support instruction. They write:

> Building public support for schools is not something an effective school administrator does "on the side." It should, in fact, be the first act of survival. (p. 49).

> School leaders must possess the skills to allocate human, material, and financial resources efficiently. (p. 171)

In his review of the literature of this decade, Murphy (1990d) also concludes that effective school leaders are more astute in "securing outside resources in support of school goals" (p. 180) than their less able peers. He discusses two specific avenues of such support. First, he finds that effective principals "are more adept in attracting funds and materials from the community" (p. 180). He also reports that more skillful administrators are more astute in garnering resources from the district.

> They use the formal and informal channels at their disposal to influence district level decision making and to "better the competitive position of their schools in the distribution of power and resources" (Kroeze, 1984, p. 2); see also Crowson & Morris, 1984; Farrar, 1987). . . . For example, Wimpelberg (1986) reports that, while their less effective colleagues often follow standard procedures in hiring and transferring staff, effective principals take assertive action to shape their staffs according to the philosophy and objectives of the school (see also Teddlie, Wimpelberg, & Kirby, 1987). (p. 180)

Principal as Visionary

In addition to functioning as instructional leader, problem solver, and resource provider, principals of the eighties are expected to cultivate and communicate a "vision" to teachers, students, and the community. Paul Bredeson (1985), after analyzing metaphors used by five principals during this decade, offers a helpful discussion of this image.

> Broadly conceived, vision is the principal's ability to holistically view the present, to reinterpret the mission of the school to all its constituents, and to use imagination and perceptual skills to think beyond accepted notions of what is practical and what is of immediate application in

present situations to speculative ideas and to, preferably, possible futures. (pp. 43-44)

Two points in this statement are especially worthy of note. The first is the need for "imagination and perceptual skills," and the second is the fact that visionary principals are oriented toward the future. The metaphorical language of this decade emphasizes both of these dimensions in discussions of administrators with vision.

Greenfield (1987) is one who links imagination and vision. Indeed, he suggests that "vision . . . results from the exercise of moral imagination" (p. 62). Elaborating on this idea, he argues that

> Moral imagination refers to the inclination of a person to see that the world, in this case the school and the associated activities and learning, need not remain as it is—that it is possible for it to be otherwise, and to be better. . . . It is the ability to see how things are and how they might be—not in terms of the ideal, but in terms of what is possible, given a particular school situation. (p. 61)

Greenfield's (1987) words suggest that principals' visions are more than lists of specific goals and objectives, for he emphasizes the importance of imagination that is distinctly moral—"rooted in an awareness of and a commitment to the standards of good practice or effective schools and good teaching, that characterize membership in the normative community of educators" (pp. 61-62). Gerald Grant (1988) offers a similar perspective. He writes of the need for leaders who hold and communicate "the enduring values of character of the school community: the spirit that actuates not just manners, but moral and intellectual attitudes, practices and ideals" (p. 172). These ideals, in his view, are at the heart of an appropriate and useful vision.

Roland Barth (1987, 1988) is another who stresses the importance of vision in education. Labeling "the continuous exercise of vision-making [as] engaging, fun, often useful, and, above all, hopeful" (1988, p. 129), he calls on teachers and principals (who, in his view, are also teachers) "to consider continuously, reflect upon, develop, and articulate their visions about how classrooms and school might become better" (1987, p. 257). Barth argues that these visions should be honor[ed]" (1987, p. 256) for three reasons.

> These are the only prescriptions for school reform that have a prayer of being taken seriously and sustained. . . .
> These rich insights [have been] hammered out of years of practice. . . .
> The excitement of working in schools, the kicks, the satisfactions, the rewards come from studying a difficult situation and then generating

one's own plan [or vision] for improving things. (1987, pp. 256–257)

Reflecting on the work of Colton (1985), Achilles (1987) also stresses the importance of administrative vision. He labels this vision as an "operational step" (1987, p. 18) in the movement toward good schools and notes:

> Vision, the ability to see feelingly, helps us in the quest for better schools. Colton (1985) describes vision as that "which establishes goals or objectives for individual and group action, which defines not what we are but rather what we *seek to be or do*." (p. 33; emphasis in original; cited in Achilles, p. 18)

Deal (1987) is yet another who uses the metaphor of the principal as visionary. He suggests that in embracing this role, school leaders "represent and embody the existential core of the school" (p. 240). In doing this, principals

> accentuate and dramatize the values of the school. . . . They give everyone someone to look up to. . . . [These leaders] articulate the important, often inaccessible dreams and visions of an organization devoted to passing on the ways of the people. They speak about their schools in artful prose, capturing the emotion and passion of the classroom or playground. They spark imagination and loyalty by connecting everyday experience with historical memories or myths and future wishes or fairy tales. (p. 241)

Excellence without vision is, in his view, an impossibility.

In his review of the work on leadership in the 1980s, Murphy (1990d) provides some clues about the specific nature of the vision found in schools with especially skillful principals. To begin with, he concludes that "more effective principals have a clear sense of direction for their schools that they are able to clearly articulate" (p. 167). In addition, these men and women, to a greater extent than their peers, translate this sense of direction into specific learning goals (Rosenholtz, 1985). The goals in schools with more able leaders tend to be student centered, while less effective schools tend to focus on adult needs and values (Rutherford, 1985; Wimpelberg, 1986). Effective leaders are more skilled at translating values into instructional goals and those stressing student achievement (Austin, 1978; Brookover & Lezotte, 1977), and in framing goals that apply to all students (Leithwood & Montgomery, 1984). Not surprisingly, they formulate ambitious goals for students, while their less effective peers "focus more on assuring that administrative and logistic requirements are attended to; that the school 'runs smoothly'" (Leithwood & Montgomery, 1984, p. 28). The major concern of the latter group is with maintaining tranquility in the here and now (Rutherford, 1985). In translating the school vision into goals, effective leaders emphasize a few coordinated objectives "around which staff energy and other school resources can be mobilized" (Murphy, 1990d, p. 168). More so than their peers, these men and women work to ensure that school goals are linked to the mission of the district (Taylor, 1986a, 1986b); "rely on a greater number of sources in developing goals and more public (and fewer private sources) (Murphy, 1990d, p. 168; see also Leithwood & Montgomery, 1984); express goals in measurable terms; and use goals in planning and decision making (Brookover, Beady, Flood, Schweitzer, & Wisenbaker 1979; Dwyer, 1986; Taylor, 1986a, 1986b). Finally, effective leaders are more successful than their colleagues in communicating goals (Louis & Cipollene, 1987; Miles, 1987; Rutherford, 1985). They employ a large variety of formal and informal mechanisms to communicate goals and, "in contrast to their less effective peers, [they] seek out opportunities to clarify goals with staff, students, parents and other members of the school community" (Leithwood & Montgomery, 1984, p. 31).

Principal as Change Agent

Writers of the eighties generally contend that holding a vision, however important, is not enough to ensure administrative success. Indeed, most suggest that good leaders will take active steps to move schools toward these visions. This invariably requires that principals work to initiate and facilitate change in education. One metaphor that begins to occur with increasing frequency at the very end of the decade is that of transformation, a word that connotes a rather dramatic kind of change.

Arguing that leadership requires the possession of "transformative power" (1984, p. 64), Bennis examines various components of this phenomenon. In so doing, he stresses that vision provides the impetus for organizational change and that powerful leaders are those able to persuade others to share their ideals. Leaders who effect change are those who can harness the energies of followers and direct these energies toward the realization of ideals.

> In sum, the transformative power of leadership . . . is the ability of the leader to reach into the souls of others in a fashion which raises human consciousness, builds meanings, and inspires human intent that is the source of power. (p. 70)

In Bennis' view, this power does not depend on "ingeniously crafted organizational structures, carefully constructed management designs and controls, elegantly rationalized planning formats, or skillfully articulated leadership tactics" (p. 70). Instead, it grows out of the administrator's ability to communicate a " 'compelling vision' [that] empowers others to excel" (p. 71).

Foster (1989) also uses a transformation metaphor in his thoughtful discussion of the types of leaders needed as schools move into the twenty-first century. He contends that administrators have the privilege and responsibility of working to bring about genuine changes within not only the school, but also the larger society. Indeed, Foster argues that schools can be agencies of change within their communities. He calls on educators to envision themselves as "agents of tranformation" (p. 21) as they strive to achieve two goals: "the democratization of the [educational] institution and the building of community" (p. 25).

Blumberg's analogy, cited earlier, between a potter and a principal also suggests that school leaders actively transform that with which they work. Just as clay becomes a pottery vessel in a craftperson's hands, so groups of students and teachers can form healthy, productive, educational organizations under the leadership of a capable principal. Blumberg's description of one principal's action in transforming an idea into reality is revealing of how this process might occur.

> This principal, though she did not conceive of herself this way, thought and acted as if she were a craftsperson at work. . . . She had an image in mind of what she wanted to "make"; she was aware of potential "bubbles in the clay"; she possessed a set of skills that enabled her to shape things the way she wanted them to look; and she was guided by some rules of thumb that enabled her, slowly, to produce the final product. Further, at one point in our interview, she noted that what had been produced . . . was not "final" in the sense that it need no longer be attended to. It would need continual attention, using a way of thinking not unlike that of the potter who talked about the problems that may occur in the process of glazing something into clay. (p. 49)

Numerous others (e.g., American Association for School Administration, 1985; Dwyer & Smith, 1987; Goodlad, 1984; National Governors' Association, 1986), speaking of change, revolution, reform, and restructuring, join with those cited above in calling on principals to lead in developing good and effective institutions. In fact, most metaphors of this decade and the discussions in which they are embedded suggest that schools are unsuccessful—often dysfunctional—organizations (see Murphy, 1990a for a review) and that fundamental changes are needed. Principals are expected to be quite active in pursuing these changes as they lead in "the search for better schools" (Achilles, 1987, p. 18).

DOMINANT TONES OF THE METAPHORS

The opening sentences of Goodlad's *A Place Called School: Prospects for the Future* (1984) nicely express the sentiment noted above. They also provide insight into an attitude that seems to have influenced the tone of the metaphors of the 1980s. He writes:

> American schools are in trouble. In fact, the problems of schooling are of such crippling proportions that many schools may not survive. It is possible that our entire public education system is nearing collapse. (p. 1)

The sense of crisis evident in these words—especially when coupled with the belief that principals could, in large measure, either avert or encourage pending disaster—leads many writers to use metaphors that have an urgent or demanding tone. The message implicit in many of the writings is that principals *must* act quickly in order to *save* or *rescue* schools.

Another theme is also central to many of the images of the eighties. Many of the metaphors dealing with specific actions principals should take or strategies they should use have a distinctly businesslike flavor. Principles of management and the jargon of the corporate world seem to have influenced educational writers as they discuss solutions to the educational and organizational problems confronting schools. As we reviewed this phenomenon in historical context, an interesting pattern emerged. In earlier chapters, we noted that in times of major educational crisis, principals tend to concern themselves with small, manageable issues—even if these issues are rather trivial. One explanation for this pattern is that educational administrators do not function well if they sense they are not in control. If this hypothesis is, in fact, correct, it would explain principals' attraction and attention to controllable problems—especially during uncertain times when leadership, even in the absence of control, is needed. This explanation might explain the presence of a businesslike tone during this decade, for as problems abound, criticisms increase, and outcomes seem less and less certain, principals may gravitate toward objective, rational management strategies, with their "proven" formulas for success.

An Urgent, Demanding Tone

Bredeson's (1985) assertion that principals use "metaphor[s] of survival" (p. 41) demonstrates one dimension of the urgent tone of this decade. He writes:

The metaphor of survival can be distinguished in that beyond a mere sense of continuance and preserving what is, the survival image must deal with the threat of not continuing on or threat to the very existence of an enterprise. The emphasis on survival for principals and for the schools in which they operate is one that focuses on meeting immediate needs and the mustering of the most vital resources available for continued existence. (pp. 40–41)

Another example of images with an urgent tone can be found in the introduction to *The World We Created at Hamilton High* (Grant, 1988). Commenting on the abandonment of interest in "either intellectual or moral virtue" (p. 1), Grant notes "a profound confusion in America today about the school's role in shaping character" (p. 10). He suggests that this confusion has led to a state where the future of schools and those who lead them is at stake. He reports: "A corrosive individualism eats away at the heart of the [educational] enterprise. . . . We are uncertain how to give form to what Michael Walzer [1983] has called our program for social survival" (p. 1). Throughout his book, Grant uses similar language to convey a sense of urgency. He writes that

a sense of emergency grew out of the fifteen-year downward slope of the SAT scores, low levels of performance revealed in the National Assessment of Education Progress, reports of drugs and disorder in public schools, and international comparisons of educational achievement. (p. 216)

And, reflecting on four reports (Business–Higher Education Task Force on Education for Economic Growth, 1983; Education Commission of the States, 1983; National Commission on Excellence in Education, 1983; Twentieth Century Fund Task Force on Federal Elementary and Education Policy, 1983), he notes that "each suggested that schools were a major reason that America was losing ground in economic competition" (p. 216).

Numerous other metaphorical phrases also exemplify the urgent and demanding tone of this decade. Burlingame (1987), for instance, writing on "Images of Leadership in Effective Schools Literature," compares the reform movement of the 1980s to "the storms that frequently sweep the rugged and beautiful coast of Oregon" and notes that the concepts of leadership in the effective schools movement "have unleashed [their] fury on the educational shoreline" (p. 3). Hoyle, English, and Steffy (1985) write of "a series of thunderclap reports [that] rolled across the nation castigating public education and educators" (p. vii) and offer suggestions for ways principals might respond. Foster (1986), in turn, discusses "a crisis in confidence in education and schooling. . . . [a crisis that has led to] the everyday erosion in the self-image of teachers and administrators" (p. 11). And Sedlack, Wheeler, Pullin, & Cusick (1986) use the words "critical, even imperative" (p. 185) to describe the challenge facing administrators in the 1980s. Each of these phrases, especially when viewed in the context of an extraordinarily large body of work on educational reform (Murphy, 1990b, 1991a), underscores the urgency of the reform of the principalship (Murphy, 1991b, 1992) and the principal's role in the reform of schooling (Murphy, 1990a, 1991a).

The Businesslike Tone

As we noted in the introduction to this section, the businesslike tone in the writings on the principalship in the 1980s is reminiscent of earlier decades when principles of scientific management influenced the thinking of educational leaders. The metaphors of the eighties also contain traces of a tone we noted in our discussion of the fifties. There is a certain objective, academic flavor to many of them. The fact that tones and themes are recapitulated—with some variations—through the years leads us to contemplate several questions. Do we, in the language of this century, have a kind of symphony in the principalship—a symphony where tunes, tones, and rhythms appear early and then re-emerge in slightly different forms at later times? If so, what are the implications for preparation and practice in the future? Can we learn from these patterns? Can we influence them? In our discussion of the metaphors of the eighties we offer several bits of evidence that some sort of evolving dialectic seems to be occurring, and, in Chapter 9, we discuss this topic and its implications more fully.

Burlingame (1987) notes that the images of leadership have tended to shift between urgent, alarmed ones and those suggesting that administrators should be more methodical in their approach to their work. He reports that in the midst of educational crises, one model of leadership had told "administrators they must lead by defining goals, creating stability, and raising expectations" (p. 9). Within this framework, "principals are told how other truly successful administrators [in business and other noneducational fields] do their work using some universal kit including all-purpose and all powerful universal and diagnostic and prescriptive tools" (p. 9). In Burlingame's view, the expectations underlying the diverse images of leadership negatively affect principals. Introducing a psychological metaphor (which is also suggestive of crisis), he warns of "leadership schizophrenia . . . [resulting from] the clash of expectations" and calls for thoughtful reflection to clarify the basic nature of educational administration.

Others apparently do not share Burlingame's concern, freely connecting metaphors of educational crisis with solution metaphors from the business world. Responding to "the spate of reports during the decade [that] cited lack of administrative leadership" as the basis for alarming educational problems, Hoyle, English, and Steffy (1985) use numerous images drawn from corporate offices and boardrooms to describe good leadership practices. They, for example, call on university-based preparation programs to "combine the best *executive* development ideas from business and from professional preparation programs to help" (pp. 5-6; emphasis added) in developing effective principals. Furthermore, these authors use business-oriented phrases in their discussion of leadership goals. They maintain that

> School leaders should . . . develop and implement effective models/modes of instructional delivery that make the best use of time, staff, advanced technologies, community resources, and financial means to maximize student outcomes . . . [and] skillfully manage school system operations and facilities. (pp. 8-9)

In his discussion of this decade, Murphy (1990b) offers a number of examples of statements offered by educational reformers that further exemplify the coexistence of urgent metaphors with those from the world of economics and business management. The following statements are illustrative (cited, p. 9):

> Sinking economic productivity, national debt, international commercial competition, trade deficits, and a declining dollar placed the nation . . . in increasing economic jeopardy. Schooling was seen as part of the problem and part of the solution. (Guthrie & Kirst, 1988, p. 4)

> Many reforms reflect the assumption that quality education is a key element in the development of a stable national economy, which in turn is a critical factor in our national security. American productivity has become a political issue, and education is seen as a major factor in improving productivity. (Association for Supervision and Curriculum Development, 1986, p. 2)

While these quotes do not specifically address the principalship, given the multitude of statements placing responsibility for education's success or failures on its leaders (see Murphy, 1990a, 1990e), linkage is clearly implied.

Two additional works offering evidence of managerial emphasis in the principalship of the 1980s are Staw's "Leadership and Persistence" (1984) and Vaill's "The Purposing of High Performing Systems" (1984). These articles, included in Sergiovanni and Corbally's *Leadership and Organizational Culture* (1984), draw analogies between leadership in business and in schools and use language usually associated with the former to discuss the latter. Straw examines "a common syndrome of behavior in investment-type decisions and [discusses] some of its determinants" (p. 82). One receiving attenion is a phenomenon called "the escalation effect. . . . [a process wherein] most individuals will wait for a valued resource beyond the point where benefits exceed costs" (p. 75). Arguing that the forces propelling this effect in business are similar to those operating in education, Staw discusses appropriate administrative responses to situations in which leaders may be tempted to persist in an activity even when it no longer offers worthwhile rewards. In turn, Vaill looks at the characteristics of "excellent . . . high-performing" (p. 85) business systems and suggests ways these might be manifested in educational organizations.

DOMINANT VALUES

Numerous values are lifted up in the educational literature of the 1980s. Two, however—effectiveness and accountability—receive special attention in discussions of the role and tasks of the principal. Clearly, these two values are related. Educators, politicians, and others throughout the decade were concerned that schools accomplish their goals, that they "work" as they should. Many argued, in turn, that a school's effectiveness is linked to and even dependent on the actions of its leader. Thus, principals are to be held accountable for education. They are expected to recognize and embrace this reality and to discover ways to monitor their work and to prove to others that they are succeeding.

We have noted that much imagery in this decade reflects themes from earlier periods. The fact that effectiveness and accountability are important values supports this contention. Early in this century, the belief emerged that principles exist that, if discovered and followed, virtually guarantee that principals can lead schools toward success. Definitions of success have changed somewhat through the years, but the assumption that there are discernible pathways to its attainment have persisted. Much of the literature on school leadership implicitly accepts this assumption and attempts to identify and illuminate these avenues to success. In the eighties, this acceptance is much more overt as scholars embrace the values of effectiveness and accountability.

Effectiveness

The high value placed on effectiveness is difficult, if not impossible, to escape in this decade. Sorting through the many phrases that exemplify the importance attached to this value and determining which to mention here presented something of a challenge to us. Because many of the metaphors noted earlier in this chapter suggest the importance of effectiveness, in this section we identify expressions from authors we have not previously cited.

DeRoche's book, *How School Administrators Solve Problems* (1985), offers insight into the value attached to effectiveness. In a brief section, this author repeats the adjective "effective" several times and underscores his belief that such a word characterizes good principals. He concludes:

> All of the problems . . . and all of the needs and concerns expressed by school principals center on the principal's effectiveness as a leader and an administrator. The belief that effective schools have effective leaders is based on the premise that the school principal is probably the most important and influential person in the school. To achieve maximum effectiveness, it is essential that [the principal] examine [her or his] performance, expectations, tasks, and responsibilities. (pp. 18–19)

Strother (1982), Persell and Cookson (1982), and Carnine, Gersten, and Green (1982) are others who write at length on the subject of effective principals. Analyzing "the many roles of the effective principal" (p. 291), Strother discusses ways preparation programs and professional organizations might better help persons "learn how to be effective through an ongoing process of growth" (p. 293). Persell and Cookson "address the question of why some principals are more effective than others in running a good school . . . [and identify] nine recurrent behaviors that good principals display" (p. 22). Taking a highly practical perspective, Carnine and his coauthors argue that a principal's effectiveness depends on her or his ability to see that "crucial, mundane, support functions" (p. 47) are carried out. They recommend delegating responsibility for these "more down-to-earth . . . [but] crucial" activities (p. 49).

Other metaphorical expressions further underscore the fact that effectiveness is an important administrative value during this decade. For example, Snyder (1983) calls on principals to strive for "greater productivity" (p. 32) in their schools. Gretchko and DeMont (1980) equate success with effectiveness, and Benjamin (1981) describes an effective leader as one who "can get things done" (discussed in Phi Delta Kappa, 1982, p. 213). In turn, Pounder (1987) admonishes administrators to make efforts to cultivate "a productive and satisfied work force [which] is the foundation for an effective school" (p. 299).

Accountability

Much of the scholarship of this decade attempts to operationalize effectiveness as it relates to education in general and to school leadership in particular (see, for example, Clark & Lotto, 1982; Hoyle, English, & Steffy, 1985; Persell & Cookson, 1982; Vaill, 1984). These efforts have resulted in lists of "behaviors that good principals display" (Persell & Cookson, 1982, p. 22), discussions of especially salient leadership qualities that correlate with effectiveness (Clark & Lotto, 1982; Strother, 1982), and checklists designed to help principals monitor their schools and themselves. Implicit in this type of literature is a belief that school leaders can and should be held accountable for what happens in their schools. Later in the chapter, we discuss standards by which principals are evaluated in the eighties. Therefore, we do not dwell here on specific yardsticks against which administrators are to be measured. Rather, we offer evidence of the high value placed on the concept of accountability during these years.

In her discussion of effective leaders, Strother (1982) offers an articulate defense of this accountability. Noting that "good principals . . . [can] learn how to be effective" (p. 293), she calls on researchers to develop tools to determine whether this learning has occurred.

> Research is suggesting new and more effective directions for the training of principals. As programs put these findings into practice, evaluations of outcomes will provide even better answers on how to improve education through principals' leadership. (pp. 293-294)

The assumption undergirding DeRoche's (1985) text is that principals are responsible for what happens in schools and that, therefore, they should be asked to account for successes and failures. He opens with a discussion of "three administrative *facts*" (p. v; emphasis added), one of which emphasizes leadership accountability.

> The school principal is *the*, not *a*, major influence on the quality of education in a school. The school principal—also known as the middle manager and the site administrator—is the major influence on whether education is effective or ineffective; whether morale is high or low; whether the school climate is positive or negative; whether personnel are satisfied or dissatisfied; whether students achieve or don't achieve; whether parents and the public are cooperative or uncooperative; and whether there is effective or ineffective management and leadership. (p. *v*; emphasis in original)

DeRoche goes on to offer a plethora of scales and checklists to assist principals in monitoring and accounting for the activities of their schools.

Similarly, Hoyle, English, and Steffy (1985) conclude nearly each chapter in *Skills for Successful School Leaders* with a "skill accomplishment checklist" (pp. 41, 77, 105, 129, 167, 205, 247) with which principals and others can identify specific strengths and weaknesses. These authors are quick to point out that these lists do not "represent a uniform, rigid standard for all to meet" (p. 3), and thus they acknowledge that accountability is not a simple value, easily achieved through the use of a few scales. This qualifying statement does not, however, discount the importance attached to this concept. Indeed, the work of Hoyle and his colleagues, with its "clear recitation and description of eight critical skill areas necessary for school leaders to master and apply" (p. 1), is predicated on the belief that principals are accountable for educational efforts and that their effectiveness or ineffectiveness can, to a large extent, be objectively determined.

THE PRINCIPAL'S RELATIONSHIP TO OTHERS

In the seventies, a disenchantment with bureaucracy appeared to influence a belief that principals should relate to others as partners and as friends and that they should use persuasive communication instead of authority to get things done. In the eighties, this movement against top-heavy educational hierarchies takes a slightly different form. In the previous decade, antibureaucratic views were often presented in rather dramatic and challenging forms, often by persons outside traditional educational establishments who wished to abolish the old ways of running schools. As the eighties wore on, these ideas began to be adopted, with some important variations, by academics and practitioners within the educational mainstream. The concern toward the end of the 1980s is with rethinking, flattening, or restructuring school governance systems, not doing away with them. Educational writers appear to be seeking new, more effective kinds of organizations to replace discredited forms. This, in turn, influences understandings of principals' relationships with others.

To Superintendents, Boards, and Other Governing Bodies

The desire to move power and authority into local schools seems to have affected conceptions of the ways principals relate to persons or groups in "superior" positions. In earlier decades, superintendents and boards are portrayed as having authority over principals in a number of areas. Principals were seen primarily as carrying out district-level policies and directives. In the 1980s, principals relate to their superordinates more as solicitors and stewards of available resources. They are expected to know their school plants, staffs, and budgets, to make needs known to persons or groups who can help meet them, and to account for the way resources are utilized.

Citing several earlier studies, Persell and Cookson (1982) claim that a central characteristic of an effective principal is the ability to function "as the resource and reward allocator" (p. 26; see also Hall, Hord, & Griffin, 1980). Snyder (1983) concurs, noting that good leaders pay much attention to "resource management," seeking to ensure that funds are "sought and provided for high-priority goal-related activities rather than spent indiscriminately in other needy areas" (p. 37). In the same vein, Crowson and Porter-Gehrie (1981) suggest that a key responsibility of principals is to "keep the school supplied with adequate resources" (p. 28). These authors specifically note that fulfilling this responsibility involves interacting with district-, state-, and federal-level administrators. Furthermore, they argue that good leaders will interact with these others in a shrewd, skillful manner. They write:

> School principals . . . have very limited formal control over the resources available for the operation of their respective schools. . . . Informally, however, we find that principals have the capacity to affect, sometimes significantly, the flow of resources to their building. . . . Two strategies observed are: (a) knowing and using "the system" to best advantage, and (b) finding discretionary resources on the outside. (pp. 46–47)

Hoyle, English, and Steffy (1985) are others who suggest that principals and their superiors chiefly interact on the question of resources. Their discussion implies that principals are expected to engage in certain activities when dealing with governing bodies. First, they are to identify needs within schools and solicit whatever is needed—time, money, personnel, and so forth—to meet those needs. Second, they are expected to account for the ways these resources are actually used. These authors offer a detailed list of skills principals need in order to successfully accomplish these activities. Starting with "a needs assessment" (p. 189), school leaders should "construct appropriate programs with proper instruction modes . . . to match a validated (agreed on) set of program objectives" (p. 189). These provide the guidelines for principals' requests for funding. Once funds are granted, Hoyle and colleagues admonish leaders to exercise careful "fiscal management and control" (p. 202). In their view, this means that the principal should serve as "the chief financial officer" (p. 202) or that she or he should be in close contact with the person in that position.

This understanding of principals' relationships to superintendents, boards, and other groups is, in our view, not surprising in light of prevailing conceptions of good and effective school leadership. It is certainly consistent with the tenets of school-based management, which were finding increasing acceptance as the decade drew to a close, for in these types of relationships, principals have a good bit of decision- and policy-making power. It is also consonant with the emphasis on accountability and with the businesslike tone of many of the metaphors of this era. In a similar way, discussions of principal–teacher relationships of this decade offer few surprises. In the next section we discuss these in some detail.

To Teachers

Early in this chapter, we noted that principals of the eighties are expected to function as instructional leaders. Consistent with this expectation, educational writers discuss, at length, the interactions between administrators and teachers, with an emphasis on improving instructional effectiveness. Two aspects of these interactions receive considerable attention. First, principals are expected to facilitate the professional development of teachers; second, they are charged with continuously monitoring the work of faculty members to see if good teaching is, in fact, occurring.

Barth (1987) asserts that the ideal principal is one who facilitates the professional development of teachers and thereby improves the instructional program. He makes a helpful distinction between "promoting institutional compliance" and "staff development" (p. 259) and argues that the second should be the administrator's goal. Barth offers an articulate discussion of the activities that, in his view, constitute good faculty development.

> Staff development for me has come to take on quite a different meaning. It is listening in a hundred different ways for a question to emanate from teachers, usually in the form, "Here's what I want to try." And staff development means being ready to supply assistance or encouragement in a hundred different ways. . . .
>
> Any initiative emanating from a teacher, whether a request to buy 1,000 tongue depressors or to deviate from the prescribed curriculum in order to build a new one based upon last summer's trip to Alaska, carries with it powerful potential for professional growth. The way to insure that a teacher becomes a deeply engrossed student [of teaching and learning] is to allow and encourage the teacher to identify the problem to be addressed. The source of the problem for adults, as for students, determines the energy and motivation that will be expended upon resolving the problem. Some call it "ownership." (p. 259)

Barth argues that unlocking teachers' energy and motivation is, in large measure, the responsibility of the principal.

> I have argued that the principal of a school occupies a position of central influence over the professionalization of teaching. Transforming relation-

ships by developing collegiality, engaging teachers in important decisions affecting their classrooms and school, developing personal visions, becoming active adult learners, serving as mentors to other teachers and prospective teachers, and maintaining quality in their own and others' performances, are all ways principals can make good use of their extraordinary influence. (p. 262)

Little and Bird (1987), McEvoy (1987), Pounder (1987), and others offer examples of specific leadership behaviors and activities that facilitate the professional development of teachers. Little and Bird suggest that principals who nurture faculty development are those who have collegial relationships with teachers, model desired commitment and enthusiasm, and spend much time in or near the classroom. In their view, this last behavior is critical. They write: "We have held that . . . leaders' influence on teaching is unlikely to be felt without a substantial investment of time spent close to the classroom" (p. 119; see also Murphy, 1990d, for a review).

In words reminiscent of Barth's, Pounder (1987) concludes:

Teachers themselves are the key resource in schools, and the basic challenge for instructional leaders is to tap and cultivate teachers as vital sources of information regarding problems and strategies for enhancing their work and the general working conditions in their schools. (p. 295)

She offers three recommendations to principals in regard to teacher development—recommendations she labels "simple and quite obvious, but [reflecting] . . . a much-neglected, yet promising set of strategies" (p. 295). In brief, she asks principals to "listen" (p. 295), "interpret" (p. 296), and "respond" (p. 298). In her discussion, she defines each of these and indicates ways principals who engage in each will, in fact, be supporting good teaching.

The first step for an instructional leader is to listen to the concerns of teachers. . . .
    In addition to listening to teachers' messages, it will sometimes be necessary to interpret or "read between the lines" of a message. . . . The ability of a school principal to interpret accurately the concerns of teachers thus often requires "ferreting-out" the more covert information and interpreting that information given his or her understanding of the individual and groups dynamics of the faculty in that particular school. . . .
    After having gathered and analyzed relevant data about teachers' concerns regarding their work or work environment, it is critical that school leaders respond appropriately, and in a timely fashion. (pp. 295–298)

Analyzing research from the 1980s, Rosenholtz and Simpson (1990) focus on a different type of action. Principals who facilitate teachers' development are those who protect (or "buffer") teachers from "classroom interruptions and managerial tasks . . . [which interfere with] their attempts to perform the core teaching tasks" (p. 245; see also Blase, 1986; Kasten, 1984; Rosenholtz, 1985, 1989). They contend:

> For school principals, these [buffering] activities may include attending to the material requirements of instructional programs, providing clerical assistance for routine paperwork, mobilizing outside resources (such as parents) to assist teachers with nonteaching tasks, and protecting classroom time from unnecessary interruption. (p. 245; see Rosenholtz, 1985, for a review)

Even more specific strategies used by effective principals to show their commitment to the professional growth of staff have been outlined by Murphy (1990d).

> They focus staff development activities on the entire staff and on the specific goals and curriculum programs of the school (Clark, Lotto, & McCarthy, 1980). . . . They are especially adept at using informal coalitions of teachers in implementing new prorams (Hanson, 1981). They take an active role in planning, participating in, and evaluating professional development activities with their staffs (Berman & McLaughlin, 1978; Clark et al., 1980; Little, 1982). Research also reveals that instructional leaders provide both direct aid (e.g., concrete technical assistance and materials) and indirect support (e.g., encouragement) to teachers as they attempt to integrate skills learned during staff development programs into their repertoire of instructional behaviors (Berman & McLaughlin, 1978; Blumberg & Greenfield, 1980; Hord & Huling-Austin, 1986; Little, 1982). Effective principals facilitate opportunities for professional growth by enabling teachers to attend conferences, establishing mechanisms that facilitate the exchange of professional dialogue, and personally sharing ideas and materials with staff (Guzzetti & Martin, 1986; McEvoy, 1987). Finally, instructional leaders are active in providing regular "incidental interventions—casual conversations, observations, suggestions of ideas—that assist teachers in their daily efforts to improve" (Phi Delta Kappa, 1983, p. 3). (p. 177)

Not only are principals expected to initiate activities to promote faculty development, they are also charged with monitoring the progress of this development, to stay on top of teachers' instructional styles and knowledge. Little and Bird (1987) argue that principals can do this only if they are frequently in classrooms. Explaining this assertion, they write:

> Previous research . . . has led us to believe that some professional interactions more than others have the potential for developing schools with the collective capacity for improvement. . . . We concentrated on certain key practices, particularly those that brought persons closest to the crucial problems of teaching and learning. Most prominent among these were practices of classroom observation and feedback. (pp. 119–120)

Hoyle, English, and Steffy (1985) devote a chapter in their text to the topic of staff evaluation and offer numerous suggestions to principals regarding the most effective ways to monitor teachers. One point, worthy of note, is their suggestion that, prior to evaluating teachers, a principal should experience an assessment of her or his own work. After this has been done, they agree that principals can and should monitor their teachers and note that this is actually one facet of responsible instructional leadership. Hoyle and colleagues discuss a number of mechanisms principals might use in this effort. They consistently remind readers to choose the strategy most appropriate to the situation. Furthermore, they emphasize that principals and teachers must view these interactions as ways to improve the overall program. These are not to be summative evaluations whereby teachers are promoted, fired, rewarded, or penalized. Rather, they are formative evaluations. Weaknesses uncovered are to be addressed by the principal and teacher working together to establish improvement strategies.

Drawing upon various research efforts, Smith and Andrews (1989) discuss several benefits to principals who carefully monitor teachers within their classrooms. Drawing upon the work of Rutherford (1985), Sapone (1985), Lipham (1981), and Fullan (1981), Smith and Andrews suggest that those who carefully and consistently observe instructional activities are in a good position to supply teachers with needed guidance, information, and resources. Additionally, Smith and Andrews note that leaders who observe classroom successes can acknowledge these to deserving instructors.

> After being out and around the school, the principal communicates praise verbally and through informal written notes.
>
> The visible presence of the principal appears to be most keenly felt when the principal serves as rewarder, giving positive attention to staff . . . accomplishments. Brookover and his associates (1982) suggest that setting up an award system that clearly "strokes" staff and students for academic success is perhaps the most important aspect of creating an effective school. Acknowledging the achievements of others is a regular practice by principals who are strong instructional leaders. (p. 19)

Finally, Smith and Andrews contend that those principals who closely monitor teachers are the ones best able to conduct effective and productive evaluations. They argue:

> The principal should wholeheartedly practice clinical supervision, "supervision up close" (Goldhammer, 1969). The purpose of frequent classroom observations and dialogues with teachers is the improvement of instruction. . . . Staff evaluation is perceived as a natural complement to the clinical supervision processes. (p. 43; see also Alfonso & Goldberry, 1982; Bolton, 1973, 1980)

Ellet (1987) is another who writes at length of "the instructional leadership role of building principals with a particular concern for more direct supervision of teaching" (p. 302). He acknowledges that this role conception is not a new one, but argues that two recent developments mandate thinking about the principal's role as supervisor or monitor in new ways. The first of these is the "research on effective schools and the instructional role of the principal" (pp. 303–304); the second is the proliferation of "a number of large-scale teacher performance assessment programs [which] have emerged in response to public demands for increased educational accountability and reform" (p. 304). In this chapter, Ellet reviews several of these systems, all of which share the assumption that principals will observe teachers regularly and will monitor their growth and development as educators.

To Students

An interesting dichotomy in discussions of principal–student relationships is evident in the literature of this period. In the more prescriptive pieces, the emphasis is typically on the principal's role in setting high standards for student performance. In so doing, principals, it is suggested, will be doing much to ensure that young people benefit from their hours in schools. In these books and articles, personal interactions between students and teachers are not highlighted. In descriptive books and articles, especially those portraying "good" or "effective" principals, a different pattern emerges. These leaders are frequently described as taking a very personal interest in individual students—in their academic performance, but also in other areas of their lives. This interest results in various direct interactions between students and principals, which occur both in and outside the school.

The belief that principals can and should serve students by seeing that high standards are set and maintained is a pervasive theme of much reform literature. Murphy (1990e), who writes that a central theme of reform literature in the eighties is the "re-emergence of [the belief] of the school administrator as a key to school and district improvement" (p. 279), notes that raising standards—for students, teachers, and administrators—is another reform theme. He underscores the fact that the prevailing belief is that each leader must attend to the standards in her or his organization. Therefore, principals are expected to support high expectations for students and teachers in their schools.

Smith and Andrews (1989) clearly state their belief that a good principal "creates a climate of high expectations in the school" (p. 8). Hoyle and colleagues (1985) concur. They call on school leaders to develop and communicate "a vision of how high school graduates should look, act, and learn" (p. 273). Then, in order to achieve that vision, they ask administrators to "identify and select the best and *most intellectually demanding* . . . educational programs (p. 273; emphasis added). Achilles and Keedy (1983–1984) similarly argue that "norm setting [is] a component of principal effectiveness" (p. 59). The norms to which they refer relate to the academic performance of students. They identify "sets of behaviors [that] comprise norm setting.

(1) setting standards of performances for teachers (K. Clark, 1968; Wellisch et al., 1978; and Brookover et al., 1979);

(2) principals working with teachers to set high learning expectations for students (Austin, 1979; and Clark et al., 1980); and

(3) coordination and sequencing of school-wide goals and objectives (University of Indiana review, 1979 [cited by] Benjamin, 1981). Ideally, the third set lends specification to sets one and two: If teachers are performing and students are meeting high expectations set by principals and teachers, students should achieve school-wide goals and objectives. (p. 59)

Snyder (1983) suggests that "raising achievement norms depends on knowledgeable leadership and collective action" (p. 37) and admonishes principals to lead teachers in establishing high standards for students. Persell and Cookson (1982) take a similar view. They write:

In higher-achieving schools, principals did not let teachers "write off" students as nonlearners, particularly because of their race or social class. In low-achieving schools, the principal helped to depress the teachers' expectations for their students. . . .

A recurrent characteristic of successful schools concerns the amount of respect shown to all the participants. The principal helps to set a tone of respect for teachers and students. . . . The principal must be a major voice in setting a tone of respect in a school. (p. 23)

Addressing the problem of low-achieving schools, Ross and MacDonald (n.d.) stress that the principal must lead the staff in holding "positive expectations for all students" (p. 3). This, in their view, means that "a common standard of instruction [should be applied] to ALL children" (p. 3; emphasis in original). Like Persell and Cookson, they stress that these high standards should apply to academics and to student behavior.

In case studies of effective leaders, principals are also portrayed as setters of high standards. This, however, is often balanced by mention of their sensitive and supportive personal interactions with students. For example, Grant (1988) praises principal Joseph Conan as a person who combined a concern for achievement with personal and compassionate relationships.

> Conan was respected intellectually for his excellence as a teacher and morally for his compassion, courage, and spirit of service to others. He rejected the language of modern management techniques. Conan was unashamed to talk to the faculty about "love of mankind" or to ask, "If we are not here to serve people, what else is there in life?" He visited students in the hospital and took school-work to homes of those who had been suspended to show that discipline was not born of hatred. He had the capacity to engage the students, faculty, and parents in dialogue about the issues that really mattered. (pp. 196–197)

Lightfoot (1983) also discusses the ways good principals relate to students. In each of the schools she describes in *The Good High School*, the principal's style of relating to students is discussed.

> Even in the schools where leaders have not expressed a clearly articulated divergence from male caricatures, we find that the leaders express a need for partnership and nurturance. . . . [Their] redefinition [of their roles] includes softer images that are based on nurturance given and received by the leader; based on relationships and affiliations as central dimensions of the exercise of power; and based on a subtle integration of personal qualities traditionally attached to male and female images. (p. 33)

For each of the principals described by Lightfoot, this redefinition involves the embracing of personal, caring relationships with teachers and students.

In Lee's (1987) discussion of leaders in one junior high school, principal Grace Lancaster is described as one whose "style [is] personable rather than business-like" (p. 83). This style clearly manifests itself in her interaction with students. Lee describes Lancaster's handling of a student who broke a school rule.

> One day . . . she encountered a small boy on the patio during class time, wearing jeans and an undershirt. Lancaster's first question was, "Honey, where's your shirt? You're supposed to be wearing a shirt." When he told her that it was in a bag that another boy had taken, she spent the next ten or fifteen minutes helping the boy locate the boy with the bag. The youngster's belongings were returned to him before he was expected to return to class. (pp. 92–93)

Lee's comments on this interchange are revealing. She writes:

> It . . . communicated to the boy the importance that the principal placed on his personal well-being. Lancaster communicated this message in numerous ways to Emerson's students. As she supervised, her exchanges with youngsters were more frequently concerned with matters other than discipline. Teasing about their social lives, asking about their families, checking on their recovery from illnesses and injuries, and inquiring about their classes and activities [are] all ways in which Lancaster indicate[s] personal knowledge of and interest in her students' lives. (p. 93)

These authors place a high value on sensitive, caring, direct interactions between principals and students. Interestingly, this does not seem to be a major concern with those who write about the evaluation of educational leaders. As we discuss in the next section, many schemes were developed for assessing principals in this decade. These, however, tend to focus on quantitative measures of academic performance rather than on the more qualitative outcomes described above.

STANDARDS FOR EVALUATION

This is a decade of accountability, one in which a prevailing assumption is that causal links between principals' competencies and school outcomes exist. This assumption has several attendant beliefs. Principals, it is assumed, should be held responsible for educational successes or failures, and they are expected to offer evidence of their abilities. Writers, therefore, argue that principals can be judged by their schools, teachers, and students. If a principal is doing her or his job, learning will, in fact, be taking place, and conversely, if learning is taking place, the principal is doing her or his job. Most seem to at least tacitly accept this view; a few, however, delve more deeply into the concept of leader evaluation and offer elaborate evaluative procedures or instruments.

Murphy (1990e) offers a nice discussion of outcome-oriented evaluations in this decade. He writes:

For much of the last quarter-century, a general belief in the professional importance of administrators has prevailed. The picture of the school superintendent or principal as the beleaguered professional who can exercise little influence over his or her organization, and who is only distally connected to important educational processes and outcomes, has been widely accepted. . . . Conditions are currently unfolding, however, that show principals . . . can exert considerable influence over their schools. (p. 279)

Murphy notes that five related literature topics—school change; school improvement; staff development; administrator as instructional leader; and school effectiveness—support the idea that school outcomes reflect the activities of school leaders and, by extension, that principals can be judged by the schools they lead. In related work, Murphy and his colleagues (1985, 1986, 1987) uncovered the strategies used to evaluate principals in instructionally effective school districts.

The belief that administrators can be assessed by school results is often expressed in reports by commissions or task forces. For example, a report from the Organization for Economic Cooperation and Development states that principals are accountable for

1. Setting quality targets and providing the means of attaining them;
2. Monitoring the implementation of appropriate strategies;
3. Conducting regular appraisals of performance in association with the schools concerned. (p. 89, cited in Boyd, 1990)

This suggests that the degree to which stated goals are achieved provides a set of standards against which principals can be judged. Furthermore, it places the onus on the school site administrator to garner evidence on the achievement of these goals. Both of these conditions were found in assessments of the evaluation of principals in instructionally effective school districts (Murphy et al., 1986, 1987).

Approaching this topic from a similar perspective, the Education Commission of the States (1983) states that "in study after study, it has been shown that one key determinant of excellence in public schooling is the leadership of the individual school principal" (p. 29). Thus, the Commission suggests that excellence (or, perhaps, the excellent achievement of goals) provides a yardstick for judging school site administrators. The National Governors' Association (1986) concurs with this view, saying in essence that schools should be places of learning; principals are responsible for seeing that this happens and should be judged accordingly.

Agreeing with this view, some scholars elaborate on mechanisms by which the degree of goal attainment can be judged. Smith and Andrews (1985), who, as we noted earlier, believe that principals must themselves be evaluated before they can judge teachers, devoted an entire chapter to the topic of "principal evaluation" (p. 88). Borrowing from Bolton, they contend that this activity involves three phases, including

Phase I: Designing the evaluation plan
Phase II: Collecting data and observing performance
Phase III: Analyzing the data and evaluating strengths and weaknesses.
   (p. 88)

Each of these phases is discussed in some detail. For example, the authors discuss a number of factors to be considered as the evaluation plan is being designed and suggest that those being evaluated should participate in establishing this plan. One key dimension of this phase is establishing educational and administrative goals that can be used as the basis for assessment. In the same way, when discussing data collection, Smith and Andrews recommend that multiple methods be used. They continue by offering a kind of protocol for analyzing evidence and for reporting the results of this analysis to involved parties.

The evaluation suggested by Smith and Andrews (1989) focuses on outcomes in the form of achieved goals. It is not, however, a summative evaluation. Rather, they note that the report emerging from this assessment process "serves as a motivator by giving relevant recognition for the principal's significant achievements. It is also a stimulus for continued efforts in targeted areas" (p. 100). Hoyle and colleagues (1985) also discuss evaluation in this fashion. Arguing that leadership is reflected by schools and that successful organizations reflect favorably on their administrators (and vice versa), these authors provide lists of needed skills against which principals can check themselves. The failure to possess these skills is not, in the view of Hoyle and colleagues, a reason to fire a leader. Rather, this assessment should be used to inspire and guide improvement.

The prevailing view of this decade is that hard-nosed, unyielding evaluations need to be conducted prior to a person's entry into the field. Many (American Association of Colleges for Teacher Education, 1988; Clark, 1988; Griffiths, Stout, & Forsyth, 1988; National Commission on Excellence in Educational Administration, 1987) argue that rigorous assessments should be conducted before a person is admitted into a preparation program and on the person's leaving the program, prior to entering the field. Indeed, they suggest that selective recruitment and high standards during the preparation stages make it possible to conduct formative, improvement-oriented evaluations on practitioners.

CONCLUSION

As we analyzed the metaphors of the 1980s, we were struck by the fact that, in this decade of reform, conceptions of the principalship did, in fact, reflect a "reforming" of earlier understandings. In the 1800s and early 1900s, the lines between administrators and teachers were indistinct. The principal's involvement in instruction was a given. Now principals are admonished to re-enter classrooms, not necessarily as teachers of children, but as teachers of teachers and as overseers and directors of the teaching/ learning enterprise. In this conception we see an expansion of an old expectation.

In a similar way, two other sets of metaphors recapitulate and expand on earlier beliefs. The metaphors used in discussions of the principal's role in establishing and cultivating a vision are not unlike those used early in this century. Spiritual, religious imagery, common in the literature of the 1920s, is reappearing as authors stress the importance of principals' upholding "the mission of the school" (Bredeson, 1985, p. 43) and "the enduring values of character" (Greenfield, 1987, p. 172). At the same time, the objective language of business, of management, and of bureaucracy, which was especially prevalent in the thirties and sixties, resurfaces. A frequent emphasis is the need for "goals and objectives . . . [which] are and should be the guideposts for program development and services as well as for evaluation and assessment" (DeRoche, 1985, p. 207). Success in instructional leadership is linked to "knowledge about how to manage technical core operations" (Murphy, 1990e, p. 283), and "cost effectiveness and program budgeting" (Hoyle, English, & Steffy, 1985, p. 127) are key administrative concerns.

This re-emergence of many earlier assumptions and metaphors suggests that the past has, indeed, influenced the present. During a decade of crisis and challenge, we do not see principals responding to calls for change by moving into "new" roles (Clinton, 1987, p. 3; National Governors' Association, 1986, p. 14). Instead, we see a recycling and reshaping of old expectations as scholars and practitioners alike react to the demands of school leadership in complex, diverse contexts.

CHAPTER EIGHT

The 1990s

We need new metaphors to describe organizations and administration.

(T. B. Greenfield, 1988, p. 151)

Just as the metaphors that help us understand the principalship of the 1980s are intricately connected to the educational reform activity of that decade—the so-called standards-raising movement—many of the metaphors being applied to the principalship in the early 1990s grow directly out of the second wave of educational reform—the restructuring movement. While in earlier chapters we applied an historical lens to the study of the metaphors associated with the principalship, in this chapter we must project into the future. We acknowledge at the outset the difficulty of this task (see Button, 1966), which is made doubly arduous both by the state of turmoil that currently characterizes education and by the contradictory, even schizophrenic, nature of the suggestions being offered for altering the principalship role and the behavior of its occupants (Boyd, 1987; Murphy, 1991a).

In the first part of this chapter, we analyze the forces that are pushing the principalship in new directions, focusing on the larger external forces that are shaping tomorrow's schools. Next we provide a portrait of schools for the twenty-first century and note how this view of education leads logically to the development of particular metaphors for the principalship in the 1990s and beyond. Based on these conclusions, we then examine the principalship in the 1990s. Using metaphorical lenses, we describe the major challenges confronting principals in the 1990s and discuss how the emerging metaphors will shape the activities of principals in this decade and into the next century.

FORCES SHAPING SCHOOLING

> Reform periods in education are typically times when concerns about the state of the society or economy spill over into demands that the schools set things straight. (Tyack, 1990, p. 174)

Consistent with one of the major themes echoed through this volume—that the principalship has been shaped extensively by larger social and historical forces—we begin with a discussion of the conditions that seem likely to have the most profound effect on education in the next century. We examine three broad trends: the perceived crisis in the economy, the changing nature of the social fabric of society, and the evolution from an industrial to a post-industrial world.

Crisis in the Economy

At the base of proposed reforms in the corporate and educational sectors is the belief that the United States is losing, and perhaps has already lost, its foremost position in the world economy—that its "once unchallenged preeminence in commerce, industry, science, and technological innovation" (National Commission on Excellence in Education, 1983, p. 5) has taken a terrible battering. Evidence of this belief is omnipresent in the reform documents that fueled the educational reform movement of the 1980s.

> Today, however, our faith in change—and our faith in ourselves as the world's supreme innovators—is being shaken. Japan, West Germany and other relatively new industrial powers have challenged America's position on the leading edge of change and technical invention. In the seventies, productivity in manufacturing industries grew nearly four times as fast in Japan, and twice as fast in West Germany and France, as in the United States.
> The possibility that other nations may outstage us in inventiveness and productivity is suddenly troubling Americans. (Education Commission of the States, 1983, p. 13)

> Already the quality of our manufactured products, the viability of our trade, our leadership in research and development, and our standards of living are strongly challenged. Our children could be stragglers in a world of technology. We must not let this happen; America must not become an industrial dinosaur. (National Science Board, 1983, p. v)

> America's ability to compete in world markets is eroding. The productivity growth of our competitors outdistances our own. The capacity of our

economy to provide a high standard of living is increasingly in doubt. (Carnegie Forum on Education and the Economy, 1986, p. 2)

As the Carnegie Forum on Education and the Economy (1986) report reveals, it did not take reformers long to draw a connection between a stagnant economy and a deteriorating educational system.

The 1980s will be remembered for two developments: the beginning of a sweeping reassessment of the basis of the nation's economic strength and an outpouring of concern for the quality of American education. The connection between these two streams of thought is strong and growing. (p. 11)

This assumption of a tight, and causal, linkage between schooling and the economy has helped to produce three outcomes. First, blame has been heaped on schools and the men and women who work in them. The language of David Kearns (1988), Chairman of Xerox Corporation, is illustrative.

Public education consumes nearly 7% of our gross national product. Its expenditures have doubled or tripled in every postwar decade, even when enrollments declined. I can't think of any other single sector of American society that has absorbed more money by serving fewer people with steadily declining service. . . .
    Public education has put this country at a terrible competitive disadvantage. The American workforce is running out of qualified people. (p. 566)

No shortage of energy has been expended to document the failure of the educational enterprise. Evidence has accumulated to show that students do not perform as well as their peers in other countries on various tests of achievement and that they are scoring considerably below the levels achieved by previous generations of students in the United States.

Second, a rationale for the failure of the educational system has been constructed. As we report elsewhere (Murphy, 1991a), investigators have begun dissecting the educational system in search of explanations. The fundamental conclusion of these analyses is that schools are characterized by intellectual softness, a lack of expectations and standards, inadequate leadership, a dysfunctional organizational structure, conditions of employment inconsistent with professional work, and the absence of any meaningful accountability. The basic infrastructure of our educational system has been found in need of serious repair. The luster has worn off the educational enterprise.

Finally, reformers have turned their attention to the very institutions they chastise, asking them to jump start the faltering economy.

> Many reforms reflect the assumption that quality education is a key element in the development of a stable national economy, which in turn is a critical factor in our national security. American productivity has become a political issue, and education is seen as a major factor in improving productivity. (Association for Supervision and Curriculum Development, 1986, p. 2)

> If only to keep and improve on the slim competitive edge we still retain in world markets, we must dedicate ourselves to the reform of our educational system. (National Commission on Excellence in Education, 1983, p. 7)

As we discuss more fully later in this chapter, the economic crisis and subsequent efforts to restructure organizations to address it promise to shape dramatically both our conception of the principalship and the language we use to describe it.

The Changing Nature of the Social Fabric

The fabric of American society is being rewoven in some places and unraveled in others, resulting in changes that promise to have a significant impact on schooling. At the core of these revisions are demographic shifts that threaten "our national standard of living and democratic foundations" (Carnegie Council on Adolescent Development, 1989, p. 27) and promise to overwhelm schools as they are now constituted. Minority enrollment in America's schools is rising as is the proportion of less advantaged youngsters. There is a rapid increase in the number of students whose primary language is other than English. The traditional two-parent family, with one parent employed and the other at home to care for the children, has become an anomaly, constituting less than one-third of American families (Kirst, McLaughlin, & Massell, 1989). A few citations from educational literature convey the extent of these demographic changes.

> Overall, more than 30 percent of students in public schools—some 12 million—are now minority. (Quality Education for Minorities Project, 1990, p. 11)
> By the year 2000, . . . nearly half of all school-aged children will be nonwhite. (Carnegie Council on Adolescent Development, 1989, p. 27)
> Forty-six percent of children live in homes where both or the only parent is working . . . about one half of all children and youth will live in a

single parent family for some period of their lives. (Kirst,
McLaughlin, & Massell, 1989, p. 4)
Between 1960 and 1987, the number of families headed by females with
children under 18 tripled. (Wagstaff & Gallagher, 1990, p. 103)

At the same time that these new threads are being woven into the fabric
of American society, a serious unraveling of other parts of that fabric is
occurring. The number of youngsters affected by the ills of the world in
which they live—for example, poverty, unemployment, crime, drug addic-
tion, malnutrition—is increasing, as is the need for a variety of more
intensive and extended services from societal organizations, especially
schools.

Today nearly 20 percent of children live in poverty, up from 14 percent
in 1969. The median family income of families in the bottom
income quintile (20 percent) has eroded over time from $9,796 to
$8,919 in 1986, and the gap between the incomes of the poorest and
wealthiest families has grown. . . . Race and ethnicity, gender, and
family structure are strongly associated with the likelihood of poverty. (Kirst, McLaughlin, & Massell, 1989, p. 3)
Another harsh statistical conclusion is that poverty has increasingly become a black, female, [urban], and youthful condition. (Wagstaff &
Gallagher, 1990, p. 104)
30% of children in metropolitan areas live in poverty; that will increase
by a third by the year 2000. Twice as high a percentage of children
aged 0–6 live in poverty as do adults aged 18–64. (Clark, 1990, p. 1)
In 1980, 2.5 million people (labeled the underclass) or 3.1 percent of all
households lived in 880 urban census-tract neighborhoods where
more than half of the men had worked less than 26 weeks. (Wagstaff
& Gallagher, 1990, p. 105)
92 percent of the high school class of 1987 had begun drinking before
graduating; of those, 56 percent had begun drinking in the 6th to
9th grades. (Carnegie Council on Adolescent Development, 1989,
p. 22)
More than half of the high school class of 1985 had tried marijuana, one
in six had used cocaine, and one in eight had used hallucinogens like
LSD. (Wagstaff & Gallagher, 1990, p. 107)
About half of the teenagers in the United States are sexually active by the
time they leave school. . . . One out of four teenage [girls] has
experienced a pregnancy. (Wagstaff & Gallagher, 1990, p. 108)

A particularly troublesome aspect of this situation is the fact that these
are the students—low-income, minority, and disadvantaged youngsters—

with whom schools have historically been the least successful (Carnegie Council on Adolescent Development, 1989).

Forty-seven percent of Black and 56% of Hispanic adults are classified as functionally illiterate or marginal readers. (Astuto, 1990, p. 1)

The gap between White and minority achievement remains unbridged. . . . By third or fourth grade, minority and nonminority achievement levels begin to diverge. . . . By the middle school years, test scores show on average that minority children are a year or more behind. By the end of high school, a three-to-four year achievement gap between minority and nonminority youth has opened on tests such as the National Assessment of Educational Progress. (Quality Education for Minorities Project, 1990, pp. 17–18)

In 1989, . . . the combined SAT verbal and mathematics scores for White students was still 27 percent higher than combined scores of Black students, 22 percent higher than scores of Puerto Rican students, and 15 percent higher than scores of American Indian and Mexican American students. (Quality Education for Minorities Project, 1990, p. 19)

In 1988, . . . about 15 percent of Black youth aged 15–24 had not graduated and were out of school . . . for Hispanic youth, the similar rate was nearly 36 percent, about three times the rate for White youth. (Quality Education for Minorities Project, 1990, p. 18)

60% of prison inmates are dropouts. 58% of all dropouts are unemployed or receiving welfare. (Hutchins, 1988, p. 76)

The job rate for high school dropouts is dismal; of the 562,000 dropouts in 1985, 54 percent were unemployed and likely to remain so. (Wagstaff & Gallagher, 1990, p. 108)

The changing demographics of America, coupled with the economic imperative to educate all youngsters to high levels of achievement, are placing tremendous strains on the country's educational system. More and more of the types of students whom educators have failed to help in the past are entering our schools. Not only are educators being asked to educate them successfully, but the definition of success has been dramatically expanded, that is, higher levels of achievement are expected. Most critics see little hope that the ever-widening goals of education can be reached in the current system of schooling. Reformers are attempting to accommodate to these demographic shifts by developing a new model of the educational enterprise—"schools for the twenty-first century"—and new types of leaders to manage these institutions.

The Evolution Toward a Post-Industrial World

The information society of the twenty-first century promises to be as different from the industrial world as the industrial era was from the agrarian age. The industrial revolution brought fundamental changes to nearly every facet of society. At the heart of these changes was a new model for the organization of work—bureaucracy. Although this word has taken on pejorative connotations over the last half century, it represents a radically different and much improved method of harnessing effort and energy to meet the needs of an industrial age.

It is, however, becoming increasingly obvious that the bureaucratic model of organizing effort is ill-suited to the demands of a technoservice society (Maccoby, 1988). What appears to be emerging to replace it is a heterarchical model of organization that has been variously described "as a constellation, as a federation, as atomized, as dispersed, as a 'membership organization,' as a network organization or as a 'shamrock organization'" (Beare, 1989, p. 16). Whatever label one chooses, one fact remains clear: Methods of performing collective activities in post-industrial organizations look considerably different from those in bureaucratic ones. There is little use for the core correlates of bureaucracy: Hierarchy of authority is often viewed as detrimental; impersonality is found to be incompatible with cooperative work efforts; specialization and division of labor are no longer considered to be assets; scientific management based on controlling the efforts of subordinates is judged to be inappropriate; and the distinct separation of management and labor is seen as counterproductive. Also coming into focus is the understanding that schools are and will continue to be increasingly shaped by the need to organize collective efforts consistent with the evolution of organizational structures in the larger environment. Just as schools have mirrored the industrial age's bureaucratic model during the twentieth century, so must they adopt a more heterarchical model as society moves into the information age. Furthermore, just as new language is being developed to describe these inchoate organizations, so too will new metaphors evolve to describe the work of the men and women who lead them.

SCHOOLING FOR THE TWENTY-FIRST CENTURY

As noted above, schools have had a fairly isomorphic relationship with the larger environmental context within which the educational process unfolds. Petrie (1990) and Schlechty (1990) have captured this evolving relationship in metaphorical terms. Along with Sykes and Elmore (1989), they have also shown how the prevailing model of schooling colors the lenses we use to view the principalship. Schlechty notes, for example, that when public education was invented, the environment of schools was white, Anglo-Saxon, rural, and agrarian. The goals of education were "to promote republican/Protestant morality and civic literacy" (p. 5). He describes the schools of the agrarian era as "tribal centers," with the teacher as "priestess" and the principal as "high priest" (pp. 18–19).

Such educational systems, however, were not well-suited to the needs of an industrial age, and as the environment in which they operated began to change, so did the schools. Industrial society was no longer either rural and agrarian or solely Anglo-Saxon Protestant. The country was becoming increasingly urban and industrial; the population was becoming increasingly heterogeneous. The purpose of schooling was also changing. Schools became places where students were sorted and packaged to meet the needs of corporate America—sorted into groups of "hands" and "heads" (see Goodlad, 1984), the former requiring a low level of skills and a good deal of socialization, and the latter needing to be educated to a much more sophisticated level. The schools of the industrial age can be described as factories in which students are the products, teachers are the workers, and principals the managers, or foremen (Button, 1966; Callahan, 1962, Petrie, 1990; Schlechty, 1990).

Schools for post-industrial society are experiencing another major metamorphosis. In its efforts both to adapt to a new world order, new ways of organizing human energy, and a rapidly changing social context at home and to address the emerging new goal of schooling—high levels of educational skills for all students—the American educational system is undergoing a frustrating, sometimes painful, and sometimes exciting transformation. This evolution is being supported by a ringing attack on the current educational system, and it is being shaped by the enumeration of emerging principles that reveal how schooling can be organized to meet the needs of a post-industrial society.

The Attack on the Current System

As we noted in our discussion of the crisis in the economy, over the past dozen years the educational system has been subjected to a barrage of criticism from nearly every quarter of society. Schools have been found wanting on almost every conceivable indicator of success—academic achievement in basic subjects, functional literacy, preparation for employment, school attendance, knowledge of specialized subject areas (such as geography), and mastery of higher-order skills (see Murphy, 1990b, for a review). While causes for these failures have been traced to a variety of conditions in schools, for our purposes here the most powerful set of explanations focuses on the inadequacy of the bureaucratic organizational structure of schooling to meet the goals of education in a post-industrial world. The most penetrating attempts to transform education being with concerns about the prevailing model of governance, organization, program delivery, and management of schools. Below we outline the major points of these critiques, which we have compiled in detail elsewhere (Murphy, 1990e; Murphy, 1991a).

Attacks on the bureaucratic model of schooling take a number of forms. Many critics conclude that bureaucratic systems inhibit initiative, creativity, and professional judgment (Chubb & Moe, 1990; Conley, 1989)—all of which are key ingredients of heterarchical organizations. These reformers maintain that the existing organizational structure of schools is simply neither sufficiently flexible nor sufficiently robust to prepare students to function in a post-industrial society (Sizer, 1984). Along these lines, a number of scholars hold that bureaucracies are counterproductive to the goal of meeting the needs and interests of educators in schools—that they are "impractical and . . . [do] not fit the psychological and personal needs of the workforce" (Clark & Meloy, 1989, p. 293). This is a critical flaw if, as Beare (1989) argues, workers in tomorrow's schools must be viewed as stakeholders rather than as employees. Other analysts have unearthed incompatibilities between the functioning of schools as bureaucracies and the goals of education for the twenty-first century. They maintain that "bureaucratic management practices have been causing unacceptable distortions in educational process" (Wise, 1989, p. 301) and that such practices are "paralyzing American education . . . [and] getting in the way of children's learning" (Sizer, 1984, p. 206; see also Cuban, 1989; Frymier, 1987; Wise, 1978). Most of these scholars perceive bureaucracy as a method of organization that inherently shifts attention away from the central activities of schooling—teaching and learning (McNeil, 1988a, 1988b, 1988c; Seeley, 1980; Wise, 1978). At a deeper level, a few critics suggest that bureaucratic management is inconsistent with the sacred values and purposes of education, and they question "fundamental ideological issues pertaining to bureaucracy's meaning in a democratic society" (Angus, 1988; Campbell et al., 1987, p. 73; Giroux, 1988). Finally, some scholars argue that bureaucracy, by its very nature, impedes the development of the types of connections between schools and their larger environments required if schools are to survive and flourish in a world that will be less well-defined, more fluid, and more market-driven than has been the case in the past (Chubb & Moe, 1990).

The Picture of the Future

Pictures of schools in the twenty-first century as well as of the principals who will lead them are already being sketched in the 1990s.[1] While it is impossible to predict the nature of the finished product, the outlines of schooling for the information age are becoming increasingly clear.

At the center of these emerging schools are new forms of school organization and management. A new "social physics" (Bell, cited in Campbell et al., 1987, p. 26) that promises to produce significant change in the nature of social relationships in schools is emerging. The hierarchical, bureaucratic organizational structures that have defined schools for the past 80 years are giving way to more decentralized (Guthrie, 1986; Murphy & Hart, 1988) and more professionally controlled systems (David, 1989; Houston, 1989)—systems that "can be thought of as a new paradigm for school management" (Wise, 1989, p. 303). In these new post-industrial school organizations, there are "very basic changes in roles, relationships, and responsibilities" (Seeley, 1988, p. 35): Traditional patterns of relationships are altered (Conley, 1989; Rallis, 1990); authority flows are less hierarchical (Calrk & Meloy, 1989); role definitions are both more general and more flexible (Corcoran, 1989); leadership is connected to competence for needed tasks rather than to formal position (American Association of Colleges for Teacher Education, 1988; Angus, 1988); and independence and isolation are replaced by cooperative work (Beare, 1989). Furthermore, the structural orientation of industrial age schools (see Callahan, 1962; Campbell et al., 1987; Tyack, 1974; and Tyack & Hansot, 1982, for reviews) is being overshadowed by a focus on the human element. The operant goal is no longer maintenance of the organizational infrastructure but rather the holistic development of persons (Mojkowski & Fleming, 1988; Schlechty, 1990; Sergiovanni, 1989). There is a good deal of emphasis on the importance of the school as a community (Barth, 1990). Developing learning climates and organizational adaptivity are replacing the more traditional emphasis on uncovering and applying the one best model of performance (Clark & Meloy, 1989; McCarthey & Peterson, 1989). The changed metaphors being applied to these restructured schools—for example, from schools as institutions to schools as communities, from principals as managers to principals as facilitators, from teachers as workers to teachers as leaders—nicely portray these fundamental revisions in our understanding of social relationships and in our views of organizations and our concep-

---

1. The material in this section is taken from J. Murphy, *Restructuring Schools: Capturing and Assessing the Phenomena* (New York: Teachers College Press, 1991).

tions of management. They reveal a reorientation in transformed schools from control to empowerment.

Some very early initiatives are underway that suggest that we may be on the threshold of major changes in the entire teaching/learning process in schools. A more robust understanding of the educational production function has begun to be translated into "dramatically different way[s] of thinking about the design, delivery, and documentation of instructional programs" (Spady, 1988, p. 8). The traditionally strongest theoretical or disciplinary influence on education—psychology—is being pushed off center stage by newer sociological perspectives. Underlying these changes are radically different ways of thinking about the "educability of humanity" (Purpel, 1989, p. 10). Schools that in the industrial era were organized to produce results consistent with the normal curve, to sort youngsters into the various strata needed to fuel the economy, are being redesigned to ensure equal opportunity and success for all learners (see Miller & Brookover, 1986).

At the center of these changes in social ecology is a not-so-subtle shift in assumptions about knowledge. As Fisher (1990) reports, the alpha paradigm of knowledge, the view that "knowledge can be assumed to be an external entity existing independently of human thought and action, and hence, something about which one can be objective . . . [which has been] dominant for so long in classroom practice, has begun to be critically examined in a new way" (pp. 82–84). A new view, one that holds knowledge to be internal and subjective, to "depend . . . on the values of the persons working with it and the context within which that work is conducted" (p. 82), is receiving serious consideration. As knowledge is becoming personal and contextualized, learning is becoming more and more a social phenomenon. New views about what is worth learning are emerging. The traditional emphasis on content coverage and rote learning of basic skills is being challenged by more in-depth treatment of topics and a focus on higher-order thinking skills (Carnegie Council on Adolescent Development, 1989). Attention is being turned to active learning, and a century-old concern for independent work and competition—a focus on the individual dimension of human existence—is slowly receding in favor of more cooperative learning relationships and a focus on the social dimensions of human existence (David, 1989). This change at the classroom level parallels the growth of community at the school level. Equally important, a long-standing concern with the technical dimensions of teaching and learning is giving way to a renewed emphasis on the need to personalize schooling. Or, as Dokecki (1990) has stated, the "centrality of caring has been recognized recently by a number of professional fields" and caring is beginning to be seen as the "regulative ideal" (p. 163) of intervention in these professions.

(See Beck, 1991, for a discussion of this phenomenon in educational leadership and Noddings, 1988, for an analysis of the ethics of caring for instructional arrangements.)

"An elevated conceptualization of teaching" (Rallis, 1990, p. 193) consistent with the epistemological change noted above is found in post-industrial schools. The importance of craft knowledge is explicitly recognized for the first time since the onslaught of scientific management (see Blumberg, 1984, for a discussion of craft knowledge in the area of school management). Rather than seeking ways to simplify instruction, education professionals are acknowledging and nurturing the complexity of teaching (Petrie, 1990). Teachers are being allotted considerable discretion over pedagogy. The teacher-centered model that is at the heart of the factory model of classroom instruction is giving way to growing demands for a learner-centered pedagogy. The model of the teacher as a "sage on a stage" (Fisher, 1990, p. 83), in which instructors are viewed as content specialists who possess relevant knowledge that they transmit to students through telling, is being replaced by an approach in which "teaching is more like coaching, where the student [as opposed to the teacher] is the primary performer" (Fisher, 1990, p. 83; see also Goodlad, 1984; Sizer, 1984). In this revised approach, teachers act as facilitators (McCarthey & Peterson, 1989), modelers (Spady, 1988), and coaches (Sizer, 1984) who invest "students with increased power and responsibility for their own learning" (Elmore, 1988, p. 3). In restructured schools students are seen as "producers of knowledge" and teachers "as managers of learning experiences" (Hawley, 1989, p. 32). The focus is on learning rather than on the delivery system (Seeley, 1980).

In this post-industrial era, education seems poised on the brink of a basic change in our view of the relationship between the school and its environment. Historically ingrained notions of schools as sheltered monopolies, or delivery systems, are breaking down under the incursions of a market philosophy into education (see Boyd, 1990; Boyd & Hartman, 1988; Chubb & Moe, 1990). The traditional dominant relationship between schools (and professional educators) and the public is being reworked in favor of more equal arrangements, that is, partnerships (Seeley, 1980, 1988). For the first time in our history, the business of schooling is being redefined in relation to those being served. Efforts to bring schools into the twenty-first century are resulting in unprecedented inroads of market forces into the governance and organization of schools (see Chubb & Moe, 1990). They are also fostering "significant changes in the way that states related to schools" (Elmore, 1988, p. 2; see also David, Cohen, Honetschlager, & Traimon, 1990; Le Tendre, 1990; Murphy, 1990c).

METAPHORS OF THE PRINCIPALSHIP IN THE 1990s

The new manager . . . will not be a classical, hierarchically oriented bureaucratic but a customized version of Indiana Jones: proactive; entrepreneurial;
communicating in various languages; able to inspire, motivate and persuade
subordinates, superiors, colleagues and outside constituents. (Gerding &
Serenhuijseur, cited in Beare, 1989, p. 19)

Up to this point, we have been considering the context that will
influence dimensions of the principalship in the 1990s and beyond. We have
examined the larger environmental forces that are shaping education as well
as the type of school that is appearing on the horizon. Throughout this
discussion, schooling has been in the foreground, with the principalship in
the background. In the next section, we re-position these elements by
analyzing the most important metaphors emerging to describe the principalship.

Principal as Leader

If there is an all-encompassing challenge for principals in the 1990s, it is
to lead the transition from the bureaucratic model of schooling, with its
emphasis on minimal levels of education for many, to a post-industrial
model, with the goal of educating all youngsters well—while at the same
time completely changing the way principals themselves operate. The first
challenge, then, is to reorient the principalship from management to leadership, and to do so in ways consistent with the principles of post-industrial
organizations. Given the penchant for society in general, and members of
organizations in particular, to look to leadership in periods of crisis (Meindl,
Ehrlich, & Dukerich, 1985), it should come as little surprise that, during
this era of unrest in education, the dominant administration-related message
of the reform reports of the 1980s is for principals to don the mantle of
leadership (Murphy, 1990a). Discounting the rhetoric and the calls for
saviors, these reports confirm a rather deep leadership void in America's
schools. The principalship has evolved to meet the clerical needs of schools,
and nearly all the pressures exerted on the role over the last 150 years have
reinforced the administrative nature of the position (March, 1978; Murphy,
1990d). Bureaucratic schools require managers and shape the activities of
the men and (to a lesser extent) women who occupy the principalship
accordingly. Competent management, however, is likely to prove insuffi-
cient to meet the challenges of leading schools into a new age. Schools need
leadership, and the principalship of the 1990s must change to meet that
need.

Principal as Servant

The challenge for principals is quite complex. Not only must they accept the mantle of leadership, changing from implementors to initiators, from a focus on process to a concern for outcomes, from risk avoiders and conflict managers to risk takers, but they must also adopt leadership strategies and styles that are in harmony with the central tenets of the heterarchical school organizations they seek to create. They must learn to lead not from the apex of the organizational pyramid but from the nexus of a web of interpersonal relationships (Chapman & Boyd, 1986). Their base of influence must be professional expertise and moral imperative rather than line authority. They must learn to lead by empowering rather than controlling others, or as Bolin (1989) puts it, leadership in the 1990s becomes "a support function for teaching rather than a mechanism for the control of teaching" (p. 8). Servant leadership will differ from more traditional styles in a number of other, more subtle, ways as well. Enabling leadership has a softer, more feminine hue to it. It is more ethereal and less direct. There is as much heart as head in this style of leading (see Lightfoot, 1983).

Principal as Organizational Architect

The metaphor of the principal as architect is designed to capture activities of principals as they address the environmental challenges confronting schools—as they both shape the evolution of post-industrial organizational forms (principal as organizational architect) and overhaul the educational system to meet the demands resulting from the changing social structure (principal as social architect). The notion of adaptive school organizations, however, is something of an oxymoron. As almost every scholar who has studied the institution of the school has concluded, schools are remarkably stable entities (see J. F. Murphy, 1989) with well-developed mechanisms to buffer their basic operations from pressures from the larger environment (see Meyer & Rowan, 1975). This ability to deflect demands for change is particularly useful for public organizations where such requests have a good deal of legitimacy regardless of their value. However, in a period of great turmoil, when the entire environment in which schools operate is being transformed, buffering strategies are likely to prove counterproductive. This appears to be the case currently. In their roles as organizational architects, principals of the 1990s will need to acknowledge the changing context in which schools must function. They will need to give voice to this new order and, to borrow a phrase from William Foster (1989), become proponents of change. They will need to learn and help others to learn about the principles of post-industrial organizations. And they will need to assist teachers, students, parents, and others as they begin to reconstruct their own schools consistent with these principles.

Principal as Social Architect

The changing social fabric discussed earlier threatens to overwhelm American society. If our response is feeble, the result is likely to be the emergence of a dual-class society not unlike that found in many third-world countries. As with many other social issues, schools will have a good deal to say about the adequacy of the nation's response. And principals, in turn, will have a large role in determining whether the efforts of our schools are successful or not. We have already noted that schools historically have not served at-risk students well. Part of this problem can be traced to the bureaucratic infrastructure of schooling, for example, the need to batch process youngsters by age cohorts (Cuban, 1989) and ability groups (Oakes, 1985). As they undertake their emerging role as organizational architects, principals will exercise considerable leverage over institutional arrangements, such as those just noted, that disproportionately disadvantage low-income students and pupils of color. Indeed, there is a good deal of effort afoot to help at-risk students by debureaucraticizing schools—as well as some encouraging signals of success in this arena (see Murphy, 1991a, for a review). Yet more is required. In their role as social architects, principals must "bridge the connection between the conditions of education and the total conditions of children" (Kirst, McLaughlin, & Massell, 1989, p. 28). They need to see education as one element of a larger attack on the problems facing at-risk children. They must also give voice to the moral imperative to address these historically nonschooling issues. To accomplish this, they will need to help design (and construct) an integrated social agency network to address the conditions confronting many of their pupils—and their families. The school may well find itself at the hub of this network. Thus principals of the 1990s will be busy not only developing integrated networks of services, but also redesigning the purposes and structures of their own institutions to better service our changing student population.

Principal as Educator

One of the interesting aspects of some of the metaphors of the principalship in the 1990s is that, in capturing the dimensions of principals' work in a new era, they hark back to a lost age and to aspects of the principalship that have atrophied over time. This is most clearly the case for the next two metaphors we describe—principal as educator and principal as moral agent.

The period of time from 1820 to 1900 has been described as an evangelical and ideological one for administrators (Glass, 1986a; Kerchner, 1988)—an era of aristocracy of character (Tyack & Hansot, 1982). The men and women who managed schools during that era have been described as teachers of teachers (Button, 1966), applied philosophers (Button, 1966), and philosopher-educators (Callahan & Button, 1964). With the growth of the business aspects of the role during the era of scientific management, the educational dimensions of the principalship lost a good deal of their luster. Principals became businesspersons rather than teachers, resulting in a net gain in status (Button, 1966) that was to make it difficult for principals to re-embrace the educational dimensions of their job. This trend toward the noneducational aspects of the administrator's role was reinforced by the rise of administrative science during the 1950s, 1960s, and 1970s (Bates, 1984; Foster, 1988, 1989; Greenfield, 1988).

There is clear evidence today that the pendulum is swinging back. Beginning with questions about and then attacks on the theory movement (see, for example, Greenfield, 1975, 1988; Harlow, 1962), and gaining momentum with the instructional leadership movement of the 1980s, practitioners and professors alike have begun to lament the lack of attention paid to educational topics in preparation and professional development programs and the inability of many principals to deal with substantive educational issues (Murphy, 1990d, 1990e; Murphy, Hallinger, Lotto, & Miller, 1987). There is a growing awareness that, in order to be educators, principals need to be well-educated themselves. The conclusion is also being formed that "educational administration must find its mission and its purpose in the purpose of schooling generally" (Foster, 1988, p. 69) and that to do this principals in the 1990s will need to be much more deeply involved with the core technology of schools than they have been in the past. Finally, in a rather dramatic shift from the role of principal as head teacher in the nineteenth century, school heads in the 1990s are being asked to demonstrate educational leadership by becoming the head learner in the organization (Barth, 1990).

Principal as Moral Agent

The behavioral science/theory movement in educational administration (see Culbertson, 1988, and Griffiths, 1988, for reviews) did for the value dimensions of the principalship what scientific management did for its educational aspects—pushed them far into the background (Greenfield, 1975, 1988). Professors of administration were at work during the 1950s and 1960s creating an "administrative science" (Culbertson, 1988, p. 15) that practitioners were to apply to solve the problems confronting their schools. Value issues were considered to be beyond the scope of this activity. In the words of Gross (cited in Culbertson, 1988), "theory must be concerned with how . . . [one] *does* behave, not with someone's opinion of how he *ought* to behave" (p. 16, emphasis in original). As Harlow (1962) notes, the entire topic of value judgments was frequently employed "as an epithet indicating intellectual contempt" (p. 66).

In the 1990s, however, a major initiative appears to be forming to address the issue of values in education and to recognize the moral dimensions of schooling in general and of the principalship in particular. In the words of T. B. Greenfield (1988), "We must understand that the new science of administration will be a science with values and of values" (p. 155). At the core of these efforts is a growing acknowledgment of what Harlow (1962) calls the central activity of administration—"purpose-defining" (p. 61)—and of the fact that "values and value judgments are the central elements in the selection, extension, and day-to-day realization of educational purpose" (p. 67). Closely aligned with this perspective is, at the basic level, a growing acceptance of the fact that the activities of principals are intertwined with critical ethical issues in schools. At a deeper level, largely due to the efforts critical theorists, feminists, Marxists, and scholars treading other less familiar territories, there are serious efforts developing to transform the principalship into an instrument of social justice.

Principal as Person in the Community

Implicit in new conceptions of leadership is the idea that every person involved in the schooling process deserves to be treated with dignity and respect. Furthermore, each individual, regardless of her or his role or function, should be afforded conditions and opportunities that allow for and encourage academic, professional, and personal growth. Leadership in the 1990s must continually bear in mind the reality that, regardless of differences in role, status, or achievements, all involved in schooling are equal in their personhood. The principal of the next decade must remember that she or he is a person whose work as an educational leader is first, foremost, and always with persons—persons who are physical, intellectual, spiritual, emotional, and social beings (Buber, 1958, 1965; Kirkpatrick, 1986; Macmurray, 1957).

If the principal is, indeed, a person among persons, the school or school system would logically and necessarily need to be viewed as a community characterized by interdependent relationships (Barth, 1990; Bryk, 1988; Buber, 1958, 1965; Dewey, 1915; Griffin & Nash, 1988; Hobbs, Dokecki, Hoover-Dempsey, Moroney, Shayne, & Weeks, 1984; Sizer, 1973). As a person in a community, the principal of the 1990s and beyond will be concerned with several things. Recognizing that communities and their occupants flourish in caring, nurturing environments, these principals will seek to utilize a caring ethic to guide their decisions and actions (Beck, 1991; Brabeck, 1989; Coegan & Raebeck, 1989; Noddings, 1984, 1988). They will strive to create schools that are, as Sizer describes in the title of his 1973 book, *Places for Learning, Places for Joy*. Principals who operate within this metaphor will strive to treat others as persons, or in Buber's words, as a "thou" (1958, p. 62) rather than as an object or "it" (p. 62). They will work to liberate teachers to engage with students and with material in exciting, innovative ways (Giroux, 1988). Indeed, they will celebrate the knowledge that they are persons who share vital, creative, caring relationships with others (Bellah, Madsen, Sullivan, Swidler, & Tipton, 1985). They will view teachers, students, parents, and others as colleagues, partners, co-learners, and friends. And they will relish the challenge of working with these groups to "[build] a community of learners" (Barth, 1990, p. 37) in which all persons can flourish.

CHAPTER NINE

Patterns in the Metaphorical Prism

Examining themes implicit in metaphors used historically to discuss the principalship has proven to be a useful method in our quest for a deeper understanding of this important role. In this chapter, we offer conclusions that, for us, represent important outcomes of this research and suggest implications for administrative scholarship, preparation, and practice. Morgan's words guide us as we shift from a decade-by-decade examination to consider the general outcomes of our study. In the concluding chapter of *Images of Organization* (1986), he notes that a thorough study of metaphors enables and requires a person to engage in a two-phased activity involving "the processes of *diagnostic reading* and *critical evaluation*" (p. 331; emphasis in original). Preparing earlier chapters, we engaged primarily in the first of these activities. Now, we turn our attention more to an evaluation of our findings as we discuss four insights on the principalship we have gained from this study.

METAPHORICAL DIVERSITY AND THE MALLEABILITY OF THE PRINCIPALSHIP

As we examine the metaphorical language through the decades, we are struck by the diversity of the images. Even a cursory glance through the preceding pages reveals comparisons between principals and

Spiritual leaders (e.g., Cubberley, 1923; Johnson, 1925; Johnston et al., 1922)

Business managers (e.g., Callahan, 1962; Strayer, 1930)

Soldiers (e.g., ASCD, 1945; Gregg, 1943; Van Til, 1946)

Social scientists (e.g., Griffiths, 1959; Hunt & Pierce, 1958; Hugget, 1950; Zirbes, 1952)

Bureaucrats (e.g., Abbott, 1969; Jones et al., 1969; Sergiovanni, 1969)

Public relations experts (e.g., Burden & Whitt, 1973; Sergiovanni &
    Carver, 1973)
Instructional leaders (e.g., Clark & Lotto, 1982; Greenfield, 1987)

Certain metaphors dominate the literature from particular eras. In the
twenties, for instance, spiritual imagery abounds. In the thirties, we find
metaphors from business management; military language is most often
found in the years before and during World War II. In a similar manner,
principals are expected to be social science experts in the 1950s; bureaucrats
during the next decade; community leaders in the seventies; and instructional leaders in the 1980s.

Examining these metaphorical emphases in the light of major social,
cultural, and political events, we are led to propose that the role of the
principal is an extremely malleable one, shaped by a diverse set of concerns
and events. In the 1930s, for example, when recovering from the depression
was a central issue in this country, principals were charged with the shrewd
and economic management of schools. During the forties, when winning
the war and establishing a democratic world order were chief national
concerns, principals were expected to lead in the "attack on wartime problems" (ASCD, 1945, p. 152). In a similar manner, the Cold War and the
alarm following Sputnik, the widespread unrest in this country in the 1960s
and 1970s, and the alarm in the last decade over America's declining
economic supremacy have all dramatically influenced expectations for
school leaders.

Worthy of note is the fact that the majority of events that have influenced educational metaphors are fundamentally noneducational in nature
and national or international in scope. This introduces new meaning to the
concept of education as an open system. It seems as if education's purposes
and the roles of those charged with carrying out those purposes are, to a
very great extent, determined by economic and political occurrences and
not, first and foremost, by concerns originating in schools. While this
reality, in and of itself, is not especially alarming, what is of some concern is
the fact that educational scholars and practitioners have apparently accepted—without much question or analysis—definitions of good schools
and good school leadership imposed on them.

Recently, some voices have begun to challenge educators to reclaim the
right and privilege to define their goals and roles (see, for example, Barth,
1990; Beck, 1992; Sergiovanni, 1992; Torbert, 1990). Our work supports
this recommendation. The principalship has been especially malleable,
being shaped by many forces. In all likelihood, it will need to remain so as
its inhabitants seek to lead diverse sets of students and teachers in quickly
changing circumstances. We assert, however, that educational leaders must

assume greater responsibility in determining how they and their schools will, in fact, respond to the demands of the future. Committed to serving the needs of students, teachers, and the larger community, they must assertively shape their profession in order to best honor that commitment. Those who fail to do this leave themselves open to the possibility of passively being shaped by a diverse set of forces, oriented to ends far removed from education.

METAPHORICAL INCONSISTENCIES AND THE MICRO-MANAGEMENT ORIENTATION OF THE PRINCIPALSHIP

Our study of metaphors has not been without its surprises. At times, we are struck by inconsistencies between the espoused images of school leadership and descriptions of principals' actual day-to-day activities. At other times, our knowledge of educational history has led us to expect certain metaphorical emphases—emphases that we do not find. Contemplating these surprises and contradictions, we realize that they occur most often when principals face major professional challenges. Especially in literature from these periods of crises, metaphors reveal a penchant for micro-management on the part of school leaders.

Through the years, many metaphors for the principalship have been rather grand in scope. School leaders are pictured as pivotal figures in local communities and in the country as a whole. On their shoulders rests responsibility not only for ensuring that young people receive excellent educations, but also for protecting and promoting global democracy and for stabilizing this country's economy (see, for example, ASCD, 1945; Burden & Whitt, 1974; Cubberley, 1923; Hitt, 1973; Murphy 1990a). Interestingly, other metaphors—often occurring concurrently with these grand ones—emphasize principals' concerns with minute details of school management. In the 1940s, for example, school leaders were expected "to help young people understand and practice the democratic way of life in a technological age" (Van Til, 1946, p. 2) and to orient their work toward "lifting the quality of living for all kinds of people" (ASCD, 1947, p. 9). The tone of these goals is not matched by language describing principals' tasks—which included formulating detailed plans for air raid drills (Limpus, 1943; Millard, 1944), teaching students how to plant victory gardens (ASCD, 1944), and the like. This type of discrepancy becomes even more pronounced in the 1950s. In this decade, as academicians began constructing a science of educational administration (Murphy, 1992), principals were charged with knowing the latest in theoretical and empirical scholarship and

applying these insights in their schools. At the same time, they were described as managers of filmstrips (Graves, 1956), providers of refreshments
at faculty meetings (Jameson, 1957), and directors of end-of-the-year parties for departing sixth-grade classes (Kyte, 1952).

After analyzing the coexistence of lofty, frequently abstract metaphors
with detailed, specific, even trivial ones, we offer a possible explanation for
this odd juxtaposition, one that, we believe, has implications for understanding the principalship. We wonder if the large number of metaphors
depicting the principal as an overseer of minute details—even in works that
emphasize the broader dimensions of the role—reveal a certain preference
on the part of school leaders and of those seeking to advise them for
situations with clear-cut courses of action and observable, controllable
outcomes. Principals driven by the charge to improve the quality of life for
all people might conceivably have difficulty knowing how to prioritize time
and activities, and they would be likely to experience frustration at not
knowing if and when goals had been accomplished because these goals were
framed in such abstract language. Similarly, authors of texts and articles
seeking to influence practice could find themselves floundering in a metaphorical sea of abstractions. Perhaps practicing principals and academicians,
when confronted with unclear goals and seemingly insoluble problems, turn
their attention to that which can be controlled, even if this takes them into
the realm of the trivial or unimportant.

This explanation gains credibility when we view micro-management
metaphors appearing at the time of some key historical occurrences. In the
1950s and 1960s, the work of educators was shaped by some monumental
events. The *Brown* decision, Sputnik, the increase in administrative research,
the Coleman report, the Civil Rights movement, the Vietnam War, and a
host of other incidents dramatically increased the complexity of educational
leadership. During these years, the metaphors emphasized the bureaucratic
nature of the principalship and virtually ignored the fact that leaders were
facing complex situations and, in all likelihood, intractable problems.

This hypothesis, if correct, has implications for the preparation of
educational administrators. Principals must lead in complicated environments and complex situations in which actions have far-reaching, long-term
political, social, cultural, and moral implications. At the same time, they
must attend to small, day-to-day details of school operations. An adequate
preparation program must address both realities. The large number of
micro-management metaphors suggests that principals are being asked to
focus on routine problems and concerns but that they are not generally
encouraged to consider the pedagogical, philosophical, cultural, and ethical
ramifications of their work (Murphy, 1992). Persons and programs con-

cerned with equipping principals must discover and implement strategies that enable school leaders to function comfortably and effectively in both worlds.

THE TIMING OF METAPHORS AND THE DEVELOPMENT OF THE PRINCIPALSHIP

As we examine the unfolding of various metaphorical emphases over time and compare these with trends in administrative scholarship, we gain yet another clue into the interplay among theories, language, and the role of the principal. Metaphorical language, it seems, has served as a vehicle for introducing concepts—usually emanating from academic circles—into the parlance of practice. In decade after decade, scholars have clothed their newly developed ideas about leadership in metaphors from earlier eras.

This pattern is discernible in the writings we studied across the decades. The twenties, for example, was a period in which religious metaphors predominated. As the writings of Cubberley (1923) and Johnston and his colleagues (1922) demonstrate, even the belief that principals should lead according to tenets of scientific management was discussed with spiritual imagery. The former writes eloquently of the need for principals to use rational, scientific strategies in order to "mould [the] life and shape [the] ideals" (p. 36) of the school and community. The latter argue that principals must be aware of the "spiritual and technical sides" (p. 18) of leadership. Others (e.g., Eaton, 1986; Tyack & Hansot, 1982), reflecting on this period, also discern that ideas about technical management competencies are often couched in religious terms.

Authors writing of principals as managers evidently introduced their concepts in terms readers could accept, for in the 1930s, the belief that principals should be effective and efficient administrators became well established. By the middle years of this decade, business metaphors replaced religious ones in the educational vernacular. Principals were expected to develop a "clear line and staff organization" (Strayer, 1930, p. 376) in order to regulate and manage schools according to rationally developed principles of efficient administration.

Military metaphors provided a linguistic vehicle for linking the 1930s and 1940s. The belief that leadership involves assuming a hierarchical position with attendant authorities and responsibilities, an assumption ingrained in the scientific management literature of the thirties, continued to find expression in many images of the forties. When the principal was compared to a soldier assuming "patriotic responsibility" (Gregg, 1943, p. 7), the forties' concern with democratic leadership was linked with the thirties' faith in the importance of operating within established hierarchical systems. Consciously or not, authors seem to introduce newer assumptions by using images consistent with accepted beliefs.

This pattern appeared again around mid-century. During the fifties and sixties, the academically based, administrative theory movement fostered the belief that principals should utilize "research and scientific evaluation" (Hunt & Pierce, 1958, p. *v*) to assist them in developing administrative skills and competencies. Many authors, explicitly accepting this assumption, go on to stress ways in which social science knowledge can help to improve principals' human relations skills. This is evident in discussions of ways research might enable leaders to use time more efficiently. In passages dealing with this topic (e.g., Department of Elementary School Principals, 1958; Yeager, 1954), authors frequently note that principals who study how to effectively manage their schedules will find they have more time to devote to the needs of teachers, staff, and students.

More recently, a similar phenomenon occurred as authors garnered earlier images to express what they considered to be current conceptions of school leadership. In the sixties, when principals were viewed as bureaucrats—executives in educational systems—metaphors from the laboratory and the factory were common. These linked emphases of earlier decades with newer assumptions. Implicit comparisons between a soundly built machine or well-designed process reinforced the belief that a rationally designed school system with persons in specific places assuming assigned responsibilities would virtually guarantee the accomplishment of goals. Still more recently, we saw authors of the eighties writing of the need to reform educational administration, taking numerous metaphors from earlier years and actually "re-forming" them to meet pressing needs and challenges.

The possibility that metaphorical language serves as a vehicle for introducing new role expectations into the vernacular of the administrative profession suggests that language may both reflect *and* shape our understanding. This idea has important implications for those hoping to influence thinking on school leadership. It suggests that wise scholars will attend to the metaphors they use. It also suggests that they will utilize images that evoke accepted concepts as they write of desirable developments in the evolution of the principal's role.

THE PATTERNS OF METAPHORS AND THE DIALECTICAL NATURE OF THE PRINCIPALSHIP

As we move through the analytical process, examining metaphors through the decades, we are struck, not infrequently, by a sense of *deja vu*.

Themes and concepts re-emerge through the years with slight twists and variations. As we think of these recurring ideas, we are struck by the presence of a dialectical pattern, apparently governing the generation of dominant metaphors and the ongoing evolution of the principal's role. We conclude our discussion of insights gained from this study by examining this dialectic on the principalship.

One of the exercises we engaged in as we analyzed our findings was the search for an all-encompassing metaphorical phrase to capture the emphasis of each decade. After some thought and discussion, we settled on the following list:

The 1920s   Values Broker
The 1930s   Scientific Manager
The 1940s   Democratic Leader
The 1950s   Theory-Guided Administrator
The 1960s   Bureaucratic Executive
The 1970s   Humanistic Facilitator
The 1980s   Instructional Leader

As the years unfold, we see, in essence, a shift between metaphors that emphasize the values base of educational leadership and those that stress the importance of technical expertise—in the areas of both corporate management and human relations. New images seem to emerge, in part, as syntheses resulting from tension between earlier conceptions of leadership.

In the twenties, a central assumption is that the principal is one who accepts and promotes certain values. We can, therefore, learn much about the role conceptions of this decade by examining the metaphors used to describe these values. Expressions offered by Johnston and coauthors (1922), Cubberley (1923), Johnson (1925), and others suggest that these ideals are viewed as absolute and certain. Johnston and his coauthors write of the importance of "love of *truth*, love of *right*, and appreciation of *the* beautiful" (p. 27; emphasis added). Additionally, they admonish principals to seek to promote these ends so that they become "eternal" (p. 27) realities in the lives of students. Tyack and Hansot (1982), commenting on the suppositions of this period, note that the driving values are also religious in that they are linked to generally accepted tenets of American Protestantism.

Absent from the writings of the twenties are lengthy, highly technical discussions of principals' work and of specific management skills. Even when lauding scientific management, authors in the twenties tend to use spiritual, religious metaphors (for a discussion, see Eaton, 1986; Tyack & Hansot, 1982). School leadership is portrayed as a lofty, important mission. In contrast, in the writings of the thirties "almost the entire emphasis is on the 'how' of administration. There is virtually no discussion of the 'why,' [with] little critical examination of education and social implications of . . . structure and procedures" (Newlon, 1934, p. 90). Language is, in large measure, technical—oriented to practical details of managing schools. Indeed, principals are expected to be professionally trained "school executives" (Strayer, 1930, p. 376) who are experts in finance, business administration, organization and administration of the curriculum, and management of school records and reports (Murphy, 1931; Newlon, 1934). Their tasks are described as quite practical in nature and include purchasing toilet tissue, paper clips, and theme paper, and devising methods for checking mail, typing correspondence, and operating mimeograph machines (Ayer, 1929; Cooper, 1933; Payne, 1931).

We suggest that conceptions of the twenties and thirties, with their respective emphases on agreed upon values and technical management details, are in effect antithetical. The vision of school leadership that emerges in the forties is, in a sense, the synthesis emerging from a dialectic between earlier understandings. In this decade, a concern with values is again evident. However, the preferred values are those related to democracy, equality, patriotism, and a concern for human relations (e.g., ASCD, 1944; Gregg, 1943; Miller, 1942; Van Til, 1946). Each of these is grounded less in an absolute sense of truth, rightness, or righteousness, and more in developed concepts of ways persons can best live together. These values, thus, are presented as having major practical benefits. Part of the synthesis we see in this era relates to the metaphorical blending of the values orientation of the twenties with the practical perspective of the thirties. We see this blending not only in analyses of the beliefs influencing principals, but also in discussions of their leadership strategies. Writers in the forties stress ways principals can and should lead their schools democratically. Many of these discussions are detailed and practical (like those from the previous decade), but they are also shaped by guiding values (in a manner reminiscent of the twenties).

In keeping with this unfolding dialectic, we suggest that ideas emanating both from academic circles and from practitioner arenas in the fifties and sixties emerge as a type of antithesis to conceptions of the principalship evident in the forties. The theory movement's emphasis on developing and empirically testing theories and hypotheses is largely a reaction to untested assumptions and anecdotal prescriptions and the heavy values orientation so evident in earlier discussions of the principalship (Murphy, 1992). Publications by the Department of Elementary School Principals (1958) and by the National Education Association (1958) and the works of Boyan (1969), Griffiths (1959), Hone (1953), Hugget (1950), Hunt and Pierce (1958), Jones and colleagues (1969), and others emphasize that principals should draw on "knowledge of [their] chosen field . . . [and] many other disciplines" (Department of Elementary School Principals, 1958, p. 5) to guide them in making sound administrative decisions. These authors also underscore the belief that legitimate knowledge is that which can be reached through logical, positivistic methods of inquiry.

The picture of leadership presented in the practitioner-oriented literature is also antithetical to the image of the principalship of the forties. In the earlier decade, practical discussions emphasized ways school leaders could establish democratic relations with others—teachers, students, parents, community members, and citizens of the nation and world. Furthermore, the goal of these interactions was to "sustain and extend [social] gains . . . compatible with the freedoms for which . . . [the country was] fighting" (ASCD, 1945, p. 154). In the fifties and sixties, principals are encouraged not to share their authority, but rather to exercise it—working through established hierarchical structures. The contrasting uses of military imagery in these two periods are quite revealing of this difference. Especially in the forties, principals were linked to soldiers heroically and sacrificially fighting for democracy. In the sixties, Jones and colleagues (1969) compare school officers to "military leaders in [the act of] making decisions, . . . taking action, [and using] the fundamentals . . . for the proper exercise of command" (p. 125). The frequent mention of the principal's role within the school bureaucracy (e.g., Abbott, 1969; Boyan, 1969; Douglass, 1963; Noar, 1961) also contrasts with the democratic facilitator role of the principal in the 1940s.

Again, we suggest that expectations for principals in the 1970s—as revealed in authors' preferred metaphors—reflect a synthesis and extension of the competing assumptions from preceding years. Now, educational leaders are portrayed as community leaders—women and men whose tasks include discovering and imparting meaning to educational efforts and encouraging positive interactions within and between the school and community. Several dimensions of this understanding and of the language in which it is embedded are reminiscent of the 1920s and 1940s. The assumption that principals can and should discover and communicate meaning to education (e.g., Berman, 1977; Hitt, 1973; Macdonald & Zaret, 1975) parallels a belief from the twenties. In the seventies, however, the foundations of meaning are different. In the early years, religious beliefs—faith in absolute conceptions of goodness, truth, and beauty—grounded understandings of the principalship. In the forties, typically American ideas—democracy and equality—provided the values foundation. In the seventies, humanism, with its emphasis on the total development of persons, has a similar influence on role conceptions of the principalship. In essence, succeeding emphases on the principal's values orientation shift from an assumption of absolute, objective, universal values to faith in relative, subjective, intensely personal ones.

The beliefs evident in the literature of the seventies also reflect the influence of the managerial and academic orientations of the thirties, fifties, and sixties. In the midst of rhetoric about humanistic schools and meaningfulness, authors also acknowledge that principals must accept the "responsibility to 'keep school' through the proper administration and management of people and things" (Roe & Drake, 1974, p. 10). Indeed, Lipham and Hoeh (1974) offer detailed lists of necessary managerial competencies, and Immegart (1971), Coleman and colleagues (1977), and Hanushek (1977) write of ways to evaluate principals' administrative competencies based on objective indicators of technical skills. The writers of the seventies also synthesize a values orientation with an academic one by frequently grounding their arguments for humanistic leadership in the theoretical framework of Abraham Maslow (1965, 1970).

The metaphors of the seventies do not focus on the principal's direct participation in instructional programs. Indeed, this emphasis has been absent from much of the literature of earlier decades. In the eighties, scholars respond to this void by writing—at length—on the expectation that principals will make teaching and learning top priorities (Hallinger & Murphy, 1985a, 1985b; Murphy, 1990d). In so doing, authors offer a mixed set of metaphors. On the one hand, they use "vision" and "visionary" images, stressing the importance of articulating "the mission of the school to all its constituents" (Bredeson, 1985, p. 43) and the importance of "moral imagination" (Greenfield, 1987, p. 61). Thus, they evoke the belief that principals' work entails recognizing and promoting nontechnical values and ethical ideals. On the other hand, scholars also portray the principal as a competent manager, one whose actions are grounded in theoretically sound organizational principles and aimed at accomplishing goals in an efficient manner. As in earlier decades, this role conception seems to emerge, in part, as a response to inadequacies of earlier understandings (Murphy, 1992). In the fifties and sixties, technique and theory dominate the metaphors. In the seventies, values and ideals assume a central place. Metaphors of the eighties indicate that educational scholars are beginning to combine and extend these emphases.

This dialectical pattern of development wherein concepts seem to reflect a synthesis and extension of images of preceding eras suggests that the principalship is a role influenced by its own history. Authors seem to choose metaphors that simultaneously emphasize strengths and respond to weaknesses of earlier views. In so doing, they hammer out expectations that are actually syntheses of already established competing views. If this assessment is correct, the principalship is a role that is influenced not only by contemporary forces within and, especially, outside education, but also by earlier conceptions of the role itself.

CONCLUDING THOUGHTS

The principalship is a complex role, one that has been shaped by numerous forces—educational and extra-educational events, language, and earlier role conceptions. Examining metaphors, from a historical perspective, has enabled us to delve into these various forces and to begin to piece together stories below the "official story" of the profession's development. This has been invaluable in our search for a more complete understanding of school site leaders. We can now situate specific research reports and case studies within a larger context. It is also possible for results from individual studies and our knowledge of the ongoing evolution of the role to mutually inform each other. Garnering insights from this and other studies, we are able to turn to questions of practice and to construct recommendations, plans, and policies that are grounded in a deeper, more robust understanding of the tasks and roles of principals.

Appendix: Procedures

DATA COLLECTION

We collected our data in a three-phased literature search and review. The first phase involved a chronological examination of books and unpublished theses and dissertations on the principalship. We read these, beginning with some of the earliest, and noted the metaphorical language used by the authors. The decade of the 1920s became, by default, the starting point for our analysis because we found little of use in books published prior to that period. Glass's (1986a) reminder that "the 1920s saw the emergence of the first real body of textbook literature written specifically for school administrators" (p. *v*) supported our decision. As we continued through the decades, because of the sheer volume of publications, we found it necessary to become more selective in choosing manuscripts for review. Generally, we focused our attention on books cited most frequently in articles and other works on the principalship (e.g., Wolcott's *The Man in the Principal's Office*, 1973; Lipham, Rankin, & Hoeh's *The Principalship: Concepts, Competencies, and Cases*, 1985; Drake & Roe's *The Principalship*, 1986).

In the second phase of the data gathering effort, we systematically examined each edition of four periodicals: the two leading academic journals—*Educational Administration Quarterly* (1965–1989) and *Journal of Educational Administration* (1964–1989); and the two leading practitioner journals—*Bulletin of the National Association of Secondary School Principals* (1920–1989) and *Principal* (1920–1989). We chose these publications because they represent both theoretical and practical perspectives on the principalship. Again, metaphorical language by contributors was noted.

During preliminary analysis of the data, several themes and patterns seemed to be emerging. We held these themes in mind as we undertook the final phase of data collection, one in which we looked at books that analyzed trends in educational administration. Six books were particularly useful in this phase: Tyack and Hansot's *Managers of Virtue* (1982); Callahan's *Education and the Cult of Efficiency* (1962); Cuban's *Urban School Chiefs Under Fire* (1976); Campbell, Fleming, Newell, and Bennion's *A History of Thought and Practice in Educational Administration* (1987); Glass' edited

volume *An Analysis of Texts on School Administration, 1820–1985* (1986a);
and Phi Delta Kappa's Center on Evaluation, Development, and Research's
The Role of the Principal (1982). The insights offered by these works helped
us to ground our discoveries in the context of other work that had been
done in the field of educational administration.

ANALYSIS

We divided metaphors about the principalship according to decades
because this seemed to be a clean and convenient, albeit arbitrary, way to
sort through the reams of materials with which we were confronted. As our
analysis continued, though, and we began to discover themes and patterns in
the language people use to write about principals, we realized that each
decade had a logic of its own—a dominant theme. It seemed that the
differences among the decades were sufficiently clear-cut to justify our
continued use of this framework to structure our analysis. We also discovered shifts in the types of metaphors used by educational writers and, at
times, conflicting metaphors operating simultaneously. Influenced by Bates
(1984), we focused especially on these shifts and contradictions, striving to
understand both their antecedents and consequences in educational thought
and practice.

As noted above, analysis took place during each phase of the literature
review. Early on, various emphases seemed to be emerging from the writings of each decade. In the twenties, for example, much of the work focused
on spiritual values; in the thirties, on businesslike efficiency in schools; the
focus of the forties was the school principal's role in war and post-war
efforts; in the fifties, the maintenance of established patterns seemed important; in the sixties, the major emphasis was on conflict; in the seventies, on
negotiation and reconciliation; and in the eighties on change.

We examined our data in light of these emphases and, after numerous
discussions and re-analyses of the metaphors, decided on the following
framework to discuss the literature of each decade: dominant metaphorical
themes; dominant tone(s); dominant values; the principal's relationship to
others; and standards for evaluation of the principal's work. Four factors
governed our choice of these categories. First, they made intuitive sense; we
had data for each category from each decade, and the data offered enough in
the way of contrast to merit discussion. Second, the categories were broad
enough to allow us to maintain our focus on understanding the principal's
role, as opposed to simply describing it. They encouraged us to search for
meaning rather than simply to chronicle facts. Third, they captured quite

nicely the dimension of the principalship that our work had led us to believe was most critical—the role of the principal in relation to others, as a key link in the development of the school community. Finally, they centered on aspects of the principal's evolving role that would be of interest and use to both practitioners and academicians.

References

Abbott, M. (1969). Hierarchical impediments to innovation in educational organizations. In F. D. Carver & T. J. Sergiovanni (Eds.), *Organizations and human behavior: Focus on schools* (pp. 42–50). New York: McGraw-Hill.

Achilles, C. M. (1987). A vision of better schools. In W. Greenfield (Ed.), *Instructional leadership: Concepts, issues, and controversies* (pp. 17–37). Newton, MA: Allyn & Bacon.

Achilles, C. M., & Keedy, J. L. (1983–1984). Principal norm setting as a component of effective schools. *National Forum of Educational Administration and Supervision, 1*(1), 58–68.

Adams, M. A., & Korber, M. K. (1943). Patriotic exercises. In *Elementary schools— The frontline of democracy: Twenty-second yearbook of the Department of Elementary School Principals* (pp. 410–416). Washington, DC: NEA.

Alexander, M. P., & Dinkel, V. C. (1952). Orienting parents and preschool children. In *Bases for effective learning: Thirty-first yearbook of the Department of Elementary School Principals* (pp. 74–75). Washington, DC: NEA.

Alfonso, R. J., & Goldberry, L. (1982). Colleagueship in supervision. In T. J. Sergiovanni (Ed.), *Supervision of teaching* (pp. 90–107). Alexandria, VA: ASCD.

American Association of Colleges for Teacher Education. (1988). *School leadership preparation: A preface for action.* Washington, DC: Author.

American Association for School Administration (AASA). (1985). *Raising standards in schools: Problems and solutions.* Arlington, VA: Author.

American Association of School Administrators. (1950). *Publications for America's schools.* Washington, DC: Author.

American Association of School Administrators. (1960). *Professional administrators for America's schools: Thirty-eighth yearbook of the American Association of School Administrators.* Washington, DC: Author.

Anderson, V., & Davies, D. R. (1956). *Patterns of educational leadership.* Englewood Cliffs, NJ: Prentice-Hall.

Anderson, W. A., & Lonsdale, R. C. (1957). Learning administrative behavior. In R. F. Campbell & R. T. Gregg (Eds.), *Administrative behavior in education* (pp. 426–463). New York: Harper & Brothers.

Angus, L. (1988, April). *School leadership and educational reform.* Paper presented at the annual meeting of the American Educational Research Association, New Orleans.

Arndt, C. O. (1945). Broadening horizons through planning. In *Group planning in education: 1945 yearbook* (pp. 116–120). Washington, DC: NEA.

Arndt, H. M. (1959). Maintenance of the school plant. In *Elementary school buildings: Design for learning: Thirty-eighth yearbook of the Department of Elementary School Principals* (pp. 164–169). Washington, DC: NEA.

Aspin, D. (1984). Metaphor and meaning in educational discourse. In W. Taylor (Ed.), *Metaphors in education* (pp. 21–38). London: Heinemann Educational Books.

Association for Supervision and Curriculum Development. (1944). *Toward a new curriculum: 1944 yearbook*. Washington, DC: NEA.

Association for Supervision and Curriculum Development. (1945). *Group planning in education: 1945 yearbook*. Washington, DC: NEA.

Association for Supervision and Curriculum Development. (1947). *Organizing the elementary school for living and learning*. Washington, DC: NEA.

Association for Supervision and Curriculum Development. (1948). *Large was our bounty: Natural resources and the schools: 1948 yearbook*. Washington, DC: NEA.

Association for Supervision and Curriculum Development. (1949). *Toward better teaching: A report of current practices: 1949 yearbook*. Washington, DC: NEA.

Association for Supervision and Curriculum Development. (1986, September). *School reform policy: A call for reason*. Alexandria, VA: NEA.

Astuto, T. (1990, September). Memo prepared for the National Center for Educational Leadership's Conference on Reinventing School Leadership. Cambridge, MA: School of Education, Harvard University.

Austin, D. B., French, W., & Hull, J. D. (1962). *American high school administration: Policy and practice*. New York: Holt, Rinehart and Winston.

Austin, G. R. (1978, February). *Process evaluation: A comprehensive study of outliers*. Baltimore: Maryland State Department of Education and Center for Research and Development, University of Maryland.

Austin, G. R. (1979). Exemplary schools and the search for effectiveness. *Educational Leadership, 37*(1), 10–14.

Ayer, F. C. (1929). The duties of public school administrators. *American School Board Journal, 78*, 39–41.

Bain, W. E. (1952). Bases for effective learning. In *Bases for effective learning: Thirty-first yearbook of the Department of Elementary School Principals* (pp. 12–17). Washington, DC: NEA.

Bair, F. H. (1934). *The social understandings of the superintendent*. New York: Teachers College.

Banks, J. A., James, M. L., Broadhead, C. A., Della-Dora, D., & House, J. E. (1974). Can educators help create an open society? In D. Della-Dora & J. E. House (Eds.), *Education for an open society: 1974 yearbook of the Association for Supervision and Curriculum Development* (pp. 189–200). Washington, DC: Author.

Barnard, C. I. (1938). *The functions of the executive*. Cambridge, MA: Harvard University Press.

Barnard, C. I. (1969). Functions and pathology of status systems in formal organizations. In F. D. Carver & T. J. Sergiovanni (Eds.), *Organizations and human behavior: Focus on schools* (pp. 51–63). New York: McGraw-Hill.

Barth, R. S. (1987). The principal and the profession of teaching. In W. Greenfield (Ed.), *Instructional leadership: Concepts, issues, and controversies* (pp. 249–270). Newton, MA: Allyn & Bacon.

Barth, R. S. (1988). School, a community of leaders. In A. Lieberman (Ed.), *Building a professional culture in schools* (pp. 129–147). New York: Teachers College Press.

Barth, R. S. (1990). *Improving schools from within: Teachers, parents, and principals can make the difference.* San Francisco: Jossey-Bass.

Bass, B. M. (1960). *Leadership, psychology, and organizational behavior.* New York: Harper & Row.

Bassett, S. G., & Cooper, R. J. (1943). Teaching pupils to care for public property. In *Elementary schools—The frontline of democracy: Twenty-second yearbook of the Department of Elementary School Principals* (pp. 361–369). Washington, DC: NEA.

Bates, R. J. (1984). Toward a critical practice of educational administration. In T. J. Sergiovanni & J. E. Corbally (Eds.), *Leadership and organizational culture: New perspectives on administrative theory and practice* (pp. 260–274). Urbana: University of Illinois Press.

Beare, H. (1989, September 25). *Educational administration in the 1990s.* Paper presented at the national conference of the Australian Council for Educational Administration, University of New England, Armidale, New South Wales, Australia.

Beck, L. G. (1991, April). *Reclaiming educational administration as a caring profession.* Paper presented at the annual meeting of the American Educational Research Association, Chicago.

Beck, L. G. (1992). Meeting the challenge of the future: The place of a caring ethic in educational administration. *American Journal of Education, 100*(3).

Beck, L. G., & Murphy, J. F. (1992). Searching for a robust understanding of the principalship. *Educational Administration Quarterly.*

Bell, G. D. (1969). Formality versus flexibility in complex organizations. In F. D. Carver & T. J. Sergiovanni (Eds.), *Organizations and human behavior: Focus on schools* (pp. 71–81). New York: McGraw-Hill.

Bellah, R. N., Madsen, R., Sullivan, W. M., Swidler, A., & Tipton, S. M. (1985). *Habits of the heart: Individualism and commitment in American life.* New York: Harper & Row.

Benjamin, R. (1981). The rose in the forest. *Principal, 60*(4), 10–15.

Bennis, W. (1984). Transformative power and leadership. In T. J. Sergiovanni & J. E. Corbally (Eds.), *Leadership and organizational culture: New perspectives on administrative theory and practice* (pp. 64–71). Urbana: University of Illinois Press.

Berliner, D. C. (1990, Spring). If the metaphor fits, why not wear it? The teacher as executive. *Theory Into Practice, 24*(2), 85–93.

Berman, L. M. (1977a). Curriculum leadership: That all may feel, value and grow. In L. M. Berman & J. A. Roderick (Eds.), *Feeling, valuing, and the art of growing: Insights into the affective: 1977 yearbook of the Association for Supervision and Curriculum Development* (pp. 249–275). Washington, DC: Author.

Berman, L. M. (1977b). A word to administrators. In L. M. Berman & J. A. Roderick (Eds.), *Feeling, valuing, and the art of growing: Insights into the affective: 1977 yearbook of the Association for Supervision and Curriculum Development* (pp. 275–299). Washington, DC: Author.

Berman, L. M., & Roderick, J. A. (Eds.). (1977). *Feeling, valuing, and the art of growing: Insights into the affective: 1977 yearbook of the Association for Supervision and Curriculum Development*. Washington, DC: Author.

Berman, P., & McLaughlin, M. W. (1978). *Federal programs supporting educational change: Vol. VIII. Implementation and sustaining innovations*. Santa Monica, CA: Rand Corporation.

Black, M. (1979). More about metaphor. In A. Ortony (Ed.), *Metaphor and thought* (pp. 19–45). Cambridge: Cambridge University Press.

Blase, J. L. (1986). A qualitative analysis of teacher stress: Consequences for performance. *American Educational Research Journal, 23*(1), 13–40.

Blau, P. M., & Scott, W. R. (1962). *Formal organizations*. San Francisco: Chandler.

Blau, P. M., & Scott, W. R. (1969). The nature and types of formal organizations. In F. D. Carver & T. J. Sergiovanni (Eds.), *Organizations and human behavior: Focus on schools* (pp. 5–18). New York: McGraw-Hill.

Blough, G. O. (1953). Science in the elementary school. In *Science for today's children: Thirty-second yearbook of the Department of Elementary School Principals* (pp. 2–10). Washington, DC: NEA.

Blumberg, A. (1984, Fall). The craft of school administration and some other rambling thoughts. *Educational Administration Quarterly, 20*(4), 24–40.

Blumberg, A. (1987). The work of principals: A touch of craft. In W. Greenfield (Ed.), *Instructional leadership: Concepts, issues, and controversies* (pp. 38–55). Newton, MA: Allyn & Bacon.

Blumberg, A., & Greenfield, W. (1980). *The effective principal. Perspectives on school leadership*. Boston: Allyn & Bacon.

Bolin, F. S. (1989, Fall). Empowering leadership. *Teachers College Record, 91*(1), 81–96.

Bolman, L. G., & Deal, T. E. (1989). *Modern approaches to understanding and managing organizations*. San Francisco: Jossey-Bass.

Bolton, D. (1973). *Selection and evaluation of teachers*. Berkeley: McCutchan.

Boyan, N. J. (1963). Common and specialized learnings for administrators and supervisors: Some problems and issues. In D. J. Leu & H. C. Rudman (Eds.), *Preparation programs for school administration: Common and specialized learnings*. East Lansing: Michigan State University.

Boyan, N. J. (1969). The emergent role of the teacher in the authority structure of the school. In F. D. Carver & T. J. Sergiovanni (Eds.), *Organizations and human behavior: Focus on schools* (pp. 200–211). New York: McGraw-Hill.

Boyd, W. L. (1987, Summer). Public education's last hurrah? Schizophrenia, amnesia, and ignorance in school politics. *Educational Evaluation and Policy Analysis, 9*(2), 85–100.

Boyd, W. L. (1990). Balancing control and autonomy in school reform: The politics of *Perestroika*. In J. F. Murphy (Ed.), *The educational reform movement of the 1980s: Perspectives and cases* (pp. 85–96). New York: Teachers College Press.

Boyd, W. L., & Hartman, W. T. (1988). The politics of educational productivity. In D. Monk & J. Underwood (Eds.), *Distributing educational resources within nations, states, school districts, and schools*. Cambridge, MA: Ballinger.

Brabeck, M. M. (Ed.). (1989). *Who cares? Theory, research, and educational implications of the ethic of care*. New York: Praeger.

Bredeson, P. V. (1985). An analysis of metaphorical perspectives on school principals. *Educational Administration Quarterly, 21*, 29–59.

Bredeson, P. V. (1987). Languages of leadership: Metaphor making in educational administration. *Administrator's Notebook, 32*(6), 1–5.

Bredeson, P. V. (1988, November). Perspectives on schools: Metaphors and management in education. *The Journal of Educational Administration, 26*(3), 293–310.

Brennan, B. (1973). Principals as bureaucrats. *Journal of Educational Administration, 11*(2), 171–178.

Bridges, E. (1982, Summer). Research on the school administrator: The state of the art, 1967–1980. *Educational Administration Quarterly, 18*(3), 12–33.

Bronfenbrenner, U. (1979). *The ecology of human development: Experiments by nature and design*. Cambridge, MA: Harvard University Press.

Brookover, W. B., Beady, C. H., Flood, P. K., Schweitzer, J. H., & Wisenbaker, J. M. (1979). *School social systems and student achievement: Schools can make a difference*. New York: Praeger.

Brookover, W. B., Beamer, L., Estin, D., Hathaway, D., Lezotte, L., Miller, S., Passalacqua, J., & Tornetzky, L. (1982). *Creating effective schools*. Holmes Beach, FL: Learning Publications.

Brookover, W. B., & Lezotte, L. W. (1977). *Changes in school characteristics coincident with changes in student achievement*. East Lansing: College of Urban Development, Michigan State University.

Brown, F. S. (1961). The in-service training of teachers toward the more effective use of test results. In A. E. Traxler (Ed.), *Measurement and research in today's schools: Report of the twenty-fifth conference of the Educational Records Bureau and the American Council on Education* (pp. 76–80). Washington, DC: American Council on Education.

Brown, R. (1976). Social theory as metaphor. *Theory and Society, 3*, 169–197.

Brown, R. (1989). *A poetic for sociology*. Chicago: University of Chicago Press.

Brown vs. Board of Education of Topeka, 347 U.S. 483. (1954).

Brubacher, J., Brownell, S. M., Childs, D. L., Cunningham, R., Kilpatrick, W. H., Ostrander, M. Q., Sanders, W. D., Threlkeld, A. L. (1944). *The public schools and spiritual values*. (Seventh yearbook of the John Dewey Society). New York: Harper & Brothers.

Bryk, A. (1989). Musings on the moral life of schools. *American Journal of Education, 96*(2), 256–290.

Buber, M. (1958). *I and thou* (2nd ed.) (R. G. Smith, Trans.). New York: Charles Scribner's Sons.

Buber, M. (1965). *Between man and man* (R. G. Smith, Trans.). New York: Macmillan.

Burden, L., & Whitt, R. L. (1973). *The community school principal: New horizons.* Midland, MI: Pendell.

Burlingame, M. (1971). The great man approach to the study of American educational leadership: Analysis of biographies. In L. Cunningham & W. J. Gephardt (Eds.), *Leadership: The art and the science today* (pp. 45–66). Itasca, IL: F. E. Peacock.

Burlingame, M. (1987). Images of leadership in effective schools literature. In W. Greenfield (Ed.), *Instructional leadership: Concepts, issues, and controversies* (pp. 3–16). Newton, MA: Allyn & Bacon.

Burton, W. (1975). Schools and sex (A tragedy in two parts). In J. B. Macdonald & E. Zaret (Eds.), *Schools in search of meaning: 1975 yearbook of the Association for Supervision and Curriculum Development* (pp. 51–78). Washington, DC: Author.

Burton, W. W. (1929). The type, the kind, the amount of supervision which elementary principals should know and be able to give. *Bulletin of the Department of Elementary School Principals, National Education Association, VIII.*

Business–Higher Education Task Force. (1983). *America's competitive challenge: The need for a national response.* Washington, DC: Business–Higher Education Forum.

Button. H. W. (1966). Doctrines of administration: A brief history. *Educational Administration Quarterly, 2*(3), 216–224.

Callahan, R. E. (1962). *Education and the cult of efficiency.* Chicago: University of Chicago Press.

Callahan, R. E., & Button, H. W. (1964). Historical change of the role of the man in the organization: 1865–1950. In D. E. Griffiths (Ed.), *Behavioral science and educational administration: 63rd yearbook of the National Society for the Study of Education, Part II.* (pp. 73–92). Chicago: University of Chicago Press.

Campbell, R. F. (1957). Situational factors in educational administration. In R. F. Campbell & R. T. Gregg (Eds.), *Administrative behavior in education* (pp. 228–268). New York: Harper & Brothers.

Cambell, R. F. (1981, Winter). The professorship in educational administration: A personal view. *Educational Administration Quarterly, 17*(1), 1–24.

Campbell, R. F., Fleming, T., Newell, L. J., & Bennion, J. W. (1987). *A history of thought and practice in educational administration.* New York: Teachers College Press.

Campbell, R. F., & Gregg, R. T. (Eds.). (1957). *Administrative behavior in education.* New York: Harper & Brothers.

Carlson, E. S., & Northrup J. (1955). An experiment in grouping pupils for instruction in reading. In *Reading for today's children: Thirty-fourth yearbook of the Department of Elementary School Principals* (pp. 53–57). Washington, DC: NEA.

Carnegie Council on Adolescent Development. (1989). *Turning points.* Washington, DC: Author.

Carnegie Forum on Education and the Economy. (1986). *A nation prepared: Teachers for the 21st century*. Washington, DC: Author.

Carnine, D., Gersten, R., & Green, S. (1982). The principal as instructional leader: A second look. *Educational Leadership, 40*(3), 47–50.

Carr, W. G. (1957). New forces in the government of the public schools. In *Parents and the schools: Thirty-sixth yearbook of the Department of Elementary School Principals* (pp. 2–10). Washington, DC: NEA.

Carter, K. (1990, Spring). Meaning and metaphor: Case knowledge in teaching. *Theory Into Practice, 24*(2), 109–115.

Carver, F. D., & Sergiovanni, T. J. (Eds.). (1969). *Organizations and human behavior: Focus on schools*. New York: McGraw-Hill.

Caswell, H. L. (Ed.). (1946). *The American high school: Its responsibility and opportunity*. New York: Harper & Brothers.

Cayce, M. D. (1931). The principalship develops supervisory status. In *Tenth yearbook of the Department of Elementary School Principals* (p. 160). Washington, DC: NEA.

Center for Community Education. (1971). *Community education*. Brochure by Texas College of Education, Texas A&M University, College Station.

Chapman, J., & Boyd, W. L. (1986, Fall). Decentralization, devolution, and the school principal: Australian lessons on statewide educational reform. *Educational Administration Quarterly, 22*(4), 28–58.

Chubb, J. E., & Moe, T. M. (1990). *Politics, markets, and America's schools*. Washington, DC: Brookings Institution.

Clapp, E. (1939). Where learning and living converge. In *Community schools in action*. New York: Viking Press.

Clark, D. L. (1988). *Charge to the study group of the National Policy Board of Educational Administration*. Unpublished manuscript, University of Virginia, College of Education.

Clark, D. L. (1990, September). Memo prepared for the National Center for Educational Leadership's Conference on Reinventing School Leadership. Cambridge, MA: Harvard University, School of Education.

Clark, D. L., & Lotto, L. S. (1982). *Principals in instructionally effective schools* (Report sponsored by the School Finance Project of the National Institute of Education). (29 pages).

Clark, D. L., Lotto, L. S., & McCarthy, M. M. (1980). *Why do some urban schools succeed?* Bloomington, IN: Phi Delta Kappa.

Clark, D. L., & Meloy J. M. (1989). Renouncing bureaucracy: A democratic structure for leadership in schools. In T. J. Sergiovanni & J. A. Moore (Eds.), *Schooling for tomorrow: Directing reform to issues that count* (pp. 272–294). Boston: Allyn & Bacon.

Clark, K. (1968). Ghetto education. *Center Magazine, 1*(7), 45–60.

Clifford, C. J. (1975). *The shape of American education*. Englewood Cliffs, NJ: Prentice-Hall.

Clinton, B. (1987). *Speaking of leadership*. Denver: Education Commission of the States.

Coegan, P. N., & Raebeck, B. S. (1989, December). Cooperation, integration, and caring in public education. *NASSP Bulletin, 73*(521), 96–100.

Cohen, E. C., & Lotan, R. A. (1990, Spring). Teacher as supervisor of complex technology. *Theory Into Practice, 24*(2), 78–84.

Coleman, J. S., Campbell, E. Q., Hobson, C. J., McPartland, J., Mood, A. M., Weinfeld, F. D., & York, R. L. (1977). Relation of school factors to achievement. In D. Erickson (Ed.), *Educational organization and administration* (pp. 131–149). Berkeley, CA: McCutchan.

Collins, E. C., & Green, J. L. (1990, Spring). Metaphors: The construction of a perspective. *Theory Into Practice, 24*(2), 71–77.

Colton, D. L. (1985). Vision. *National Forum, 65*(2), 33–35.

Combs, A. W. (1972). *Educational accountability: Beyond behavioral objectives.* Washington, DC: Association for Supervision and Curriculum Development.

Conley, S. C. (1989, March). *Who's on first? School reform, teacher participation, and the decision-making process.* Paper presented at the annual meeting of the American Educational Research Association, San Francisco.

Cook, D. A. (1962). Programmed instruction and the aims of education. In A. E. Traxler (Ed.), *Improving the efficiency and quality of learning: Report of the twenty-sixth conference of the Educational Records Bureau* (pp. 21–29). Washington, DC: American Council on Education.

Cooke, D. H. (1939). *Administering the teaching personnel.* Chicago: Benjamin H. Sanborn.

Cooper, B. S. (1979). The future of middle management in education. In D. A. Erickson & T. L. Reller (Eds.), *The principal in metropolitan schools* (pp. 272–299). Berkeley, CA: McCutchan.

Cooper, B. S., & Boyd, W. L. (1987). The evolution of training for school administrators. In J. Murphy & P. Hallinger (Eds.), *Approaches to administrative training* (pp. 3–27). Albany: State University of New York Press.

Cooper, N. C. (1953). Unit concepts in elementary school science. In *Science for today's children: Thirty-second yearbook of the Department of Elementary School Principals* (pp. 146–149). Washington, DC: NEA.

Cooper, W. J. (1933). *Economy in education.* Washington, DC: United States Commissioner of Education.

Corcoran, T. B. (1989). Restructuring education: A new vision at Hope Essential High School. In J. M. Rosnow & R. Zager (Eds.), *Allies in educational reform* (pp. 243–274). San Francisco: Jossey-Bass.

Corey, S. M. (1945). Principles of cooperative group work. In *Group planning in education: 1945 yearbook of the Department of Supervision and Curriculum Development* (pp. 130–138). Washington, DC: NEA.

Cottrell, D. P. (1946). The influence of basic social trends. In H. L. Caswell (Ed.), *The American high school: Its responsibility and opportunity* (pp. 31–48). New York: Harper & Brothers.

Cox, P. W. L., & Langfitt, R. E. (1934). *High school administration and supervision.* New York: American Book Co.

Crow, L. D., & Crow, A. (1947). *Introduction to education: Fundamental principles and modern practices*. Atlanta: American Book Co.

Crowson, R. L., & Morris, V. C. (1984, April). *Administrative control in large-city school systems: An investigation in Chicago*. Paper presented at the annual meeting of the American Educational Research Association, New Orleans.

Crowson, R. L., & Porter-Gehrie, C. (1981). The urban school principalship: An organizational stability role. *Planning and Changing, 12*(1), 26–53.

Cuban, L. (1976). *Urban school chiefs under fire*. Chicago: University of Chicago Press.

Cuban, L. (1984). *How teachers taught: Constancy and change in American classrooms, 1890–1980*. New York: Longman.

Cuban, L. (1989). The "at-risk" label and the problem of urban school reform. *Phi Delta Kappan, 79*(10), 780–784, 789.

Cubberley, E. P. (1914). *State and county educational reorganization: The revised constitution and school code of the state of Osceola*. New York: Macmillan.

Cubberley, E. P. (1916). *Public school administration*. Boston: Houghton Mifflin.

Cubberley, E. P. (1923). *The principal and his school*. Boston: Houghton Mifflin.

Cubberley, E. P. (1927). *State school administration: A Textbook of principles*. Boston: Houghton Mifflin.

Culbertson, J. A. (1964). The preparation of administrators. In D. E. Griffiths (Ed.), *Behavioral science and educational administration* (63rd yearbook of the National Society for the Study of Education, Part II) (pp. 303–330). Chicago: University of Chicago Press.

Culbertson, J. A. (1988). A century's quest for a knowledge base. In N. J. Boyan (Ed.), *Handbook of research on educational administration* (pp. 3–26). New York: Longman.

Cunningham, L., & Gephardt, W. J. (1971). Preface. In L. Cunningham & W. J. Gephardt (Eds.), *Leadership: The art and the science today* (pp. xv–xvi). Itasca, IL: F. E. Peacock.

David, J. L. (1989). *Restructuring in progress: Lessons from pioneering districts*. Washington, DC: National Governors' Association.

David, J. L., Cohen, M., Honetschlager, D., & Traimon, S. (1990). *State actions to restructure schools: First steps*. Washington, DC: National Governors' Association.

Davies, D. R. (1952). Educational administration at mid-century. *Teachers College Record, 54*(3), 128–129.

Davis, F. B. (Ed.). (1966). *Modern educational developments: Another look: Report of the thirtieth conference of the Educational Records Bureau*. New York: Educational Records Bureau.

Davis, H. S. (1974). How to organize an effective team teaching program. In *Handbook of successful school administration* (pp. 147–195). Englewood Cliffs, NJ: Prentice-Hall.

Dawson, D. T. (1955). Some issues in grouping for reading. In *Reading for today's children:Thirty-fourth yearbook of the Department of Elementary School Principals* (pp. 48–52). Washington, DC: NEA.

Deal, T. E. (1987). Effective school principals: Counselors, engineers, pawnbrokers, poets . . . or instructional leaders? In W. Greenfield (Ed.), *Instructional leadership: Concepts, issues, and controversies* (pp. 230–248). Newton, MA: Allyn & Bacon.

Della-Dora, D., & House, J. E. (1974). Education for an open society. In D. Della-Dora & J. E. House (Eds.), *Education for an open society: 1974 yearbook of the Association for Supervision and Curriculum Development* (pp. 1–10). Washington, DC: Author.

Department of Elementary School Principals. (1943). *Elementary schools: The frontline of democracy: Twenty-second yearbook of the Department of Elementary School Principals.* Washington, DC: NEA.

Department of Elementary School Principals. (1954). *Time for the job.* Washington, DC: NEA.

Department of Elementary School Principals. (1957). *Parents and the schools: Thirty-sixth yearbook of the Department of Elementary School Principals.* Washington, DC: NEA.

Department of Elementary School Principals. (1958). *So now you're a principal! A guide for the elementary school administrator in his initial principalship.* Washington, DC: NEA.

Department of Elementary School Principals. (1961). *Better principals for our schools: A cooperative approach to competence.* Washington, DC: NEA.

DeRoche, E. F. (1985). *How school administrators solve problems.* Englewood Cliffs, NJ: Prentice-Hall.

Dewey, J. (1915). *The school and society.* Chicago: University of Chicago Press.

Dewey, J. (1916). *Democracy and education.* New York: Macmillan.

Dewey, J. (1946). *Problems of men.* New York: Philosophical Library.

Dodd, P. C. (1965). *Role conflicts of school principals: Final report no. 4 of the National Principalship Study.* Washington, DC: Department of Health, Education, and Welfare.

Dodson, D. W. (1974). Authority, power and education. In D. Della-Dora & J. E. House (Eds.), *Education for an open society: 1974 yearbook of the Association for Supervision and Curriculum Development* (pp. 99–108). Washington, DC: Author.

Dokecki, P. R. (1990, May). On knowing the person as agent in caring relations. *Person-Centered Review, 5*(2), 155–169.

Donmoyer, R. (1985, Spring). Cognitive anthropology and research on effective principals. *Educational Administration Quarterly, 21*(2), 31–57.

Dorsey, S. M. (1930). *Ninth yearbook of the Department of Elementary School Principals* (pp. 174–190). Washington, DC: NEA.

Doughtery, J. H., Gorman, F. A., & Phillips, C. A. (1936). *Elementary school organization and management.* New York: Macmillan.

Douglass, H. R. (1945). *Organization and administration of secondary schools.* New York: Ginn.

Douglass, H. R. (1963). *Modern administration of secondary schools: Organization and administration of junior and senior high schools.* New York: Blaisdell.

Downing, J. (1963). Experiments with an augmented alphabet for beginning readers in British schools. In A. E. Traxler (Ed.), *Frontiers of education: Report of the twenty-seventh conference of the Educational Records Bureau* (pp. 99–157). Washington, DC: American Council on Education.

Drake, T. L., & Roe, W. H. (1986). *The principalship* (3rd ed.). New York: Macmillan.

Drake–Des Moines Institute. (1971). *How a community planned two inner-city schools.* Des Moines: Drake University and the Des Moines School Board.

Dreeben, R., & Gross, N. (1965). *The role behavior of school principals: Final report no. 3 of the National Principalship Study.* Washington, DC: Department of Health, Education, and Welfare.

Drews, E. M. (1961). A critical evaluation of approaches to the identification of gifted students. In A. E. Traxler (Ed.), *Measurement and research in today's schools: Report of the twenty-fifth educational conference of the Educational Records Bureau and the American Council on Education* (pp. 109–121). Washington, DC: American Council on Education.

Dugan, E. M. (1954). Divide and conquer. In *Time for the job* (pp. 24–25). Washington, DC: NEA.

Dunn, J. O., LeBaron, W. A., & Young, W. E. (1952). The principal pacesetter. In *Bases for effective learning: Thirty-first yearbook of the Department of Elementary School Principals* (pp. 37–44). Washington, DC: NEA.

Dunn, M. (1952). As we give people cause to think. In *Bases for effective learning: Thirty-first yearbook of the Department of Elementary School Principals* (pp. 112–114). Washington, DC: NEA.

Durrell, D. D. (1955). Some 'musts' in reading research. In *Reading for today's children: Thirty-fourth yearbook of the Department of Elementary School Principals* (pp. 17–21). Washington, DC: NEA.

Dwyer, D. C. (1986, Fall). Understanding the principal's contribution to instruction. *Peabody Journal of Education, 63*(1), 3–18.

Dwyer, D. C., Lee, G. V., Rowan, B., & Bossert, S. T. (1983, March). *Five principals in action: Perspectives on instructional management.* San Francisco: Far West Laboratory for Research and Development.

Dwyer, D. C., & Smith, M. (1987). The principal as explanation of school change: An incomplete story. In W. Greenfield (Ed.), *Instructional leadership: Concepts, issues, and controversies* (pp. 155–178). Newton, MA: Allyn & Bacon.

Eaton, W. (1986). From ideology to conventional wisdom: School administration texts 1915–1933. In T. E. Glass (Ed.), *An analysis of texts on school administration 1820–1985: The reciprocal relationship between the literature and the profession* (pp. 23–39). Danville, IL: Interstate.

Education Commission of the States Task Force on Education for Economic Growth. (1983). *Action for excellence: A comprehensive plan to improve our nation's schools.* Washington, DC: Education Commission of the States.

Ellet, C. D. (1987). Emerging teacher performance assessment practices: Implications for the instructional supervision role of school principals. In W. Greenfield (Ed.), *Instructional leadership: Concepts, issues, and controversies* (pp. 302–327). Newton, MA: Allyn & Bacon.

Elliot, R. K. (1984). Metaphor, imagination and conceptions of education. In W. Taylor (Ed.), *Metaphors in education* (pp. 38–53). London: Heinemann.

Elmore, R. F. (1988). *Early experience in restructuring schools: Voices from the field.* Washington, DC: National Governors' Association.

Elsbree, W., & McNally, H. J. (1951). *Elementary school administration and supervision.* Atlanta: American Book Co.

Erickson, D. A. (Ed.). (1977). *Educational organization and administration.* Berkeley, CA: McCutchan.

Etzioni, A. (1964). *Modern organizations.* Englewood Cliffs, NJ: Prentice-Hall.

Etzioni, A. (1965). Organizational control structure. In D. G. March (Ed.), *Handbook of organizations* (pp. 650–676). Chicago: Rand McNally.

Farmer, F. M. (1948). The public high school principalship. *Bulletin of the National Association of Secondary School Principals, 32*(154), 82–91.

Farquhar, R. H. (1977). Preparatory programs in educational administration. In L. L. Cunningham, W. G. Hack, & R. O. Nystrand (Eds.), *Educational administration: The developing decades* (pp. 329–357). Berkeley, CA: McCutchan.

Farrar, E. (1987, April). *The role of leadership at the school and district level.* Paper presented at the annual meeting of the American Educational Research Association, Washington, DC.

Fenollosa, G. M., Kendrick, S. A., Lennon, R. T., North, R. D., Seashore, H., Spencer, L. M., & Turnbull, W. W. (1961). How may schools best meet the problems and pressures related to the many available testing programs. In A. E. Traxler (Ed.), *Measurement and research in today's schools: Report of the twenty-fifth educational conference of the Educational Records Bureau and the American Council on Education* (pp. 41–64). Washington, DC: American Council on Education.

Fenske, P. E. (1956). Make your own filmstrips. In *Instructional materials for elementary schools: Thirty-fifth yearbook of the Department of Elementary School Principals* (pp. 154–157). Washington, DC: NEA.

Fernandez, D. W. (1986). *Persuasions and performances: The play of tropes in culture.* Bloomington: Indiana University Press.

Finch, A. (1974). Growth in-service programs that work. In *Handbook of successful school administration* (pp. 97–146). Englewood Cliffs, NJ: Prentice-Hall.

Fisher, C. W. (1990, January). The research agenda project as prologue. *Journal for Research in Mathematics Education, 21*(1), 81–89.

Fisk, R. S. (1957). The task of educational administration. In R. F. Campbell & R. T. Gregg (Eds.), *Administrative behavior in education* (pp. 200–227). New York: Harper & Brothers.

Fitzpatrick, D. (1945). Good neighbors and good citizens plan. In *Group planning in education: 1945 yearbook of the Department of Supervision and Curriculum Development* (pp. 38–47). Washington, DC: NEA.

Foster, W. (1986). *Paradigms and promises: New approaches to educational administration.* Buffalo, NY: Prometheus.

Foster, W. (1988). Educational administration: A critical appraisal. In D. E. Griffiths, R. T. Stout, & P. B. Forsyth (Eds.), *Leaders for America's schools* (pp. 68–81). Berkeley, CA: McCutchan.

Foster, W. (1989, March). *School leaders as transformative intellectuals: A theoretical argument*. Paper presented at the annual meeting of the American Educational Research Association, San Francisco.

Frymier, J. (1987, September). Bureaucracy and the neutering of teachers. *Phi Delta Kappan, 69*(1), 9–14.

Fullan, M. G. (1981). *The meaning of educational change*. New York: Teachers College Press.

Getzels, J. W. (1952). A psychosociological framework for the study of educational administration. *Harvard Educational Review, 22*(4), 235–246.

Giles, H. H. (1945). What group planning means. In *Group planning in education* (pp. 139–153). Washington, DC: NEA.

Giroux, H. A. (1988). *Teachers as intellectuals: Toward a critical pedagogy of learning*. Granby, MA: Bergin & Garvey.

Gist, A. S. (1924). Evolution of the principal. In *Third yearbook of the Department of Elementary School Principals* (p. 205). Washington, DC: NEA.

Gist, A. S. (1926). *Elementary school supervision*. New York: Charles Scribner's Sons.

Glass, T. E. (Ed.). (1986a). *An analysis of texts on school administration 1820–1985: The reciprocal relationship between the literature and the profession*. Danville, IL: Interstate.

Glass, T. E. (1986b). Factualism to theory, art to science: School administration texts 1955–1985. In T. E. Glass (Ed.), *An analysis of texts on school administration: The reciprocal relationship between the literature and the profession* (pp. 93–114). Danville, IL: Interstate.

Glass, T. E. (1986c). An overview: 1820–1985. In T. E. Glass (Ed.), *An analysis of texts on school administration 1820–1985: The reciprocal relationship between the literature and the profession* (pp. 115–133). Danville, IL: Interstate.

Goldhammer, K. (1963). *The social sciences and the preparation of educational administrators*. Columbus, OH: University of Alberta, Division of Educational Administration and the University Council for Educational Administration.

Goldhammer, K. (1983, Summer). Evolution in the profession. *Educational Administration Quarterly, 19*(3), 249–272.

Goldhammer, K., Becker, G., Withycombe, R., Doyel, F., Miller, E., Morgan, C., Delorretto, L., & Aldridge, B. (1971). *Elementary principals and their schools— Beacons of brilliance and potholes of pestilence*. Eugene, OR: Center for the Advanced Study of Educational Administration.

Goldhammer, R. (1969). *Clinical supervision*. New York: Holt, Rinehart and Winston.

Goodlad, J. I. (1984). *A place called school: Prospects for the future*. New York: McGraw-Hill.

Graff, O. B., & Street, C. M. (1957). Developing a value framework for educational administration. In R. F. Campbell & R. T. Gregg (Eds.), *Administrative behavior in education* (pp. 120–152). New York: Harper & Brothers.

Grant, G. (1988). *The world we created at Hamilton High.* Cambridge, MA: Harvard University Press.

Graves, H. (1956). Producing motion pictures and slides. In *Instructional materials for elementary schools: Thirty-fifth yearbook of the Department of Elementary School Principals* (pp. 146–149). Washington, DC: NEA.

Graves, R. (1989). Preface. In E. Van Bellingham and L. F. Ludwig (Eds.), *LIFE through the sixties.* New York: United Technologies and Time Magazine.

Greenfield, T. B. (1975). Theory about organization: A new perspective and its implications for schools. In M. Hughes (Ed.), *Administering education: International challenge* (pp. 71–99). London: Author.

Greenfield, T. B. (1988). The decline and fall of science in educational administration. In D. E. Griffiths, R. T. Stout, & P. B. Forsyth (Eds.), *Leaders for America's schools* (pp. 131–159). Berkeley, CA: McCutchan.

Greenfield, W. (1987). Moral imagination and interpersonal competence. Antecedents to instructional leadership. In W. Greenfield (Ed.), *Instructional leadership: Concepts, issues, and controversies* (pp. 56–75). Newton, MA: Allyn & Bacon.

Gregg, R. T. (February 1943). The principal and his school in wartime. *Bulletin of the National Association of Secondary School Principals, 27*(112), 7–19.

Gregg, R. T. (1957). The administrative process. In R. F. Campbell & R. T. Gregg (Eds.), *Administrative behavior in education* (pp. 269–317). New York: Harper & Brothers.

Gregg, R. T. (1960). Administration. In C. W. Harris (Ed.), *Encyclopedia of educational research* (3rd ed) (pp. 19–24). New York: Macmillan.

Gregg, R. T. (1969). Preparation of administrators. In R. L. Ebel (Ed.), *Encyclopedia of educational research* (4th ed.) (pp. 993–1004). London: Macmillan.

Gretchko, S., & DeMont, R. A. (1980). *The principal makes the difference.* Paper presented at the National School Boards Association, San Francisco.

Griffin, R. S., & Nash, R. J. (1988, February). Individualism, community, and education: An exchange of views. *Educational Theory, 40*(1), 1–18.

Griffiths, D. E. (1956). *Human relations in school administration.* New York: Appleton-Century-Crofts.

Griffiths, D. E. (1957). Toward a theory of administrative behavior. In R. F. Campbell & R. T. Gregg (Eds.), *Administrative behavior in education* (pp. 354–392). New York: Harper & Brothers.

Griffiths, D. E. (1959). *Administrative theory.* New York: Appleton-Century-Crofts.

Griffiths, D. E. (1969). Viable alternatives to the status quo. In F. W. Lotz & Q. Azzarelli (Eds.), *The struggle for power in education.* Englewood Cliffs, NJ: Prentice-Hall.

Griffiths, D. E. (1982). *Theories: Past, present, and future.* Paper presented at the Fifth International Intervisitation Program, Lagos, Nigeria.

Griffiths, D. E. (1988). Administrative theory. In N. J. Boyan (Ed.), *Handbook of research in educational administration* (pp. 27–51). New York: Longman.

Griffiths, D. E., Stout, R. T., & Forsyth, P. B. (1988). The preparation of educational administrators. In D. E. Griffiths, R. T. Stout, & P. B. Forsyth (Eds.), *Leaders for America's schools* (pp. 284–304). Berkeley, CA: McCutchan.

Gross, N., & Herriot, R. E. (1964). *The professional leadership of elementary school principals: Final report no. 1 of the National Principalship Study*. Washington, DC: Department of Health, Education, and Welfare.

Gross, N., & Trask, A. E. (1964). *Men and women as elementary school principals: Final report no. 2 of the National Principalship Study*. Washington, DC: Department of Health, Education, and Welfare.

Gudgeon, C. (1989, Spring). Mother, father, sister, friend: Metaphor and the craft of child care. *Child and Youth Care Quarterly, 18*(1), 17–22.

Guthrie, J. W. (1986, December). School-based management: The next needed education reform. *Phi Delta Kappan, 68*(4), 305–309.

Guthrie, J. W., & Kirst, M. W. (1988). *Conditions of education in California 1988*. Berkeley: Policy Analysis for California Education.

Guzzetti, B., & Martin, M. (1986, April). *A comparative analysis of elementary and secondary principals' instructional leadership behavior*. Paper presented at the annual meeting of the American Educational Research Association, San Francisco.

Habern, R. (1956). Picturing ourselves at work. In *Instructional materials for elementary schools: Thirty-fifth yearbook of the Department of Elementary School Principals* (pp. 150–153). Washington, DC: NEA.

Hagman, H. L., & Schwartz, A. (1955). *Administration in profile for school executives*. New York: Harper & Brothers.

Hall, G., Hord, S. M., & Griffin, T. H. (1980). *Implementation at the school building level. The development and analysis of nine mini-case studies*. Paper presented at the annual meeting of the American Educational Research Association.

Hall, R. M., & McIntyre, K. E. (1957). The student personnel program. In R. F. Campbell & R. T. Gregg (Eds.), *Administrative behavior in education* (pp. 393–425). New York: Harper & Brothers.

Hallinger, P., & Murphy, J. (1985a). Instructional leadership and school socioeconomic status: A preliminary investigation. *Administrator's Notebook, 31*(5), 1–4.

Hallinger, P., & Murphy, J. (1985b, November). Assessing the instructional management behavior of principals. *Elementary School Journal, 86*(2), 217–247.

Hallinger, P., & Murphy, J. (1986, May). The social context of effective schools. *American Journal of Education, 94*(3), 328–355.

Hallinger, P., & Murphy, J. (1987). Instructional leadership in the school context. In W. Greenfield (Ed.), *Instructional leadership: Concepts, issues, and controversies* (pp. 179–203). Newton, MA: Allyn & Bacon.

Hallinger, P., Murphy, J., Weil, M., Mesa, R. P., & Mitman, A. (1983, May). School effectiveness: Identifying the specific practices and behaviors for principals. *NASSP Bulletin, 67*(463), 83–91.

Halpin, A. W. (1957). A paradigm for research on administrative behavior. In R. F. Campbell & R. T. Gregg (Eds.), *Administrative behavior in education* (pp. 155–200). New York: Harper & Brothers.

Hanft, E. H., & Sutton, M. A. (1955). Solving problems of public relations. In *Instructional material for elementary schools: Thirty-fifth yearbook of the Department of Elementary School Principals* (pp. 115–121). Washington, DC: NEA.

Hanley, G. H., & Schiesser, E. (1953). A point of view for science. In *Science for today's children: Thirty-second yearbook of the Department of Elementary School Principals* (pp. 17–21). Washington, DC: NEA.

Hanna, L. A. (1948). Characteristics of a democratic school. In *Group processes in supervision: 1946 yearbook of the Association for Supervision and Curriculum Development* (pp. 9–19). Washington, DC: NEA.

Hanson, E. M. (1981). Organizational control in educational systems: A case study of governance in schools. In S. B. Bacharach (Ed.), *Organizational behavior in schools and school districts*. New York: Praeger.

Hanson, M. (1984). Exploration of mixed metaphors in educational administration research. *Issues in Education, 2*, 167–185.

Hanushek, E. (1977). The production of education, teacher quality, and efficiency. In D. Erickson (Ed.), *Educational organization and administration* (pp. 150–169). Berkeley, CA: McCutchan.

Harding, L. W. (1952). Minor adjustments but major morale boosters. In *Bases for effective learning: Thirty-first yearbook of the Department of Elementary School Principals* (pp. 23–26). Washington, DC: NEA.

Harlow, T. G. (1962). Purpose-defining: The central function of the school administrator. In J. A. Culbertson & S. P. Hencley (Eds.), *Preparing administrators: New perspectives* (pp. 61–71). Columbus, OH: University Council for Educational Administration.

Hawley, W. D. (1989). Looking backward at educational reform. *Education Week, 9*(9), 32–35.

Hedges, W. P., & Martinello, M. L. (1977). What the schools might do: Some alternatives here and now. In L. M. Berman & J. A. Roderick (Eds.) *Feeling, valuing, and the art of growing: Insights into the affective: 1977 yearbook of the Association of Supervision and Curriculum Development* (pp. 229–248). Washington, DC: Author.

Hemphill, D. K., Richards, J. M., & Peterson, R. F. (1965). *Report of the senior high school principalship: Vol. 1. The study of the secondary-school principalship*. Washington, DC: National Association of Secondary School Principals.

Hemphill, J., Griffiths, D., & Frederickson, N. (1962). *Administrative performance and personality*. New York: Bureau of Publications, Teachers College, Columbia University.

Henderson, R. L. (1952). Reflections of a beginning principal. *Bases for effective learning: Thirty-first yearbook of the Department of Elementary School Principals* (pp. 45–51). Washington, DC: NEA.

Hitt, W. D. (1973). *Education as a human enterprise*. Worthington, OH: Charles A. Jones.

Hobbs, N., Dokecki, P. R., Hoover-Dempsey, K. V., Moroney, R. M., Shayne, N. W., & Weeks, K. H. (1984). *Strengthening families*. San Francisco: Jossey-Bass.

Homans, G. C. (1950). *The human group*. New York: Harcourt, Brace.

Hone, E. (1953). Ideas for the administrator. In *Science for today's children: Thirty-*

second yearbook of the Department of Elementary School Principals (pp. 24–27). Washington, DC: NEA.

Hord, S. M., & Huling-Austin, L. (1986, September). Effective curriculum implementation: Some promising new insights. *The Elementary School Journal, 87*(1), 97–115.

House, R. J. (1968). Leadership training: Some dysfunctional consequences. *Administrative Science Quarterly, 12*(4), 560–561.

Houston, H. M. (1989, March). *Professional development for restructuring: Analyses and recommendations.* Paper presented at the annual meeting of the American Educational Research Association, San Francisco.

Howard, E. R., & Bardwell, R. W. (1974). How to organize a non-graded school. In *Handbook of successful school administration* (pp. 196–234). Englewood Cliffs, NJ: Prentice-Hall.

Howard, G. G. (1958). The children we teach. In *The elementary school principalship: A research study: Thirty-seventh yearbook of the Department of Elementary School Principals* (pp. 1–12). Washington, DC: NEA.

Hoyle, J. R., English, F. W., & Steffy, B. F. (1985). *Skills for successful school leaders.* Arlington, VA: American Association for School Administrators.

Huebner, D. (1975). The contradiction between the recreative and the established. In J. B. Macdonald & E. Zaret (Eds.), *Schools in search of meaning: 1975 yearbook of the Association for Supervision and Curriculum Development* (pp. 27–38). Washington, DC: Author.

Huggett, A. J. (1950). *Practical school administration.* Champaign, IL: Gerrard.

Hunt, D. (1952). Factors in good staff relationships. In *Bases for effective learning: Thirty-first yearbook of the Department of Elementary School Principals* (pp. 52–56). Washington, DC: NEA.

Hunt, H. C., & Pierce, P. R. (1958). *The practice of school administration.* Boston: Houghton Mifflin.

Hutchins, C. L. (1988). Redesigning education: A report of a task force on new directions for regional educational laboratories. In Far West Laboratory, *The redesign of education* (Vol. 1, pp. 73–78). San Francisco: Far West Laboratory for Research and Development.

Immegart, G. L. (1971). Suggestions for leadership research: Toward a strategy for the study of leadership in education. In L. Cunningham & W. J. Gephardt (Eds.), *Leadership: The art and the science today* (pp. 219–251). Itasca, IL: F. E. Peacock.

Inbar, D. B. (1977, May). Perceived authority and responsibility of elementary school principals in Israel. *Journal of Educational Administration, 15*(1), 80–91.

Jameson, M. (1957). Include the nonprofessional staff, too. In *Parents and the schools: Thirty-sixth yearbook of the Department of Elementary School Principals* (pp. 57–61). Washington, DC: NEA.

Johnson, F. W. (1925). *The administration and supervision of the high school.* New York: Ginn.

Johnston, C. H., Newlon, D. H., & Pickell, F. G. (1922). *Junior–senior high school administration.* Atlanta: Charles Scribner's Sons.

Jones, J. L., Salisbury, C. J., & Spencer R. L. (1969). *Secondary school administration*. New York: McGraw-Hill.

Jordan, R. E. (1970). Love in administration. In L. E. Bradfield & L. E. Kraft (Eds.), *The elementary school principal* (pp. 3–19). Scranton, PA: International Textbook.

Kasten, K. L. (1984). The efficacy of institutionally based rewards in elementary school teaching. *Journal of Research & Development in Education, 17*(4), 1–13.

Katz, D., & Kahn, R. L. (1966). *The social psychology of organizations*. New York: John Wiley.

Kearns, D. L. (1988, April). An education recovery plan for America. *Phi Delta Kappan, 69*(8), 565–570.

Keller, C. R. (1963). The "cutting edge" of education. In A. E. Traxler (Eds.), *Frontiers of education: Report of the twenty-seventh conference of the Educational Records Bureau* (pp. 158–165). Washington, DC: American Council on Education.

Kelley, B. F., & Bredeson, P. V. (1987). *Principals as symbol managers: Measures of meaning in schools*. Paper presented at the annual meeting of the American Educational Research Association, Washington, DC.

Kerchner, C. T. (1988, November). Bureaucratic entrepreneurship: The implications of choice for school administration. *Educational Administration Quarterly, 24*(4), 381–392.

Kilpatrick, W. H., & Van Til, W. (1947). *Intercultural attitudes in the making: Parents, youth leaders, and teachers at work*. (9th yearbook of the John Dewey Society). New York: Harper & Brothers.

Kirkpatrick, F. G. (1986). *Community: A trinity of models*. Washington, DC: Georgetown University Press.

Kirst, M. W., McLaughlin, M., & Massell, D. (1989). *Rethinking children's policy: Implications for educational administration*. Stanford, CA: Stanford University, Center for Educational Research at Stanford.

Koopman, G. R., Miel, A., & Misner, P. J. (1943). *Democracy in school administration*. New York: Appleton-Century-Crofts.

Koos, L. V. (1924). *The high-school principal: His training, experience, and responsibilities*. New York: Houghton Mifflin.

Koos, L. V., Hughes, D. M., Hudson, P. M., & Reavis, W. C. (1940). *Administering the secondary school*. New York: American Book Co.

Kopp, A. W. (1958). Challenges facing the principalship. In *The elementary school principalship: A research study: Thirty-seventh yearbook of the Department of Elementary School Principals* (pp. 200–220). Washington, DC: NEA.

Kroeze, D. J. (1984). Effective principals as instructional leaders: New directions for research. *Administrator's Notebook, 30*(9), 1–4.

Kyte, G. C. (1952). *The principal at work*. Boston: Ginn.

Lakoff, G., & Johnson, M. (1980). *Metaphors we live by*. Chicago: University of Chicago Press.

Law, D., & Lodge, P. (1984). *Science for the social scientist*. Chicago: University of Chicago Press.

Le Tendre, B. (1990, April). *Implementing accelerated schools: Issues at the state level.* Paper presented at the annual meeting of the American Educational Research Association, Boston.

Lee, G. V. (1987). Instructional leadership in junior high school: Managing realities and creating opportunities. In W. Greenfield (Ed.), *Instructional leadership: Concepts, issues, and controversies* (pp. 77–99). Newton, MA: Allyn & Bacon.

Leithwood, K. A., & Montgomery, D. J. (1982). The role of the principal in program development. *Review of Educational Research, 52*(3), 309–339.

Leithwood, K. A., & Montgomery, D. J. (1984, April). *Patterns of growth in principal effectiveness.* Paper presented at the annual meeting of the American Educational Research Association, New Orleans.

Leithwood, K. A., & Montgomery, D. J. (1986). *Improving principal effectiveness: The principal profile.* Toronto: Ontario Institute for Studies in Education.

Lewis, A. J., Grant, W. R. F., King, R. N., Reynolds, G. P., & Robinson, H. W. (1954). Checklist for the principal. In *Time for the job* (pp. 19, 21). Washington, DC: NEA.

Lightfoot, S. L. (1983). *The good high school: Portraits of character and culture.* New York: Basic Books.

Limpus, A. M. (1943). Air-raid drills as citizenship experiences. In *Elementary schools—The frontline of democracy: Twenty-second yearbook of the Department of Elementary School principals* (pp. 451–456). Washington, DC: NEA.

Lindquist, R. D. (1933). *Effective instructional leadership: A study of the problem of integration.* New York: Bureau of Publications, Teachers College, Columbia University.

Lipham, J. M., Rankin, R. E., & Hoeh, J. A. (1985). *The principalship: Concepts, competencies, and cases.* New York: Logan.

Lipham, J. M. (1981). *Effective principals, effective schools.* Reston, VA: National Association for Secondary School Principals.

Lipham, J. M., & Hoeh, J. A. (1974). *The principalship: Foundations and functions.* New York: Harper & Row.

Little, J. W. (1982, Fall). Norms of collegiality and experimentation: Work place conditions of school success. *American Educational Research Journal, 19*(3), 325–340.

Little, J. W., & Bird, T. (1987). Instructional leadership "close to the classroom" in secondary schools. In W. Greenfield (Ed.), *Instructional leadership: Concepts, issues, and controversies* (pp. 118–138). Newton, MA: Allyn & Bacon.

Litwak, E. (1969). Models of bureaucracy which permit conflict. In F. D. Carver & T. J. Sergiovanni (Eds.), *Organizations and human behavior: Focus on schools* (pp. 82–90). New York: McGraw-Hill.

Lortie, D. C. (1961). *Craftsmen and colleagueship.* Paper presented at the annual meeting of the American Sociological Association, St. Louis.

Lotto, L. S., & Murphy, J. (1990). Making sense of schools as organizations: Cognition and sensemaking in schools. In P. W. Thurston & L. S. Lotto (Eds.), *Advances in educational administration* (Vol. IB, pp. 201–240). Greenwich, CT: JAI Press.

Louis, K. S., & Cipollene, A. (1987, April). *Causal model of the change process.* Paper presented at the annual meeting of the American Educational Research Association, Washington, DC.

Maccoby, M. (1988, November–December). A new model for leadership. *Research Technology Management, 31*(6), 53–54.

Macdonald, J. B. (1975). The quality of everyday life in schools. In J. B. Macdonald & E. Zaret (Eds.) *Schools in search of meaning: 1975 yearbook of the Association for Supervision and Curriculum Development* (pp. 78–94). Washington, DC: Author.

Macdonald, J. B., & Zaret, E. (Eds.). (1975). *Schools in search of meaning: 1975 yearbook of the Association for Supervision and Curriculum Development.* Washington, DC: Author.

Macmurray, J. (1957). *The self as agent.* London: Faber.

Manning, P. (1979). Metaphors of the field varieties of organizational discourse. *Administrative Science Quarterly, 24,* 660–671.

March, J. G. (1978, February). American public school administration: A short analysis. *School Review, 86,* 217–250.

March, J. G., & Simon, H. A. (1969). Dysfunctions in organizations. In F. D. Carver & T. J. Sergiovanni (Eds.), *Organizations and human behavior: Focus on schools* (pp. 63–70). New York: McGraw-Hill.

Marshall, H. H. (1990a, Spring). Beyond the workplace metaphor: The classroom as a learning setting. *Theory Into Practice, 24*(2), 94–101.

Marshall, H. H. (1990b, Spring). Metaphor as an instructional tool in encouraging student teacher reflection. *Theory Into Practice, 24*(2), 128–132.

Maslow, A. (1965). *Eupsychian management: A journal.* Homewood, IL: Richard D. Irwin.

Maslow, A. (1970). *Motivation and personality.* New York: Harper & Row.

Mason, R. (1986). From idea to ideology: School administration texts 1820–1914. In T. E. Glass (Ed.), *An analysis of texts on school administration 1820–1985: The reciprocal relationship between the literature and the profession* (pp. 1–21). Danville, IL: Interstate.

Maxwell, F. M. (1954). Ten ways the principal guides. In *Guidance for today's children. Thirty-third yearbook of the Department of Elementary School Principals* (pp. 25–29). Washington, DC: NEA.

Mayo, E. (1933). *The human problems of an industrial civilization.* Boston: Harvard University Press.

Mayo, E. (1945). *The social problems of an industrial civilization.* Boston: Harvard University Press.

McCarthey, S. J., & Peterson, P. L. (1989, March). *Teacher roles: Weaving new patterns in classroom practice and school organization.* Paper presented at the annual meeting of the American Educational Research Association, San Francisco.

McClure, W. (1956, May). Seven keys to leadership. *Nation's Schools, 57,* 47.

McEvoy, B. (1987, February). Everyday acts: How principals influence development of their staffs. *Educational Leadership, 44*(5), 73–77.

McNeil L. M. (1988a, January). Contradictions of control, part 1: Administrators and teachers. *Phi Delta Kappan, 69*(5), 333–339.

McNeil, L. M. (1988b, February). Contradictions of control, part 2: Teachers, students, and curriculum. *Phi Delta Kappan, 69*(6), 432–438.

McNeil, L. M. (1988c, March). Contradictions of control, part 3: Contradictions of reform. *Phi Delta Kappan, 69*(7), 478–485.

McQuade, W. (1959). The site and its climate. In *Elementary school buildings: Design for learning: Thirty-eighth yearbook of the Department of Elementary School Principals* (pp. 103–109). Washington, DC: NEA.

McSwain, E. T. (1945). Misunderstandings of teacher–pupil planning. In *Group planning in education: 1945 yearbook of the Department of Supervision and Curriculum Development* (pp. 11–19). Washington, DC: NEA.

Meindl, J. R., Ehrlich, S. B., & Dukerich, J. M. (1985, March). The romance of leadership. *Administrative Science Quarterly, 30*, 78–102.

Messinger, M. G. (1939). *The non-teaching elementary school principal in the state of New Jersey.* Unpublished dissertation, Temple University, Camden, NJ.

Meyer, J. W., & Rowan, B. (1975). *Notes on the structure of educational organizations: Revised version.* Paper presented at the annual meeting of the American Sociological Association, San Francisco.

Miel, A. (1944). Living in a modern world. In *Toward a new curriculum: Extending the educational opportunity of children, youth, and adults: 1944 yearbook of the Department of Supervision and Curriculum Development* (pp. 11–22). Washington, DC: NEA.

Miles, M. B. (1987, April). *Practical guidelines for school administrators: How to get there.* Paper presented at the annual meeting of the American Educational Research Association, Washington, DC.

Miles, R. E. (1965). Human relations or human resources. *Harvard Business Review, 43*, 148–163.

Millard, M. C. (1944). A make-believe air raid. In *Creative schools: Twenty-third yearbook of the Department of Elementary School Principals* (pp. 144–149). Washington, DC: NEA.

Miller, L. R. (1952). Identifying the outsider. In *Bases for effective learning: Thirty-first yearbook of the Department of Elementary School Principals* (pp. 156–161). Washington, DC: NEA.

Miller, S. I., & Fredericks, M. (1988). Uses of metaphor: A qualitative case study. *Qualitative Studies in Education, 1*(3), 263–272.

Miller, S. K., & Brookover, W. B. (1986, April). *School effectiveness versus individual differences: Paradigmatic perspectives on the legitimation of economic and educational inequalities.* Paper presented at the annual meeting of the American Educational Research Association, San Francisco.

Miller, V. (1957). Assessment and projection. In R. F. Campbell & R. T. Gregg (Eds.), *Administrative behavior in education* (pp. 513–530). New York: Harper & Brothers.

Miller, V. (1963). *Common and specialized learnings for educational administration* (UCEA position paper). Columbus, OH: The University Council for Educational Administration.

Mintzberg, H. (1973). *The nature of managerial work.* New York: Harper & Row.

Moeller, G. H., & Charters, W. W. (1969). Relation of bureaucratization to sense of power among teachers. In F. D. Carver & T. J. Sergiovanni (Eds.), *Organizations and human behavior: Focus on schools* (pp. 235–249). New York: McGraw-Hill.

Mojkowski, C., & Fleming, D. (1988, May). *School-site management: Concepts and approaches*. Andover, MA: Regional Laboratory for Educational Improvement of the Northeast and Islands.

Montagu, A. (1955). *The direction of human development*. New York: Harper & Brothers.

Moore, H. A. (1964). The ferment in school administration. In D. E. Griffiths (Ed.), *Behavioral science and educational administration* (63rd yearbook of the National Society for the Study of Education, Part II) (pp. 11–32). Chicago: University of Chicago Press.

Morgan, G. (1986). *Images of organization*. Beverly Hills, CA: Sage.

Morris, V. C., Crowson, R. L., Porter-Gehrie, C., & Hurwitz, E. (1984). *Principals in action: The reality of managing schools*. Columbus, OH: Charles E. Merrill.

Morris, W. A. (1955). Reducing reading problems through organization. In *Reading for today's children: Thirty-fourth yearbook of the Department of Elementary School Principals* (pp. 58–62). Washington, DC: NEA.

Munby, H. (1986). Metaphor in the thinking of teachers: An exploratory study. *Journal of Curriculum Studies, 18*, 197–209.

Munby, H. (1987). Metaphor and teachers' knowledge. *Research in the Teaching of English, 21*, 377–397.

Munby, H., & Russell, T. (1990, Spring). Metaphor in the study of teachers' professional knowledge. *Theory Into Practice, 24*(2), 116–121.

Murdy, L. L. (1962). *Perceptions of interpersonal relationships among secondary school administrators*. Unpublished doctoral dissertation, University of Southern California, Los Angeles.

Murphy, A. B. (1931). *Basic training for city school superintendents*. Unpublished doctoral dissertation, University of California, Berkeley.

Murphy, J. F. (1988, Summer). Methodological, measurement, and conceptual problems in the study of administrator instructional leadership. *Educational Evaluation and Policy Analysis, 10*(2), 117–139.

Murphy, J. F. (1990a). Preparing school administrators for the twenty-first century: The reform agenda. In B. Mitchell & L. L. Cunningham (Eds.), *Educational leadership and changing contexts of families, communities, and schools* (pp. 232–251). Chicago: University of Chicago Press.

Murphy, J. F. (1990b). The educational reform movement of the 1980s: A comprehensive analysis. In J. Murphy (Ed.), *The reform of American public education in the 1980s: Perspectives and cases* (pp. 3–55). Berkeley: McCutchan.

Murphy, J. F. (1990c, August). *Restructuring America's schools*. Charleston, WV: Appalachia Educational Laboratory.

Murphy, J. F. (1990d). Principal instructional leadership. In P. W. Thurston & L. S. Lotto (Eds.), *Recent advances in educational administration* (Vol. IB, pp. 163–200). Greenwich, CT: JAI Press.

Murphy, J. F. (1990e). The reform of school administration: Pressures and calls for change. In J. Murphy (Ed.), *The reform of American public education in the 1980s: Perspectives and cases* (pp. 277–303). Berkeley, CA: McCutchan.

Murphy, J. F. (1991a). *Restructuring schools: Capturing and assessing the phenomena.* New York: Teachers College Press.

Murphy, J. F. (1991b, Spring). The effects of the educational reform movement on departments of educational leadership. *Educational Evaluation and Policy Analysis, 13*(1), 49–65.

Murphy, J. F. (1992). *The landscape of leadership preparation: Patterns and possibilities.* Beverly Hills, CA: Corwin.

Murphy, J. F., Hallinger, P., Lotto, L. S., & Miller, S. K. (1987, December). Barriers to implementing the instructional leadership role. *Canadian Administrator, 27*(3), 1–9.

Murphy, J. F., Hallinger, P., & Peterson, K. D. (1985, October). Supervising and evaluating principals: Lessons from effective school districts. *Educational Leadership, 43*(2), 78–82.

Murphy, J. F., Hallinger, P., & Peterson, K. D. (1986). The administrative control of principals in effective school districts: The supervision and evaluation functions. *The Urban Review, 18*(3), 149–175.

Murphy, J. F., Hallinger, P., Peterson, K. D., & Lotto, L. S. (1987, Summer). The administrative control of principals in effective school districts. *Journal of Educational Administration, 25*(2), 161–192.

Murphy, J. F., Hallinger, P., Weil, M., & Mitman, A. (1983, Fall). Instructional leadership. A conceptual framework. *Planning and Changing, 14*(3), 137–149.

Murphy, J. F., Weil, M., Hallinger, P., & Mitman, A. (1982, December). Academic press: Translating high expectations into school policies and classroom practices. *Educational Leadership, 40*(3), 22–26.

Murphy, M. J., & Hart, A. W. (1988, October). *Preparing principals to lead in restructured schools.* Paper presented at the annual meeting of the University Council for Educational Administration, Cincinnati.

Nash, P. (1970). *Motivation and authority.* Paper presented at the Centennial Conference on Human Motivation, Ohio State University, Cleveland, OH.

National Commission on Excellence in Education. (1983). *A nation at risk: The imperative for educational reform.* Washington, DC: Government Printing Office.

National Commission on Excellence in Educational Administration. (1987). *Leaders for America's schools.* Tempe, AZ: University Council for Educational Administration.

National Conference of Professors of Educational Administration. (1948). *Educational leaders—Their function and preparation* (Report of the second conference). Madison, WI: Author.

National Education Association. (1958). *The elementary school principalship: A research study: Thirty-seventh yearbook of the Department of Elementary School Principals.* Washington, DC: Author.

National Education Association Research Division. (1958a). School resources available to the principal. In *The elementary school principal: A research study: Thirty-seventh yearbook of the Department of Elementary School Principals.* Washington, DC: NEA.

National Education Association Research Division. (1958b). The principal's average workweek. In *The elementary school principalship: A research study: Thirty-seventh yearbook of the Department of Elementary School Principals* (pp. 97–104). Washington, DC: NEA.

National Governors' Association. (1986). *The governors' 1991 report on education—time for results—1991.* Washington, DC: Author.

National Science Board. (1983). *Educating Americans for the 21st century.* Washington, DC: National Science Board, National Science Foundation.

National Society for the Study of Education. (1953). *The community school.* Chicago: University of Chicago Press.

Newell, C. A. (1978). *Human behavior in educational administration.* Englewood Cliffs, NJ: Prentice-Hall.

Newlon, J. H. (1934). *Educational administration as social policy.* San Francisco: Charles Scribner's Sons.

Noar, G. (1961). *The junior high school: Today and tomorrow.* Englewood Cliffs, NJ: Prentice-Hall.

Noddings, N. (1984). *Caring: A feminine approach to ethics and moral education.* Berkeley: University of California.

Noddings, N. (1988, February). An ethic of caring and its implications for instructional arrangements. *American Journal of Education, 12*(2), 215–230.

Noll, V. (1961). Preservice preparation of teachers in measurement. In A. E. Traxler (Ed.), *Measurement and research in today's schools: Report of the twenty-fifth conference of the Educational Records Bureau and the American Council on Education* (pp. 65–75). Washington, DC: American Council on Education.

Norton, J. K. (1957). The contemporary scene. In R. F. Campbell & R. T. Gregg (Eds.), *Administrative behavior in education* (pp. 41–82). New York: Harper & Brothers.

Nultan, L. (1954). Administration is sharing. In *Time for the job* (pp. 29–33). Washington, DC: NEA.

Oakes, J. (1985). *Keeping track: How schools structure inequality.* New Haven: Yale University Press.

Ogbu, J. U. (1981). School ethnography: A multilevel approach. *Anthropology and Education Quarterly, 12*(1), 23–29.

Ohlsen, M. M., Anderson, S., Sides, R. W., Roose, M., & Litterick, W. S. (1963). Better interpretation of test results. In A. E. Traxler (Ed.), *Frontiers of education: Report of the twenty-seventh conference of the Educational Records Bureau* (pp. 84–98). Washington, DC: American Council on Education.

Ortony, A. (1979). *Metaphor and thought.* Cambridge, MA: Cambridge University Press.

Owens, R. G., & Shakeshaft, C. (1987, October). *Teaching administrative theory: The educational reform movement of the 1980's.* Paper presented at the convention of the University Council for Educational Administration, Charlottesville, VA.

Owens, R. G., & Steinhoff, C. R. (1989). Toward a theory of organizational culture. *Journal of Educational Administration, 27*(3), 6–16.

Paivio, A. (1979). Psychological processes in the comprehension of metaphor. In A. Ortony (Ed.), *Metaphor and thought* (pp. 150–171). Cambridge, MA: Cambridge University Press.

Parker, D. C. (1986). From conventional wisdom to concept: School administration texts 1934–1945. In T. E. Glass (Ed.), *An analysis of texts on school administration 1820–1985: The reciprocal relationship between the literature and the profession* (pp. 39–75). Danville, IL: Interstate.

Patina, P. (1988). *Metaphor and the high school principalship.* Unpublished doctoral dissertation, Hofstra University, Hempstead, NY.

Patterson, C. H. (1977). Insights about persons: Psychological foundations of humanistic and affective education. In L. M. Berman & J. A. Roderick (Eds.), *Feeling, valuing, and the art of growing: Insights into the affective: 1977 yearbook of the Association for Supervision and Curriculum Development* (pp. 145–181). Washington, DC: Author.

Payne, A. C. (1931, September). Buying supplies on scientific lines. *School Executive Magazine, 21,* 16.

Pearson, E. M. (1952). A newsletter for parents. In *Bases for effective learning: Thirty-first yearbook of the Department of Elementary School Principals* (pp. 126–128). Washington, DC: NEA.

Perkins, B. (1974). Getting better results from substitutes, teacher aides, and volunteers. In *Handbook of successful school administration* (pp. 1–48). Englewood Cliffs, NJ: Prentice-Hall.

Perrin, S. (1987). Metaphorical revelations: A description of metaphor as the reciprocal engagement of abstract perspectives and concrete phenomena in experience. *Metaphor and Symbolic Activity, 2,* 251–280.

Persell, C. H., & Cookson, P. W. (1982). The effective principal in action. In *The effective principal: A research summary* (pp. 22–29). Reston, VA: National Association for Secondary School Principals.

Peterson, K. D. (1987). Administrative control and instructional leadership. In W. Greenfield (Ed.), *Instructional leadership: Concepts, issues, and controversies* (pp. 139–154). Newton, MA: Allyn & Bacon.

Petrie, H. G. (1990). Reflections on the second wave of reform: Restructuring the teaching profession. In S. L. Jacobson & J. A. Conway (Eds.), *Educational leadership in an age of reform* (pp. 14–29). New York: Longman.

Phi Delta Kappa. (1982). *The role of the principal.* Bloomington, IN: Author.

Phi Delta Kappa. (1983, March). Inservice education. *Practical Applications for Research, 5*(3), 1–4.

Phillips, H. W. (1952). It's fun to play together. In *Bases for effective learning: Thirty-first yearbook of the Department of Elementary School Principals* (pp. 235–241). Washington, DC: NEA.

Pierce, P. R. (1935). *The origin and development of the public school principalship.* Chicago: University of Chicago Press.

Postel, H. H. (1955). Motivating reading thru the school newspaper. In *Reading for today's children: Thirty-fourth yearbook of the Department of Elementary School Principals.* Washington, DC: NEA.

Pounder, D. G. (1987). The challenge for school leaders: Attracting and retaining good teachers. In W. Greenfield (Ed.), *Instructional leadership: Concepts, issues, and controversies* (pp. 287–301). Newton, MA: Allyn & Bacon.

Powell, A. G., Farrar, E., & Cohen, D. (1985). *The shopping mall high school: Winners and losers in the educational marketplace.* Boston: Houghton Mifflin.

Prall, C. (1944). Community organization and cooperation. In *Toward a new curriculum: 1944 yearbook of the Department of Supervision and Curriculum Development.* Washington, DC: NEA.

Prosser, C. (1939). *Secondary education and life.* Cambridge, MA: Harvard University Press.

Purpel, D. E. (1989). *The moral and spiritual crisis in education: A curriculum for justice and compassion in education.* Granby, MA: Bergin & Garvey.

Quality Education for Minorities Project. (1990). *Education that works: An action plan for the education of minorities.* Cambridge: Massachusetts Institute of Technology.

Rallis, S. F. (1990). Professional teachers and restructured schools: Leadership challenges. In B. Mitchell & L. L. Cunningham (Eds.), *Educational leadership and changing contexts of families, communities, and schools* (pp. 184–209). Chicago: University of Chicago Press.

Ransberger, M. (1946). Supervision in the American scene. In *Leadership through supervision: 1946 yearbook of the Association for Supervision and Curriculum Development* (pp. 17–26). Washington, DC: NEA.

Ravitch, D. (1974). *The great school wars: New York City, 1905–1973: A history of the public schools as battlefield of social change.* New York: Basic Books.

Ravitch, D. (1983). *The troubled crusade, American education, 1945–1989.* New York: Basic Books.

Reavis, W. C., Pierce, R., & Stullken, E. H. (1931). *The elementary school, its organization and administration.* Chicago: University of Chicago Press.

Reber, D. D. (1948). The principal interprets his school. *Bulletin of the National Association of Secondary School Principals, 32*(152), 73–80.

Reiffel, S. M. (1952). Helping children achieve emotional stability. In *Bases for effective learning: Thirty-first yearbook of the Department of Elementary School Principals* (pp. 201–204). Washington, DC: NEA.

Rich, L. M. (1954). Clerical help for principals. In *Time for the job* (pp. 33–36). Washington, DC: NEA.

Roberts, D. (1952). Improving the status of isolates. In *Bases for effective learning: Thirty-first yearbook of the Department of Elementary School Principals* (pp. 183–188). Washington, DC: NEA.

Rock, D. A., & Hemphill, D. K. (1966). *Report of the junior high-school principalship: Vol. 2. The Study of the Secondary School Principalship.* Washington, DC: National Association of Secondary School Principals.

Roderick, J. A. (1977). Describing persons in settings: Making the affective explicit. In L. M. Berman & J. A. Roderick (Eds.), *Feeling, valuing, and the art of growing: Insights into the affective: 1977 yearbook of the Association for Supervision and Curriculum Development* (pp. 203–228). Washington, DC: Author.

Roe, W. H., & Drake, T. L. (1974). *The principalship.* New York: Macmillan.

Roethlisberger, F. J. (1941). *Management and morale.* Cambridge, MA: Harvard University Press.

Roethlisberger, F. J., & Dickson, W. J. (1939). *Management and the worker.* Cambridge, MA: Harvard University Press.

Rogers, C. R. (1961). *On becoming a person.* Boston: Houghton Mifflin.

Rogers, V. M. (1945). We all plan. In *Group planning in education: 1945 yearbook of the Department of Supervision and Curriculum Development* (pp. 110–115). Washington, DC: NEA.

Rosenblatt, L. M. (1963). Reappraisal of the English curriculum. In A. E. Traxler (Ed.), *Frontiers of education: Report of the twenty-seventh conference of the Educational Records Bureau* (pp. 63–73). Washington, DC: American Council on Education.

Rosenholtz, S. J. (1985, May). Effective schools: Interpreting the evidence. *American Journal of Education, 93*(2), 352–387.

Rosenholtz, S. J. (1989). *Teachers' workplace: The social organization of schools.* New York: Longman.

Rosenholtz, S. J., & Simpson, C. (1990). Workplace conditions and the rise and fall of teachers' commitment. *Sociology of Education, 63*(4), 241–257.

Ross, D. A., & MacDonald, J. D. (n.d.). *Principals do make a difference.* ORE Series on Effective Schools: Successful Instruction (Publication No. 81.32). Austin Independent School District, Office of Research and Evaluation.

Rushton, E. W. (1963). Experimentation with three methods of instruction in high school mathematics. In A. E. Traxler (Ed.), *Frontiers of education: Report of the twenty-seventh conference of the Educational Records Bureau* (pp. 74–78). Washington, DC: American Council on Education.

Rutherford, W. (1985). School principals as effective leaders. *Phi Delta Kappan, 67*(1), 31–34.

Sapone, C. O. (1985). Curriculum: The basis for instructional leadership, the principal's role. *Catalyst for Change, 14*(2), 4–7.

Sarason, S. (1971). *The culture of the school and the problem of change.* Boston: Allyn & Bacon.

Sargent C., & Belisle, E. L. (1955). *Educational administration: Cases and concepts.* Boston: Houghton Mifflin.

Schlechty, P. C. (1990). *Schools for the twenty-first century: Leadership imperatives for educational reform.* San Francisco: Jossey-Bass.

Schön, D. A. (1979). Generative metaphor: A perspective on problem-setting in social policy. In A. Ortony (Ed.), *Metaphor and thought* (pp. 254–283). Cambridge, MA: Cambridge University Press.

Schott, A. H. (1956). Adventure in arithmetic. In *Instructional materials for elementary schools: Thirty-fifth yearbook of the Department of Elementary School Principals* (pp. 86–90). Washington, DC: NEA.

Scott, G. (1952). Leadership in studying behavior problems. In *Bases for effective learning: Thirty-first yearbook of the Department of Elementary School Principals* (pp. 56–60). Washington, DC: NEA.

Searle, J. R. (1979). Standard approaches to metaphor and a proposal for literary metaphor. In A. Ortony (Ed.), *Metaphor and thought* (pp. 92–123). Cambridge, MA: Cambridge University Press.

Sedlack, M. W., Wheeler C. W., Pullin, D. C., & Cusick, P. A. (1986). *Selling students short: Classroom bargains and academic reform in the American High School.* New York: Teachers College Press.

Seeley, D. S. (1980, February). *The bankruptcy of service delivery.* Paper presented at the Foundation Lunch Group: Panel on Children, Edwin Gould Foundation for Children, New York.

Seeley, D. S. (1988, February). A new vision for public education. *Youth Policy, 10*(2), 34–36.

Senate Select Committee on Equal Educational Opportunity. (1970). *Toward equal educational opportunity: The report of the Senate Select Committee on Equal Educational Opportunity.* Washington, DC: Government Printing Office.

Sergiovanni, T. J. (1989). Value-driven schools: The amoeba theory. In H. T. Walberg & J. J. Lane (Eds.), *Organizing for learning: Toward the 21st century.* Reston, VA: National Association of Secondary School Principals.

Sergiovanni, T. J. (1992). *Moral leadership: Getting to the heart of school improvement.* San Francisco: Jossey-Bass.

Sergiovanni, T. J., Burlingame, M., Coombs, F. S., & Thurston, P. W. (1980). *Educational governance and administration.* Englewood Cliffs, NJ: Prentice-Hall.

Sergiovanni, T. J., & Carver, F. D. (1973). *The new school executive: A theory of administration.* New York: Dodd, Mead.

Sergiovanni, T. J., & Corbally, J. E. (Eds.) (1984). *Leadership and organizational culture: New perspectives on administrative theory and practice.* Urbana: University of Illinois Press.

Sergiovanni, T. J., & Starratt, R. J. (1971). *Emerging patterns of supervision: Human perspectives.* New York: McGraw-Hill.

Sheets, W. W. (1986). *The perceptions and expectations of principals, teachers, and parents from selected public elementary schools regarding the role of the elementary school principal.* Unpublished doctoral dissertation, George Peabody College, Nashville, TN.

Shields, V. L. (1955). Local and state cooperation for improved reading. In *Reading for today's children: Thirty-fourth yearbook of the Department of Elementary School Principals* (pp. 227–234). Washington, DC: NEA.

Shuell, T. J. (1990). Teaching and learning as problem solving. *Theory Into Practice, 24*(2), 102–109.

Simon, H. A. (1950). *Administrative behavior.* New York: Macmillan.

Simpson, E. L. (1977). The person in community: The need to belong. In L. M. Berman & J. A. Roderick (Eds.), *Feeling, valuing, and the art of growing: Insights into the affective: 1977 yearbook of the Association for Supervision and Curriculum Development* (pp. 181–201). Washington, DC: Author.

Sizemore, B. A. (1974). Community power and education. In D. Della-Dora &

J. E. House (Eds.), *Education for an open society: 1974 yearbook of the Association for Supervision and Curriculum Development* (pp. 109–136). Washington, DC: Author.

Sizer, T. R. (1973). *Places for learning, places for joy: Speculations on American school reform.* Cambridge, MA: Harvard University Press.

Sizer, T. R. (1984). *Horace's compromise: The dilemma of the American high school.* Boston: Houghton Mifflin.

Small, J. F. (1974). Initiating and responding to social change. In J. A. Culbertson, C. Henson, & R. Morrison (Eds.), *Performance objectives for school principals: Concepts and instruments* (pp. 18–53). Berkeley, CA: McCutchan.

Smircich, L. (1983, September). Concepts of culture and organizational analysis. *Administrative Science Quarterly, 28*(3), 339–388.

Smith, M. B. (1955). Reading "musts" contribute to living. In *Reading for today's children: Thirty-fourth yearbook of the Department of Elementary School Principals* (pp. 7–12). Washington, DC: NEA.

Smith, W. F., & Andrews, R. L. (1989). *Instructional leadership: How principals make a difference.* Alexandria, VA: Association for Supervision and Curriculum Development.

Snyder, D. C. (1957). Leadership in staff relationships. In *Parents and the school: Thirty-sixth yearbook of the Department of Elementary School Principals* (pp. 52–56). Washington, DC: NEA.

Snyder, K. J. (1983). Instructional leadership for productive schools. *Educational Leadership, 40*(5), 32–37.

Solberg, J. (1968, September). Community relations, I want them to know that we care. *School Management,* 36–44.

Spady, W. G. (1988, October). Organizing for results: The basis of authentic restructuring and reform. *Educational Leadership, 46*(2), 4–8.

Starkey, M. L. (1952). Meeting the needs of children. In *Instructional materials for elementary schools: Thirty-first yearbook of the Department of Elementary School Principals* (pp. 215–219). Washington, DC: NEA.

Staw, B. (1984). Leadership and persistence. In T. J. Sergiovanni & J. H. Corbally (Eds.), *Leadership and organizational culture: New perspectives on administrative theory and practice* (pp. 72–84). Urbana: University of Illinois Press.

Steinhoff, C. R., & Owens, R. G. (1989). The organizational culture assessment inventory: A metaphorical analysis in educational settings. *Journal of Educational Administration, 27*(1), 17–23.

Stevens, A. (1974). Techniques for handling problem parents. In *Handbook of successful school administration* (pp. 607–650). Englewood Cliffs, NJ: Prentice-Hall.

Stoddard, G. D. (1963). An exciting time to be in education. In A. E. Traxler (Ed.), *Frontiers of education: Report of the twenty-seventh conference of the Educational Records Bureau* (pp. 13–22). Washington, DC: American Council on Education.

Stodgill, R. M. (1971). The trait approach to the study of educational leadership. In L. Cunningham & W. J. Gephardt (Eds.), *Leadership: The art and the science today* (pp. 83–107). Itasca, IL: F. E. Peacock.

Story, B. (1952). The "good life" in the elementary school. In *Bases for effective learning: Thirty-first yearbook of the Department of Elementary School Principals* (pp. 18–22). Washington, DC: NEA.

Strayer, G. (1930). Progress in city school administration during the past twenty-five years. *School and Society, 32*, 375–378.

Street, S. W. (1957). How far can parents go? In *Parents and the schools: Thirty-sixth yearbook of the Department of Elementary School Principals* (pp. 11–21). Washington, DC: NEA.

Strother, D. P. (1982). The many roles of the effective school principal. *Phi Delta Kappan, 65*(4), 291–294.

Study, H. P. (1945). Administration takes a step forward. In *Group planning in education: 1945 yearbook Department of Supervision and Curriculum Development* (pp. 121–129). Washington, DC: NEA.

Sykes, A. J. M. (1962). The effect of a supervisory training course in changing supervisors' perceptions and expectations of the role of management. *Human Relations, 15*, 227–243.

Sykes, G., & Elmore, R. F. (1989). Making schools manageable: Policy and administration for tomorrow's schools. In J. Hannaway & R. Crowson (Eds.), *The politics of reforming school administration*. New York: Falmer.

Taggart, L. A., & Evans, M. C. (1946a). Analyzing our problems. In *Leadership through supervision: 1946 yearbook of the Association for Supervision and Curriculum Development* (pp. 27–76). Washington, DC: NEA.

Taggart, L. A., & Evans, M. C. (1946b). A look at our best. In *Leadership through supervision: 1946 yearbook of the Association for Supervision and Curriculum Development* (pp. 77–114). Washington, DC: NEA.

Tannenbaum, R. (1950). Managerial decision-making. *Journal of Business, 23*(1), 22–29.

Taylor, B. O. (1986a, April). *Metasensemaking: How the effective elementary principal accomplishes school improvement*. Paper presented at the annual meeting of the American Educational Research Association, San Francisco.

Taylor, B. O. (1986b, April). *How and why successful elementary school principals address strategic issues*. Paper presented at the annual meeting of the American Educational Research Association, San Francisco.

Taylor, F. (1911). *The principles of scientific management*. New York: Harper & Row.

Taylor, H. (1962). Experiment at the Frontier. In A. E. Traxler (Ed.), *Frontiers of education: Report of the twenty-seventh conference of the Educational Records Bureau* (pp. 40–54). Washington, DC: American Council on Education.

Taylor, W. (1984). Metaphors of educational discourse. In W. Taylor (Ed.), *Metaphors in education* (pp. 4–20). London: Heinemann.

Teddlie, C., Wimpelberg, R., & Kirby, P. (1987, April). *Contextual differences in effective schools in Louisiana*. Paper presented at the annual meeting of the American Educational Research Association, Washington, DC.

Thompson, V. A. (1969). Hierarchy, specialization, and organizational conflict. In F. D. Carver & T. J. Sergiovanni (Eds.), *Organizations and human behavior: Focus on schools* (pp. 19–41). New York: McGraw-Hill.

Tobin, K. (1990, Spring). Changing metaphors and beliefs: A master switch for teaching. *Theory Into Practice, 24*(2), 122–127.

Torbert, W. R. (1990). Reform from the center. In B. Mitchell & L. L. Cunningham (Eds.), *Educational leadership and changing contexts of families, communities, and schools* (pp. 252–263). Chicago: University of Chicago Press.

Traxler, A. E. (Ed.). (1961). *Measurement and research in today's schools: Report of the twenty-fifth conference of the Educational Records Bureau and the American Council on Education.* Washington, DC: American Council on Education.

Traxler, A. E. (Ed.). (1962). *Improving the efficiency and quality of learning: Report of the twenty-sixth conference of the Educational Records Bureau and the American Council on Education.* Washington, DC: American Council on Education.

Traxler, A. E. (Ed.). (1965). *Innovation and experiment in modern education: Report of the twenty-ninth educational conference of the Educational Records Bureau.* Washington, DC: American Council on Education.

Trump, D. L. (1962). Quality education of the future. In A. E. Traxler (Ed.), *Frontiers of education: Report of the twenty-seventh conference of the Educational Records Bureau* (pp. 23–39). Washington, DC: American Council on Education.

Twentieth Century Fund Task Force on Federal Elementary and Educational Policy. (1983). *Making the grade.* New York: Twentieth Century Fund.

Tyack, D. B. (1974). *One best system.* Cambridge, MA: Harvard University Press.

Tyack, D. B. (1990, Winter). "Restructuring" in historical perspective: Tinkering toward utopia. *Teachers College Record, 92*(2), 170–191.

Tyack, D. B., & Hansot, E. (1982). *Managers of virtue: Public school leadership in America, 1920–1980.* New York: Basic Books.

United Community Services of Metropolitan Boston. (1971). *The community school—What it is and what it attempts to become.* Boston: Author.

Vaill, P. B. (1984). The purposing of high performing systems. In T. J. Sergiovanni & J. H. Corbally (Eds.), *Leadership and organizational culture: New perspectives on administrative theory and practice* (pp. 85–104). Urbana: University of Illinois Press.

Van Til, W. (1946). Exploring educational frontiers. In *Leadership through supervision: 1946 yearbook of the Association for Supervision and Curriculum Development* (pp. 1–16). Washington, DC: NEA.

Wagstaff, L. H., & Gallagher, K. S. (1990). Schools, families, and communities: Idealized images and new realities. In B. Mitchell & L. L. Cunningham (Eds.), *Educational leadership and changing contexts of families, communities, and schools* (pp. 91–117). Chicago: University of Chicago Press.

Walter, R. (1957). The parent–school team. In *Parents and the schools: Thirty-sixth yearbook of the Department of Elementary School Principals* (pp. 114–120). Washington, DC: NEA.

Walters, H. G. (1943). Better half a loaf than none. In *Elementary schools: The frontline of democracy: Twenty-second yearbook of the Department of Elementary School Principals* (pp. 417–422). Washington, DC: NEA.

Walzer, M. (1983). *Spheres of justice: A defense of pluralism and equality.* New York: Basic Books.

Weade, R., & Ernst, G. (1990, Spring). Pictures of life in classrooms, and the search for metaphors to frame them. *Theory Into Practice, 24*(2), 133–140.

Webb, H. A. (1953). Nine reasons why. In *Science for today's children: Thirty-second yearbook of the Department of Elementary School Principals* (p. 22). Washington, DC: NEA.

Weick, K. (1976). Educational organizations as loosely coupled systems. *Administration Science Quarterly, 2,* 1–19.

Weinberg, C. (1971). *Education and social problems.* New York: Free Press.

Wellisch, J. B., MacQueen, A. H., Carriere, R. A., & Duck, G. A. (1978, July). School management and organization in successful schools. *Sociology of Education, 51,* 211–226.

Wilhelms, F. T. (1946). Tomorrow's assignment. In *Leadership through supervision: 1946 yearbook of the Association for Supervision and Curriculum Development* (pp. 115–122). Washington, DC: NEA.

Wilhelms, F. T. (1963). *Teacher education and mental health.* Report of the Teacher Education Project sponsored by the National Institute of Mental Health.

Wimpelberg, R. K. (1986, April). *Bureaucratic and cultural images in the management of more and less effective schools.* Paper presented at the annual meeting of the American Educational Research Association, San Francisco.

Wise, A. E. (1978, February). The hyper-rationalization of American education. *Educational Leadership, 35*(5), 354–361.

Wise, A. E. (1989). Professional teaching: A new paradigm for the management of education. In T. J. Sergiovanni & J. H. Moore (Eds.), *Schooling for tomorrow: Directing reforms to issues that count* (pp. 301–310). Boston: Allyn & Bacon.

Witty, P. (1955). The principal and the classroom teacher of reading. In *Reading for today's children: Thirty-fourth yearbook of the Department of Elementary School Principals* (pp. 13–16). Washington, DC: NEA.

Wolcott, H. F. (1973). *The man in the principal's office: An ethnography.* New York: Holt, Rinehart and Winston.

Wolfe, D. P. (1974). Woman power and education. In D. Della-Dora & J. E. House (Eds.), *Education for an open society: 1974 yearbook of the Association for Supervision and Curriculum Development* (pp. 175–186). Washington, DC: Author.

Woodruff, M. (1957). Important elements in parent participation. In *Parents and the schools: Thirty-sixth yearbook of the Department of Elementary School Principals* (pp. 21–27). Washington, DC: NEA.

Woodruff, M. (1958) Part two: In the days ahead. In *The elementary school principals: A research Study: Thirty-seventh yearbook of the Department of Elementary School Principals* (pp. 90–97). Washington, DC: NEA.

Worden, J. (1971). *A tool kit for community-school development.* Unpublished manuscript, Drake University, Des Moines.

Wramp, H. M. (1944). Handwork stimulated by a war emergency. In *Creative schools: Twenty-third yearbook of the Department of Elementary School Principals* (pp. 218–221). Washington, DC: NEA.

Wynn, R. (1957). Organization and administration of the professional program. In

R. F. Campbell & R. T. Gregg (Eds.), *Administrative behavior in education* (pp. 464–512). New York: Harper & Brothers.

Yauch, W. A. (1949). *Improving human relations in school administration.* New York: Harper & Brothers.

Yeager, W. A. (1954). *Administration and the teacher.* New York: Harper & Brothers.

Zaret, E. (1975). Woman/schooling/society. In J. B. Macdonald & E. Zaret (Eds.), *Schools in search of meaning: 1975 yearbook of the Association for Supervision and Curriculum Development* (pp. 38–51). Washington, DC: Author.

Zirbes, L. (1952). The principal's challenge. In *Bases for effective learning: Thirty-first yearbook of the Department of Elementary School Principals* (pp. 28–36). Washington, DC: NEA.

Index

About the Authors

Lynn G. Beck is an Assistant Professor of Education at the University of California at Los Angeles and the author of *Reclaiming Educational Administration as a Caring Profession* (forthcoming, Teachers College Press). Her research and teaching interests include ethical dimensions of educational leadership, the socio-cultural contexts of education, and administrator preparation programs.

Joseph Murphy is Professor and Chair, the Department of Educational Leadership, Peabody College of Vanderbilt University. He is also a Senior Research Fellow with the National Center for Educational Leadership. His work focuses on the issue of school improvement, with particular interest in the role that school administrators can play in that process.

257